Historically Black Colleges and Universities in a Globalizing World

Historically Black Colleges and Universities in a Globalizing World

The Past, Present, and Future

Edited by

Alem Hailu
Mohamed S. Camara
Sabella Ogbobode Abidde

LEXINGTON BOOKS
Lanham • Boulder • New York • London

Published by Lexington Books
An imprint of The Rowman & Littlefield Publishing Group, Inc.
4501 Forbes Boulevard, Suite 200, Lanham, Maryland 20706
www.rowman.com

86-90 Paul Street, London EC2A 4NE

British Library Cataloguing in Publication Information Available

Library of Congress Cataloging-in-Publication Data

Library of Congress Cataloging-in-Publication DataNames: Hailu, Alem, editor. | Camara, Mohamed Saliou, editor. | Abidde, Sabella Ogbobode, 1962- editor.
Title: Historically Black colleges and universities in a globalizing world : the past, present, and future / edited by Alem Hailu, Mohamed S. Camara, and Sabella Ogbobode Abidde.
Description: Lanham : Lexington Books, 2022. | Includes bibliographical references and index. | Summary: "This book examines the unique contribution of HBCUs, arguing that through their distinct public education, engagement, and activism, they have been at the forefront of leading global transformations. The book also argues that HBCUs can do more by paying more attention to the issue of enrollment, leadership, finances, and graduation standards"— Provided by publisher.
Identifiers: LCCN 2022034598 (print) | LCCN 2022034599 (ebook) | ISBN 9781666902747 (cloth) | ISBN 9781666902761 (paper) | ISBN 9781666902754 (ebook)
Subjects: LCSH: African American universities and colleges—History. | African American universities and colleges—Social aspects.
Classification: LCC LC2781 .H5722 2022 (print) | LCC LC2781 (ebook) | DDC 378.1/982996073—dc23/eng/20220727
LC record available at https://lccn.loc.gov/2022034598
LC ebook record available at https://lccn.loc.gov/2022034599

Contents

Abbreviations

AMA	American Missionary Association
AME	African Methodist Episcopal Church
ASU	Alabama State University
BECC	Black Emergency Cultural Coalition
BLM	Black Lives Matter
BSI	Institute for the Study of the History, Life, and Culture of Black People
CAU	Clark Atlanta University
CDC	Centers for Disease Control and Prevention
COFO	Council of Federated Organizations
CORE	Congress for Racial Equality
COVID-19	Coronavirus Disease 2019
CRM	Civil Rights Movement
CTEE	Current Term Enrollment Estimates
ERT	Emergency Remote Teaching
FAMU	Florida Agricultural & Mechanical University
FVSU	Fort Valley State University
HBCU	Historically Black College and Universities
HWUS	Historically White Universities
ICC	Interstate Commerce Commission
ISD	Instructional Design

IT	Information Technology
JSC	Jackson State College
LGBTQIA	lesbian, gay, bisexual, transgender, queer or questioning, intersex, or
MIAS	Mississippi Improvement Association of Students
MSI	Minority Serving Institutions
MWC	Margaret Walker National Research Center
NAACP	National Association for the Advancement of Colored People
NBCS	National Black Communications Society
NC A&T	North Carolina Agricultural and Technical University
NDEA	National Defense Education Act
NEH	National Endowment for the Humanities nonbinary, and asexual or aromantic.
NSCRC	National Student Clearinghouse Research Center
PWI	Predominantly White Institutions
PWI	Predominately White Institution
SARS-Co V-2	Syndrome Coronavirus 2
SCLC	Southern Christian Leadership Conference
SNCC	Student Nonviolent Coordinating Committee
TSU	Texas Southern University
UNIA	Universal Negro Improvement Association
WHO	World Health Organization
WPC	Women's Political Council
YMCA	Young Men's Christian Association

Preface

The need for this book was broached many years ago by Professor Alem Hailu. This was his idea. However, nothing was done because he was busy with other scholarly assignments and commitments. By the Spring of 2020, however, he decided that the time was right to embark on this scholarly journey—to examine the totality of the Historically Black Colleges and Universities (HBCUs). Public records indicate that HBCUs were founded years before the American Civil War; established primarily to serve the African American population who were mostly excluded from and or denied higher education. Then, and now, most of the HBCUs are concentrated in the southern region of the United States. The earliest institutions included the Cheyney University of Pennsylvania, the University of the District of Columbia, Lincoln University, Wilberforce University, Clark Atlanta University, Shaw University, and Storer College.

It should be noted some of the earliest institutions are either no longer in existence, merged to form larger institutions, or underwent a name change. Nonetheless, several decades after their founding, many have become storied institutions that cater to students from all races, nationalities, and socio-economic backgrounds. The globally recognized HBCUs include Howard University, Spelman College, Morgan State University, Florida Agricultural and Mechanical University, Philander Smith College, Tougaloo College, Hampton University, Dillard University, Xavier University of Louisiana, Tuskegee University, Morehouse College, Bowie State University, Jackson State University, Fisk University, Prairie View A&M University, and North Carolina Agricultural and Technical State University.

In the last decade, more than three dozen scholarly books regarding the HBCUs have been published. Many of these books dealt with sports and marching band, the dearth of transformative leadership, and the mounting problems and challenges facing many HBCUs i.e., declining enrollment, rising tuition, and retention. These are legitimate topics undertaken mostly by first-rate scholars and public intellectuals. And indeed, their works have advanced our knowledge of the inner workings, the roles, and responsibilities of these institutions. However, this volume—*Historically Black Colleges and Universities in a Globalizing World: The Past, Present and the Future*—takes a different approach. It is comprehensive in that it examines the HBCUs from both a national and international perspective.

But more importantly, it examines the immeasurable contribution of HBCUs to education, creativity, activism, politics, and society that goes far beyond the spatial frontiers of the United States—arguing that through their distinct public engagement and partnership models they have been at the forefront of leading global transformations. Nonetheless, the book also argues that HBCUs can do more by paying singular attention to the issue of enrollment, transformative leadership, funding, and graduation standards. While no single book can adequately and satisfactorily cover all the dimensions and dynamics of the HBCU, this is a reasonable attempt at doing so. Even so, readers and critics may find that the book does not cover some obvious topics. That is true. It is true because some contributors did not submit their chapters.

Overall, there are a dozen or more questions we wanted to examine. Among them were: Would the HBCUs survive—survive and thrive in an ever-interconnected and interrelated world? Are the students who attend these institutions being trained and educated to meet the challenges of an ever more complex and evolving American economic, social, and political environment? Do the graduates of the HBCUs have the skill set to meet and exceed the challenges of the twenty-first century, of a globalizing world? More than a century after their early beginnings, are these sorts of institutions still needed? A follow-up book will be devoted to these and other salient questions that are not addressed here.

Alem Hailu, PhD (Howard University)
Mohammed S. Camara, PhD (Howard University)
Sabella O. Abidde, PhD (Alabama State University)
Spring 2022

Acknowledgments

The structure, tone, and thrust of this book are slightly different from what we had planned because some scholars and public intellectuals withdrew their commitment to being a part of this project. But more importantly, political conditions in the Horn of Africa delayed the editing process; hence, we were not able to submit the manuscript at the scheduled time. Nonetheless, "all's well that ends well."

We owe many people a world of gratitude. Shelby Russell was instrumental in securing the book contract for us (but has since moved on to other endeavors). She was succeeded by the able Sydney Wedbush. To our delight, Sydney has been a joy to work with. She has been very patient and understanding even after several missed deadlines.

We are also appreciative of the anonymous reviewers and colleagues who penned endorsements and blurbs in support of our work. And of course, others supported us by engaging us in intellectual discussions.

This book couldn't have been completed without the enduring support and kindness of friends and colleagues in our various departments: The Department of African Studies (Howard University), and the Department of History and Political Science (Alabama State University).

And finally, our profound appreciation to all the scholars—the chapter contributors --- who remained and responded to our supplications despite the many months of postponements and uncertainties. Thank you, thank you, and thank you so very much. We did this together. Thanks!

Introduction

Expanded Paradigm of Higher Education through Inclusive Public Engagement, Activism, and Social Change

Alem Hailu, Mohammed S. Camara,
and Sabella O. Abidde

Historically Black Colleges and Universities (HBCUs) are public and private institutions that were established in the late 1800s to educate people of African descent who had been mainly prevented by enslavement and segregation from accessing higher education before the legislation of the Civil Rights Act of 1964. Mainly created out of the Christian tradition that aimed at uplifting emancipated slaves through spiritual and secular education, HBCUs have, thus, been institutions that have nurtured diverse faiths, cultures, races, creeds, and persuasions.[1]

The historical record of their achievements, however, shows how they have played key educational and social change roles for individuals and nations extending to the far corners of the earth. Until the mid-1960s, over 90 percent of African American students enrolled in higher education were educated by the HBCUs. However, after desegregation in higher education, the percentage of students enrolling in the HBCUs fell to 17 percent. From the high number of 121 HBCUs in the 1930s, the number fell to 101 in 2018, spread across nineteen states, the District of Columbia, and the U.S. Virgin Islands. Of these, fifty are private nonprofits, and fifty-one are public institutions. But the significance and relevance of the institutions for African Americans, the United States, and the world have continued to grow in numerical terms and scope.[2]

The wide and profound impact of HBCUs ranges from their imprint on producing a huge professional labor force to providing paths of professional development in medicine, business, and science to strengthening communities and building great material and social wealth for the nation and the globalized world. The disproportionate impact of the HBCUs, relative to their small share of the educational pie, is again underscored by the astounding statistics of just the two medical institutions of Howard University and Meharry Medical College accounting for nearly 80 percent of medicine and dentistry degrees awarded to Black students. The impact of the HBCUs in America and the world extends to the wider areas of the economy, finance, society, and politics.[3]

HBCUs were conceived as ideal institutions of learning dedicated to serving the economically disadvantaged, socially excluded, and politically marginalized. Following the principles of valuing all members of the human family, women, members of indigenous populations, low-income whites, and international students from nations in Africa, Asia, and Latin America were given opportunities. That this noble policy had mutually beneficial results is illustrated not only by the efforts HBCUs undertook to fight racism but also by the conditions they created to welcome displaced populations that sought refuge from the racial and xenophobic persecutions in Europe and nations around the world. When racism, Nazism, and Antisemitism reigned in the decades before World War II, HBCUs helped mobilize and prepare young men to fight on the war fronts. A large number of intellectual Jews and persecuted scholars who could not work in predominantly white universities were embraced as valued members of the academic communities.[4]

The open-door policy of HBCUs to offer access to all, regardless of gender, race, religion, or ethnic origin, has made them forerunners to the thenceforth widely accepted principle of providing opportunities to all groups across the wide socioeconomic spectrum. Although they are defined as institutions established to train African Americans, HBCUs have adopted open enrollment policies that provide equal opportunities to individuals across racial, ethnic, religious, and gender identities and socioeconomic backgrounds. Starting from the early times when a good number of female students were accepted and trained to be trailblazers in education, medicine, law, business, and other areas, their share of the academic community has even far outpaced the percentage growth of males.[5] Female enrollment grew from 53 percent in 1976 to 63 percent in 2019 and 64 percent in 2020.[6] Hence, most recipients of the degrees awarded by HBCUs are Black women. The diversity extended to faith and civic units housed in these institutions, as well as to the faculty, staff, and community organizations affiliated with the HBCU system.

Moreover, the sense of purpose and responsibility developed in the HBCU milieu of service and that of commitment to public welfare has been epitomized by the years of student civic engagement in activism and community service for the advancement of social justice and related common goods. In addition to their engagements in assisting local and regional efforts to address poverty, social displacement, and ill-health in the communities, students of Historically Black Colleges and Universities took the time to challenge colonialism, sociopolitical exclusion, apartheid, and political marginalization.[7]

The iconic image of the four A&T students who took a historic stand against racism on February 1, 1960, by sitting at the segregated Woolworth lunch counter in Greensboro, North Carolina, is a monument to the pivotal role HBCUs played in social change. Luminary leaders of the civil rights movement such as Dr. Martin Luther King Jr. (Morehouse College), Rosa Parks (Alabama State University), Medgar Evers (Alcorn State University), and Stokely Carmichael (Howard University), had their roots in the HBCU intellectual, moral, and civic environment. Following their leadership, thousands of students on the various campuses actively participated in the struggle for equality and justice. Contemporary HBCU students proudly and dedicatedly carry the torch of excellence in academia and civic engagement that their predecessors kept alive for decades. Using varied sources ranging from archival materials, oral history recordings, film clips, and journal and newspaper articles, as well as social media and electronic information systems, HBCU students now work autonomously and collectively to learn from their forebears and find ways in which to strengthen their agency and actions and bring about vital social change.

HBCUs have been evaluated and critiqued on various academic, economic, and social metrics. Critiques have emphasized the shortcomings related to the low level of their resources, the predominance of economically challenged student populations, and the philosophical or political legitimacy of their establishment, particularly in the wake of the post-legalized segregation era when all constraints on African American students are believed to have been lifted. Accordingly, politicians and self-appointed experts have questioned the relative value or continued relevance of HBCUs in these "post-segregation" times. Policymakers in Mississippi, for example, have called for closures or mergers between HBCUs and Historically White Colleges and Universities(HWCUs). Moreover, some African American students and their parents, along with other constituencies, have expressed concerns about the relative value of attending an HBCU as opposed to an HWCU. A balanced examination of the records, however, reveals a long list of benefits that students, the communities in which HBCUs are embedded, and the larger global constituency have derived and continue to derive from their services. These are among the many salient issues that the authors of the eleven chapters contained in this book document and analyze.[8]

In chapter 1, "Howard University and the African World," Alem Hailu argues that Howard University has served as an institution of higher education for people of African descent with an enduring commitment to education, research, and public engagement for over a century and a half. The historic mission of HBCUs to expand the orthodox boundaries of knowledge, training, and socio-political change has been enshrined by their stated goal of "not only educating but also liberating; of not only discovering but also reconstructing" the multiple ways they helped shape the constructs of power, academic discipline and scholarship are illustrated not just by the tens of citizens they have educated and trained for the United States. Their institutions of teaching, research, and public engagement have been open to young people from Africa and nations around the world. Global movements for independence, equality, dignity and equal rights have been greatly influenced by the scholarly and public service commitments of the prominent scholars at these institutions. Many African leaders, in all spheres of endeavor, graduated from HBCUs and went on to become pillars of their society.

In chapter 2, "The Creation of a University: Dr. John Manuel Gandy and Virginia State University, 1914–1943," Oscar R. Williams highlights the leadership of the third president of Virginia State University (VSU) and his efforts to make the institution the leading place for higher learning for African Americans in Virginia. Adjacent to Petersburg, Virginia, VSU was founded in 1882 largely thanks to the efforts of Alfred Harris, an African American member of the Virginia House of Delegates. Established as a college, the institution faced opposition from those who rejected the idea of higher education for African Americans. In 1902, the Virginia State Legislature revised the charter of VSU to sharply reduce the collegiate program. Faced with this challenge, Dr. Gandy would embark on a vigorous campaign to lead VSU into a new era. Born in Mississippi to African American sharecroppers in 1870, Dr. Gandy overcame odds and dedicated his life to the education and uplift of African Americans during an age of racial segregation in America. Dr. Gandy's accomplishments include the restoration of VSU's college status; the improvement of the campus infrastructure; the recruitment of faculty and staff from Fisk, Columbia, and the University of Chicago; and the addition of a graduate program. Under his leadership, VSU became firmly established as the land grant college for African Americans in the Commonwealth of Virginia until racial desegregation in the 1960s.

In Chapter 3, "'The Struggle Staggers Us': The Institute for the Study of the History, Life, and Culture of Black People at Jackson State, 1968–1979 that in 1968," Rico Devara Chapman and D. Caleb Smith assert that Margaret

Walker Alexander established the Institute for the Study of the History, Life and Culture of Black People at Jackson State College. Alexander's Black Studies program was truly one of a kind at the time. To date, histories of higher education speak little to the development of Black Studies programs at HBCUs. Instead, scholarly attention is typically placed on the establishment of such programs at universities where African American students were the minority of the overall campus population. In predominantly white institutions (PWIs), Black Studies programs were a result of student protests which stemmed from broader calls for Black nationalism. However, Jackson State College's Black Studies Institute was an administratively led initiative that centered around the resilience of Margaret Walker Alexander. In this chapter, furthermore, the authors chronicle the evolution of Alexander's Institute amid Mississippi's burgeoning Black freedom movement and offer an analysis of the growth and decline of the Black Studies Institute by detailing its structure, personnel, campus activities, and curriculum.

In chapter 4, "Art and Activism as HBCU Tradition," Elizabeth Carmel Hamilton contends that HBCUs produce world-caliber artists that are not only prepared to create art, but also agitate for social change in the lives of Black people in the United States. Among them, she cites Elizabeth Catlett (1915–2012), Benny Andrews (1930–2006), and the members of Otabenga Jones and Associates. Art departments at HBCUs trained black artists and raised their social consciousness. Because of their unique founding to educate Black people, the missions of these academic departments were intertwined with the political imperative to improve the lives of the people and communities they served. Catlett trained at Howard University (Washington, D.C.), Andrews trained at Fort Valley State University (Fort Valley, Georgia), and Otabenga Jones and Associates trained at Texas Southern University (Houston, Texas). Through her research, Elizabeth demonstrates that artists trained at HBCUs had a unique orientation toward art-making that allowed them to create works that were not just beautiful but also stood out as significant records of the civil rights movement that promoted social change.

In "Keeping It Real" On the Decline of HBCU Student Enrollment: A Content Analysis on Rhetoric in Practice" (chapter 5), Ivon Alcime, Ashla Hill Roseboro, and Carlos Morrison examine statements of prospective, current, and former students of Clark Atlanta University, Morehouse College, and Spelman College, the three HBCUs that are part of the Atlanta University Center. The authors also examine the communication format to identify ineffective statements that contribute to the declining enrollment of students at HBCUs. To this end, they gathered data from a collection of articles published in scholarly journals, newspapers, and magazines, as well as materials from social media forums spanning the period of 2015 to 2020. The data were coded based on types of communication format and types of messages from the students (i.e., paralanguage, nonverbal communication, jargon, and text). The assumption was that the communication of HBCUs' administrators and faculty contributes to low enrollment.

Chapter 6, "Twenty-First- Century HBCU Students: Living in An Era of Oppression," by Carla Brown is original research that exposes the effects of Black oppression on HBCU students. The chapter highlights the current systematic and institutionalized racism that is still heavily prevalent. Black students who attend HBCUs are forced to focus on their academics and career paths while having to also witness a world that is oppressing Black people. This is the same world that HBCU students must enter upon the completion of their degree and must navigate to the best of their abilities. Black oppression has been a lingering issue for centuries, for although policies and laws have been established to protect Black people, severe discrepancies persist.

In chapter 7, "Historically Black Colleges and Universities: Laboratories for Social and Political Activism," Regina M. Moorer examines how the history and practices of HBCUs shaped students' social and political activism. This chapter focuses specifically on four HBCUs: Alabama State University, Albany State University, Bennett College, and North Carolina A&T University. It, therefore, examines how these distinctly American institutions sparked and fueled the Civil Rights Movement's (CRM) drive for racial equality. The study of these historically significant institutions exposes the social environment that engulfed and continues to engulf HBCUs and transformed them into agents of social change. Though often ignored in the available CRM literature, HBCUs played a significant role in the sociopolitical arena. They each made a significant contribution to the fight for civil rights in their respective states.

According to Patrice W. Glenn Jones, in chapter 8, "Academic Outbreak: Safety, Psychosocial, Enrollment, and Learning Challenges Facing HBCU As a Result of Covid-19," the spread of COVID-19 was unprecedented. As the medical community scrabbled to mitigate the health-related effects of the virus, the pandemic spread with a feverous intensity, threatening not only the physical health of individuals throughout the world but also our mental wellness, ways of life, and even our education. Because HBCUs are, among post-secondary institutions, institutions that serve largely disadvantaged populations, they and their stakeholders were faced with many challenges, and as the restrictions associated with COVID-19 begin to lift, some of these challenges will remain. The chapter specifically identifies select challenges about safety, psychosocial conditions and mental health, enrollment, and learning that HBCUs face because of the COVID-19 pandemic. The chapter also provides general suggestions to address these challenges.

In chapter 9, "HBCU Medical Programs in a Globalizing World," Tabitha Morton, Tamika Baldwin-Clark, and Tiffany Thomas contend that Historically Black Colleges and Universities continue to increase the number of underrepresented minorities in medicine (URMM) by providing African American students opportunities to earn medical degrees previously denied to them at PWIs. Although they are the leading producers of African American physicians and healthcare professionals, HBCUs still only have two medical schools (Howard and Meharry) and suffer from a lack of funding, advancements, and related types of support. This chapter begins by discussing HBCUs' historical importance to medicine and the contributions they have made to healthcare. It goes on to detail the benefits that the African American community has obtained from the presence of African American medical professionals, and how those benefits can be enhanced if various organizations work to increase support and funding. The chapter also examines policy frameworks to be considered and steps that HBCUs themselves are taking to address the perduring challenges. The authors conclude with an argument that underscores the relevance of HBCU medical programs in the global world.

In chapter 10, "Black College Renaissance: My Decision to Create the First HBCU History Course and 2020 Proposal for Interdisciplinary HBCU Studies Curricula En Masse." Cheryl Mango proposes a Black College Renaissance through a novel conceptual model termed the HBCU Studies interdisciplinary academic discipline. The focus is on explaining the justification for institutionalizing HBCU Studies courses across the K-12 and higher education landscapes, particularly at Black colleges, to stimulate the systematic study of HBCUs. Priority is given to providing the schools with self-imposed methodical fortification, from deep-seated challenges rooted in inequity from which they will rise and earn reimbursements for their democratizing contributions in a racially discriminatory America. In the end, the project explains why the national reception to the 2020 creation of the first HBCU History course, HIST-349 at Virginia State University, is only the first step toward HBCU Studies serving as the next frontier for Black colleges.

Finally, in chapter 11, "Critical Reflections on Race, Social Justice and Historically Black Colleges and Universities," Felix Kumah-Abiwu states that race and social justice issues have continued to be intensified after the death of Mr. George Floyd in 2020, with a renewed debate on racial injustice in America. There is no question that many Americans were traumatized by watching the demise of another human being in the disturbing video of George Floyd's murder. Mr. Floyd, an unarmed African American man, was denied justice, basic human rights, and dignity as he was killed in public by a white police officer. As scholar-activists who have dedicated their careers to interrogating issues of race, racism, and social injustice would argue, the public death of Mr. Floyd might be new to some, but not out of the norm for scholars who have been exposing systemic/institutionalized racism, anti-Blackness, and Black suffering in America. We also know that the quest for total emancipation has been at the center of the Black struggle with support from civil rights movements and core institutions such as the HBCUs. While recognizing the importance of HBCUs in the Black struggle movement, important questions have also been raised on the role of these historic institutions in the broader study of race and social justice issues. For some scholars, HBCUs not only embody Black culture and identity but also arguably encompass race and racial justice within their "natural domain." At the same time, key questions need to be asked about how race and social justice issues occupy the intellectual space of HBCUs. In other words, how integral are race and social justice systematically studied and researched at HBCUs? The chapter explores these important questions with a view to better understanding HBCUs and their role in the systematic study of race, racism, and social justice issues.

At this point, two recommendations are in order if HBCUs are to continue to prosper. First, while they continue to be relevant domestically and globally, we recommend that they expand their sphere of function and influence. For instance, they should engage in bilateral and multilateral cooperation with colleges and universities in Africa and the Caribbean. If properly designed, pursued, and implemented, such engagements would benefit all sides. While there are student and faculty exchange programs with a handful of universities on the African continent, for example, they should go a step further by either establishing satellite campuses or establishing joint campuses. Howard University could, for instance, establish autonomous or semiautonomous campuses in The Gambia, Tanzania, Liberia, or Botswana. Alabama State University could, for instance, establish joint campuses in Côte d'Ivoire, Angola, or Madagascar.

Second, instead of continuing to place disproportionate emphasis on the liberal arts, the social sciences, and the humanities that many HBCUs are known for, we suggest that they also adapt their degree and course offerings to meet the demands of the twenty-first century. To be competitive in a globalizing world—and to meet the demands of an ever-changing and complex workforce—HBCUs must offer specialized programs and advanced degrees in the areas of science, technology, engineering, and math, including computer science (STEM+CS). And of course, in geospatial technologies such as geography, geographic information science (GIS), global positioning systems (GPS), and remote sensing. These programs are a better bulwark against economic recession, cutbacks, and poor compensation. While some schools are making the changes, the numbers are not high enough and neither are they making the change at a rapid pace. Also, they should offer programs in law (with specialization in environmental law, oil and gas, corporate law, and international law).

In these STEM+CS recommendations we, by no means, imply that the liberal arts, the social sciences, and the humanities should be neglected or weakened. Far from it! What we are recommending, instead, is a strategic balancing of them with STEMS+CS that will make HBCUs more competitive in the twenty-first century by being better equipped to prepare future generations of graduates to enter the global job market with the relevant skills, expertise, and self-confidence they need to succeed.

NOTES

1. Anderson, James D. *Education of Blacks in the South, 1860–1935.* Chapel Hill, North Carolina: The University of North Carolina Press, 1988.

2. "Historically Black Colleges and Universities." National Center for Education Statistics (NCES). U.S. Department of Education. Accessed May 30, 2022. https://nces.ed.gov/fastfacts/display.asp?id=667

3. "At a Glance: Black and African American Physicians in the Workforce." AAMC, February 20, 2017. https://www.aamc.org/news-insights/glance-black-and-african-american-physicians-workforce.

4. LeMelle, Tilden J. "The HBCU: yesterday, today and tomorrow." *Education* 123, no. 1 (2002): 190+. *Gale Academic OneFile* (accessed May 30, 2022. https://link.gale.com/apps/doc/A94265120/AONE?u=naal_asum&sid=googleScholar&xid=4a655bfc.

5. Esters, Lorenzo L., and Terrell L Strayhorn. "Demystifying the Contributions of Public Land-Grant Historically Black Colleges and Universities: Voices of HBCU Presidents." *Negro Educational Review* 64, no. 1–4 (2013): 119–34.

6. Biddle, Sekous, and Naomi Shelton. "The Value of Historically Black Colleges and Universities." UNCF/National Association for College Admission Counseling. Accessed May 30, 2022. https://www.nacacnet.org/globalassets/documents/professional-development/school-counselor-pd-day/loudoun-county/the-value-of-hbcus.pdf.

7. Ibid

8. Clayton, Dave, Melissa Leavitt, and Nichole Torpey-Saboe. "The Significant Value of Historically Black Colleges and Universities." Center for Education Consumer Insights, February 16, 2022. https://cci.stradaeducation.org/pv-release-feb-16-2022/.

REFERENCES

Anderson, James D. *Education of Blacks in the South, 1860–1935.* Chapel Hill, NC: The University of North Carolina Press, 1988.

"At a Glance: Black and African American Physicians in the Workforce." AAMC, February 20, 2017. https://www.aamc.org/news-insights/glance-black-and-african -american-physicians-workforce.

Biddle, Sekous, and Naomi Shelton. "The Value of Historically Black Colleges and Universities." UNCF/National Association for College Admission Counseling. Accessed May 30, 2022. https://www.nacacnet.org/globalassets/documents/ professional-development/school-counselor-pd-day/loudoun-county/the-value-of -hbcus.pdf.

Clayton, Dave, Melissa Leavitt, and Nichole Torpey-Saboe. "The Significant Value of Historically Black Colleges and Universities." Center for Education Consumer Insights, February 16, 2022. https://cci.stradaeducation.org/pv-release-feb-16 -2022/.

Esters, Lorenzo L, and Terrell L Strayhorn. "Demystifying the Contributions of Public Land-Grant Historically Black Colleges and Universities: Voices of HBCU Presidents." *Negro Educational Review* 64, no. 1–4 (2013): 119–34.

"Historically Black Colleges and Universities." National Center for Education Statistics (NCES). U.S. Department of Education. Accessed May 30, 2022. https:// nces.ed.gov/fastfacts/display.asp?id=667.

LeMelle, Tilden J. "The HBCU: yesterday, today and tomorrow." *Education* 123, no. 1 (2002): 190+. *Gale Academic OneFile* (accessed May 30, 2022. https://link .gale.com/apps/doc/A94265120/AONE?u=naal_asum&sid=googleScholar&xid =4a655bfc.

PART I

A Rich and Consequential Heritage

Chapter 1

Howard University and the African World

A Commentary

Alem Hailu

HOWARD'S LEGACY OF STRUGGLE AGAINST RACISM, BIGOTRY, AND INEQUALITY

Howard University, armed with the knowledge and dedication of its scholars and the principles and visions of its institution, has been at the forefront of the momentous changes of the twentieth century. In partnership with other universities, public and private organizations, and movements in the nation and the world, Howard has been instrumental in inducing structural and policy changes on the issues of race, independence, ethnicity, civil rights, democracy, and governance. The problems that confronted the African World—racism, colonialism, segregation, exclusion, bigotry, and repression—were addressed with rigorous scholarship and active gown-town models of engagement with actors in the broader society.

Howard University's leading role in the sociopolitical change in the African World is symbolized by the struggle for human dignity that inspired people to resist. However, the dynamics of transformation have expanded to have an impact on all members of global society with movements against totalitarianism, nuclear war, environmental degradation, national oppression, gender, disability or age discrimination, and a myriad of human and civil rights causes animated by the knowledge as well as practical examples of collaborative, peaceful alliances, embodied in the institutions legacy. In tracing the long roads to global changes, the concerns of the African World comprising the political and economic realities of oppression and exploitation as well as the socioeconomics of ideologies, cultures, and knowledge systems that denigrated the worth of Africans are recounted in comparative narratives.

Howard University and HBCUs as the academic arms of the advocacy and public policy engagement dimensions of the African world have demonstrated the power of ideas, alliance, and broad partnership in bringing about profound transformation within nations and at global levels.

Howard University as the leading historically Black institution is taken as an agency for spreading light embodying the characteristics of the candle and the mirror. When Howard was established as a venue of higher education in 1867, the world had registered great strides in science, technology, and human knowledge. Yet as Alexander Pope's description of nature and nature's laws that lay hidden in the night before the divine summoning words of "let there be light," large portions of human thoughts and practices were shrouded in ignorance and bigotry as well.

HOWARD UNIVERSITY AND
GLOBAL TRANSFORMATION

The modern world embracing the industrial revolution, and a new era of science, technology and advances in human thought held up a vision of enlightenment, peace and prosperity for all peoples around the earth. Lofty promises to vanquish the age-old challenges of starvation, disease and distance were accordingly delivered as anticipated by the exponents of change. Nevertheless, the revolutions in science and cognition not only fail to address human conditions of inequality, injustice and prejudice it also exacerbated persisting problems and even created conditions of large-scale cruelty, persecution and annihilation of whole societies. The dubbing of the twentieth century as the most deadly period of history that claimed the lives of over 250 million people is evidence of the two faces of modern progress.

Confronting the negative aspect of this development have been great men and women of vision and institutions of principle and integrity. Howard University has been one such institution that has advanced this cause through the two modes of spreading light indicated by Edith Wharton: By being both the candle of scholars and members of the academic community and the mirror of reflection and engagement with leading figures and organizations in the country and all other nations. Howard University in its 155 years of history has been at the center of global transformations by assuming the role of not the proverbial ivory tower isolated from the concerns of society but rather by adopting the alternate responsibility of the gown-town metaphor whereby scholars, administrative personnel and students have been engaged in the worldwide quest for human dignity, freedom and respect for all peoples, races, social groups and individuals.

Drawing students from the United States, Africa, the Caribbean, and all other regions, Howard has produced over 150,000 graduates in degrees and certificates over its long history sending missionaries of change into all corners of society. Among its notable alumni are Supreme Court justices, such as Thurgood Marshall; senators, such as Edward Brooke; UN ambassadors, such as Andrew Young; prominent singers such as Roberta Flack; outstanding actors such as Ossie Davis; Kamala Harris and Phylicia Rashad; Nobel laureate and writers as Toni Morrison as well as a host of political figures, musicians, educators, film producers, civic and corporate leaders. The combined impact of these "social engineers" in transforming the goals, principles, and visions of political and socioeconomic structures in America and around the world cannot be exaggerated. Howard University's power to change the world can be appraised in terms of the foremost ideas and institutional transformations that have led to the betterment of the human condition at national, regional and global levels. The transformations include the enshrining of civil and human rights as universal laws, the adoption of nonviolent approaches as civilized strategies of change, the affirmation of races, cultures, and civilizations as having equal worth and the valorization of individuals, social groups, and neglected human assets. Using the individual actors as the human stories indicating the vitality and significance of institutions and movements these particular agents of change are traced along the following subheadings to demonstrate the contributions of Howard University to global transformations.

LINKING THE STRUGGLES AGAINST SEGREGATION, COLONIALISM, FASCISM, AND APARTHEID

When scholars such as Toynbee unashamedly asserted with purported volumes of research to assert that "the only primary race that has not made a creative contribution to any civilization is the black race," many scientists conducted elaborate research to establish similar theses, popular culture and sociopolitical institutions erected structures of discrimination, repression and violence. Howard University in collaboration with progressive thinkers and truly democratic institutions waged a long and hard-fought battle to counter the pernicious effects of the ideas and policies.

Frederick Douglass who along with Booker T. Washington sat on the governing board of Howard University went further than merely countering white supremacist denials of Africa's contribution to assert that "the arts, appliances and blessings of civilization flourished in the very heart of Ethiopia, at a time when all Europe floundered in the depths of ignorance and barbarism."[1] Scholarly and mass movements represented by the ideas and practices of the era from Edward Wilmot Blyden, Alexander Crummell and Martin Delany to W. E. B. Du Bois, Marcus Garvey, Sylvester Williams and George Padmore resonated in the academic works and activist engagements of scholars at Howard. During the dark hours of colonialism and the world's deadly battle against Nazism and fascism, Rayford Logan together with Du Bois and Walter White "published books in 1944–45 that focused on the international character of racial inequality and the need for its demise."[2]

Earlier, the return of Fascist Italy to undertake its invasion of Ethiopia in 1935 had galvanized the African World with uncommon determination to stand in solidarity against the victimization of one of the only two independent nations in Africa. Ethiopia, as a synonym for Black Africa and the first non-European nation to defeat an imperialist power, stood as a symbol of freedom for people of African descent. The invasion, therefore, coming at a time when millions had begun to put their aspirations for a nonracial free world, rose in indignation and a historic sense of shared history and destiny. This event is believed to have created a very strong sense of kinship among Ethiopia, African Americans, and the African World in general. The renowned history professor at Howard University observed how the brutal Fascist Italian campaign had the strong impact of "electrifying a wide array of African Americans who had long treasured, from a distance, Ethiopia's peculiar prestige." As W. E. B. Du Bois wrote about the interconnection of the fate of Africans and African Americans, John Franklin underscored the depth of the change in the global awareness by noting that "almost overnight, even the most provincial among Negro Americans became international-minded."[3]

Yet this transformation did not take place automatically by itself; a great deal of scholarly and public mobilization had to be carried out long before and during the event. The university's president, Mordechai Johnson; Charles Houston, dean of the Law School; Charles Wesley, Ralph Bunche, and Leo Hansberry expressed their solidarity with Ethiopia. When Italy's violation of African sovereignty with its Fascist ideology became clearer, scholars in the university formed an organization named the Ethiopian Research Council and conducted research, public education, and mobilization that influenced African Americans around the country to express their indignation while many volunteered resources, logistical support, and their lives.[4]

The active involvement of scholars and other members of the university community in African affairs extended to linking struggles against racial injustices on all continents and fighting against Fascism and Nazism and mobilizing for independence and pan-African movements. Rayford Logan's association with Du Bois and experience with the Pan African Congress in the 1940s and 1950s enabled him to have an observer status for the NAACP at the Paris United Nations General Assembly.[5] His published work on Haiti and the Dominican Republic indicating the issue of race and sovereignty in international relations is considered to be a notable example of the broad impact the university's scholars have had on the African World. Edward Franklin Frazier's study of Brazil and Ralph Bunche's research in Togoland and Dahomey (Benin) and later works culminating in his association with the United Nations in decolonization policies in Africa are among the long list of contributions Howard University has achieved in confronting racism, colonialism, and apartheid on the world stage.[6]

CIVIL RIGHTS MOVEMENTS AS PROTOTYPES FOR GLOBAL TRANSFORMATION

One major facet of the long struggle waged by people of African descent has been the civil rights movement, which served as the embodiment of the quest for dignity, tolerance, independence, pluralism, and shared humanity. From the earliest scholars and leaders of movements who articulated the human worth of the African World's descendants and called for institutions of justice and equality to their followers over the decades who strove to translate the visions into practicable policies, the civil rights movement has been undertaken by a combination of foresight and popular engagement. While the immediate objectives of the movement were the realization of conditions of fairness, equal opportunity, and justice for members of the constituency, its broader goals incorporated much loftier principles that would be of common concern to all members of the human family.

Since the civil rights movements covered the entire range of human affairs, few individuals or institutions can be selected as the only agents behind the forces of transformation. The collective contributions of scholars, religious leaders, civic institutions, artists, and just plain folks involved in mass activities over prolonged periods cannot be understated. It is, nonetheless, important to recognize the far-sighted knowledge and dedication of individuals and institutions in leading the charges of enlightenment and mobilization. Howard University, again, has been one of the institutions that has played a critical role in shaping the goals as well as the dynamics of the movements.

The impact of visionaries on raising social awareness, the effects of world war on citizens who took up arms to defend the liberty of other nations and the influence of the Cold War or the independence of African nations are among the myriad factors believed to be the causes behind the civil rights movements. Howard's role, therefore, cannot be viewed as the case of a single institution stage-managing such a giant social project. Howard's historical role has been one of lighting the fire of knowledge or reflecting it to others through the engagement of the issues of the times. The ideas, far from being monolithic, often assisted in resolving dilemmas through debates carried out even within the members of the academic community.

HISTORICALLY BLACK COLLEGES
AND UNIVERSITIES

While a large number of independent intellectuals and citizens have contributed to the development of African Studies, Historically Black Colleges and Universities, in partnership with independent scholars and movements, have been the real vanguards of the enterprise. The identity of the African and the African World was established by the interplay of self-definitions as well as external conceptualizations. Europe like other regions was defined by its self-image as much as its interactions with the world. Disparate and national groupings estimated to be five hundred at the start of the state-building initiative forged a sense of cultural unity under the newly constructed identity of Europe. Africa before its strong interconnections with the international system, similarly, did not have a self-perception of continental or global cultural identity. As the integration by the United States of the particular identities of European and other nationalities into a single system worked as an impetus for reversing Europe's history of feuding fiefdoms and states into the promise of a common union or home, people of African descent in the diaspora provided the dream and task of forging the African world as well.

Historically Black Colleges and Universities (HBCUs) played leading roles in the definition of Africa's identity and future by educating people of African descent with professional skills and a sense of shared history on the one hand and the vigorous pursuit of research, public education and mobilization on the African World at national and global scales on the other. W. E. B. Du Bois illustrated the heavy responsibilities HBCUs shouldered with their graduation of 1,941 students of African descent by 1900 compared to the white colleges' record of merely 390 students. Nationwide, even decades later, calls for integrating African Studies into the educational system registered huge gains but still left a lot of shortcomings. In response to the demands for African Studies over 250 of America's 2,100 four-year institutions had developed programs. Whereas celebrated scholars such as Rayford Logan saw to the actual implementation of the programs according to activist Amiri Baraka, who led in the great marches, success "came only as a result of student struggles. . . . Black studies would not yet be on these campuses, nor will it remain, if it had to depend solely on the efforts of Redding type intellectuals and their pleas for 'moral uplift' among the bourgeoisie. Black studies came only as a result of struggle and confrontation."[7] The exact apportioning of the credit for the changes can be debated but the larger point of the collective efforts of senior intellectuals, students, and activists in the larger public that brought about the transformations cannot be exaggerated.

The combined impact of scholarship, public education, and engagement of students and the public in social change and the institutionalization of African Studies is indisputable. Students at Howard University, the flagship of HBCUs, as in many American universities in the late 1960s, demanded and won the enhancement of African Studies programs and curricula. The uphill battles waged by these generals and field warriors of social revolutions are demonstrated by the lingering gaps between projected ideals and realized goals. According to statistical figures from the *Chronicle of Higher Education*, the proportion of Black faculty members in 2000–2003 at U.S. universities and colleges was just 4.9 percent, far below the national population share of 12.3 percent. In contrast, Asians with only 3 percent of the population outnumbered Black faculty by almost five thousand. Noting the unchanged statistics of the 2.3 percent Black faculty representation of predominantly white universities for the last twenty years, Paul Tiyambe Zeleza makes the ironic observation that "Black faculty continue to find themselves marginalized in the Historically White Universities (HWUS), despite all the rhetoric about affirmative action in the aborted promises of civil rights." Still from the early times of the segregation era to the later period of the post-civil rights era, HBCUs have been the driving forces behind the education of the African World. Studies clearly indicate the centrality of HBCUs not only in scholarship on the African world but also in the training of Africans symbolized by the education of Kwame Nkrumah, Nnamdi Azikwe, and Hastings Kamuzu Banda in these institutions.[8]

HBCUs along with intellectuals and activists in the broader community has nurtured African Studies in different forms. Nevertheless, despite the strong interests of HBCUs in Africa, the institutions were generally unable to fully develop the infrastructures needed for full-fledged African Studies. Howard University is singled out as the towering institution that has risen to the historic challenge. Going back to the dark ages when ideologies of imperialism, scientific racism, and social Darwinism reigned supreme, scholars at Howard defiantly challenged the dogmas that vilified the African World. Frederick Douglass wrote against supremacist claims. In the early decades of the twentieth century, Kelly Miller and Alain Locke led curriculum proposals on Negro history to be incorporated into the educational system. With the coming of Carter G. Woodson as a faculty member, this work was supplemented by two other prominent scholars, Charles H. Wesley and William Leo Hansberry, who offered courses on Africa.[9] The monumental significance of these visionaries in laying the groundwork for African Studies can be appraised both by the foresight of the ideas adopted by other academic institutions thirty and forty years after their pioneering contributions and the depth of their intellectual works. Woodson's scholarly initiatives included the organization of associated publishers designed to print books on the African world, the establishment of Negro History Week and the integration of textbooks relating to Africa in school systems. His argument, that there was no such thing as "Negro History" only a missing segment of world history, anticipated paradigms of pluralism recognized years after Woodson's time.[10]

William Leo Hansberry is recognized as the leading architect of African Studies who, along with W. E. B. Du Bois, combined great scholarship with activism on Africa and the African World. His extensive research on Nile Valley civilizations spawned great interest and appreciation for Africa's heritage. Yet his passion extended to nurturing African students such as Nnamdi Azikiwe who returned the favor when he became president of Nigeria by having Hansberry officially open the Hansberry College of African Studies in Nigeria. Working in close association with another protégé, Melaku Beyan, the first medically trained Ethiopian alumnus of Howard, Hansberry helped galvanize African American public opinion against the Fascist Italian invasion of Ethiopia.

Alain Locke, together with other colleagues in the university, led the launch of the Harlem Renaissance with the culture, arts and literature of Africa and the African World promoted to awaken movements for human dignity, independence and pluralism around the globe. Ralph Bunche complemented these extraordinary traditions again with the combination of research in West and East Africa along with activist engagement as a diplomat in the United Nations influencing the framing of the U.N. human rights and facilitating the decolonization of Africa. The long list of the giant intellectuals at Howard extends from Kelly Miller and Frazier Edward Franklin to successors such as Joseph E. Harris, who not only enhanced African knowing with his research on the African World but also organized and edited the works of Leo Hansberry which was posthumously published.

Scholars at Howard and other HBCUs have played vital roles in advancing African Studies, influencing public policies, and mobilizing citizens. Despite their extraordinary contributions, however, far from being honored for their work, they have been ignored and even at times maligned for their focus on the dimensions of culture, race, and civilization raised as important issues in understanding Africa and the African World.

While acknowledging the establishment of the African Studies Association in 1959 as a major milestone and "a boon for the broader field of African Studies," Robert O. Collins and James M. Burns, lamented that "it ignored the historically black colleges, which had been in the vanguard of establishing African Studies curricula."[11] Similarly, underscoring Allen F. Isaacman's

2002 annual address of the African Studies Association meeting when he mentioned that African Studies "all too often ignored the pioneering work on Africa by African American scholars in HBCUs such as Howard University," Edward A. Alpers and Allen F. Roberts lament the less-than-full recognition of the fundamental contributions of scholars such as W. E. B. Du Bois and William Leo Hansberry to shaping American understanding of Africa during the twentieth century.[12]

Against the background of historical accounts that credit the far-reaching influence of scholars in HBCUs on leaders, education, and intellectual movements spanning the centuries and the primary roles these institutions shouldered, Paul Tiyambe Zeleza echoed the voices by emphasizing: "It was at these colleges and universities that the serious and systematic study of Africa was pioneered, courses on African peoples established, and monographs and journals published, long before the historically white universities, in pursuit of national security, disciplinary excitement, or belated multiculturalism, discovered African Studies or diaspora studies."[13]

The vital roles Historically Black Colleges and Universities played in the development of African Studies have been highlighted. This should not, however, obscure the fact that intellectuals, institutions, movements, and policies outside the HBCUs around the world have also been key players in shaping the content and direction of the field. The complementarity of the two observations is clear when we realize that the pioneering institutions advanced the cause in constant communication and engagement with the broader forces of transformation.

HOWARD—THE MECCA

Howard University, "described as the only truly comprehensive predominantly black institution of higher education in the world" is taken as a case example symbolizing the pivotal role people of African descent have played in bringing about profound transformations around the world. Howard University, leading African American citizens and institutions espoused the momentous challenges of freedom, emancipation, independence and civil liberties to help define the course of human events in the twentieth century.

At the turn of the twentieth century, the world was a different place. Ideologies and governmental policies unashamedly upheld the tenets of racial hierarchy, social separation, colonialism, imperialism, and segregation. Pseudoscientific doctrines proclaimed whole racial groups as less intelligent and unworthy of respect or equal justice. In Africa and large parts of the African World, the systems of colonialism and exploitation were the material institutions manifesting the doctrines of supremacy. In the United States, slavery and segregation were the legal expressions of the creeds. When people of African descent confronted these entrenched ideas and practices, extraordinary visions and wills had to be summoned. Appreciation of the courage of their convictions and foresight can be attained only when the realities of the period are weighed against the magnitude of the problems they confronted.

Scientific racism, eugenics, and diverse sociopolitical dogmas of racial supremacy polarized differences, and exclusion were championed and practiced by elites at the highest echelons of society. Not only African Americans but also ethnic groups from Native Americans, Chinese and Jews to Southern Europeans and Slavs were defined as inferior races. In fact, public opinion-makers of the period openly expressed antipathies even to immigrants from Southern and Eastern Europe on the alleged grounds of racial defect that could degrade the United States. Women, likewise, were largely excluded from public participation.

Howard University's critical role in global transformations becomes clear when we consider the time and exceptional contributions of its members in helping pave the way for pluralism, tolerance, and social justice in America and the world. Since prominent names serve as the signposts of historic changes, recapitulating some of the figures could demonstrate the significance of the far-reaching changes. The change agents that played on Howard's public stage differ from figures such as Rayford Logan, who served the university's community for over four decades, to others who were associated for shorter periods. Carter G. Woodson's vital if brief tenure, deemed to be his most intellectually fruitful period, is given as evidence for the institution's academic environment as the key laboratory for the profound transformations.

The background for the changes was set early by pioneers such as Frederick Douglass and Booker T. Washington who served as members of the university's board of trustees. Carter G. Woodson is acknowledged as one of the exceptional scholars who blazed the trail with his work and conviction declaring that the achievements of people of African descent would enrich all human civilization. Rayford Logan's contributions amalgamated scholarship with engagements in international causes including collaboration with W. E. B. Du Bois epitomized by his service in the Pan-African Congress of the 1940s and 1950s. Ralph J. Bunche led with his colossal intellectual and diplomatic commitment to the African World demonstrated by his field research, United Nations decolonization efforts and association with the leading independent and rights advocates of the day. His function in the institutionalization of the United Nations, partnership with Eleanor Roosevelt in enshrining human rights on the U.N. Charter as well as personal ties with Martin Luther King Jr., are examples of his vast impact in bringing about revolutions on the global scale.

Alain Locke's avant-garde leadership in establishing African civilizations' ties with the worlds of art, literature, folklore, and culture in the Harlem Renaissance also had a far-reaching impact on the Caribbean, Africa and Europe by restoring the dignity of the African World. The influence extended to political and social movements for self-determination and nobility in artistic endeavors. William Leo Hansberry, along with his colleagues took the historic responsibility of debunking all the negative stereotypes about Africa and rebuilding African Studies as an academic pursuit for teaching and research. In the tradition of Howard's scholars, he combined his relentless efforts to authenticate Africa's civilizations with engagements in supporting positive sociopolitical changes and mentoring African students.

Mordechai Johnson helped chart the course of global transformation through his profound influence on the world outlook of young Martin Luther King Jr. The seeds of a nonviolent paradigm of social change planted by Johnson were nurtured by Howard Thurman's philosophical teachings and the collective work of African Americans who synthesized African traditions with Mahatma Gandhi's principles, relaying the heritage to King's civil rights movement. In parallel with the spiritual and philosophical modalities of transformation, Charles Houston launched the legal strategy of change in which numerous colleagues and students at the Howard Law School were mobilized as "social engineers" to dismantle structures of segregation and exclusion.

Kelly Miller as a professor and dean of the College of Arts and Sciences helped reinforce the paths of scholarship and social engagement for the African World. The refrain crediting Howard as the venue whereby all people of note in influencing social revolution either devoted extended stay or passed through its halls is corroborated by the historical records of prodigious intellectuals such as Melville Herskovits, who carried out extensive pioneering research on the African World, Edward Franklin Frazier, whose scholarship on similar areas was rewarded with a 1954 Ford Foundation grant for Howard and John Hope Franklin, whose extensive scholarship is judged as a continuation of the great works of Du Bois and Woodson. If the additional contributions of the countless students and graduates who led in the vast movements of transformation are too long for the scope of this recount, Stokley Carmichael's role might serve to illustrate the case. As an active leader in the Student Nonviolent Coordinating Committee (SNCC), he symbolized the depth in the reversal of negative images of Africa and Africaness championed by Africanist scholars of the previous century in the 1960s embracing of African culture, clothing, food, history, music, and spirituality with his bold proclamation that people of African descent did not have to wait to be judged by standards outside their culture, arguing that we will not wait for judgment—we are beautiful. He lived his radical convictions by standing for pan-Africanism and resettling in the continent.

One of the major outcomes of the community-engaged scholarship model of change undertaken by Howard has been the strong impact on African Studies as an indispensable instrument for waging battles against prejudice and dogmatism. Furthermore, knowledge of and in Africa that enriched humankind over the centuries was embraced as a major way of knowing and living that would be part of human knowledge and be of great worth for all humankind.

IN SUMMATION

The African World and global transformation are brought together by the example of Howard University as an institution that played a central role along the four major avenues of change: (1) through scholarship and partnership with other agents of change, Africa and the African World's contributions to civilizations, cultures and the wellbeing of all human societies have been established; (2) knowledge of the African world has been translated in terms of restoring its place in the global market place of ideas and paradigms. The town-gown model of engaging academia with the day-to-day concerns of people was employed to assist the alliance of political movements for democracy and liberty symbolized by the organization of support activities against Fascist Italy's invasion of Ethiopia, colonial and apartheid rules in the continent; (3) cultural revolutions. Reconceptualizing paradigms of race, identity, creativity, and community launched by Alain Locke's leadership of the Harlem Renaissance have been instrumental in redefining art, literature, folklore and poetry for the African World and all humanity as reflected by the creative ideas of Céesaire, Senghor, and Sartre and others; (4) closely related to the foregoing ideas and victories in the civil rights movement's crowning battle cry of "we shall overcome" that came to symbolize for the world the struggles of African Americans not only for social justice and equality before the law but for the total transformation of society.

We shall overcome, the battle cry of the civil rights movement, thus came to crown the struggles of African Americans for social justice and equality before the law for the total transformation of society. The Civil Rights Movement has often been cast as the quest confined to the goals of access to service and institutions. It was a visionary movement that embodied the synthesis of great heritages from African, Asian and European civilizations. The movement addressed the philosophical, moral and existential foundations of both industrial and nonindustrial societies. It sought to greatly expand the moral, legal, and political basis for human rights, justice and equality. Rooted in its African heritage of justice, the American experiences of democratic perseverance in the face of adversity and interactions with humanity's quest for meaning, it marked a significant paradigm shift in the universal search for viable answers for the human condition.

Its profound impact on America is illustrated by the revolutions it brought about in the economic and political institutions but also in the deeper way it transformed the social terms of dialogue, change, and growth. American society was transformed by its vision. Contrary to the efforts many observers made to cast it as the narrow preserve gained for African Americans, its mandates touched all aspects of society. Civil rights struggles for housing made it possible for disenfranchised groups to benefit from the laws spawned by its provisions. The quest for dignity and equality extended to numerous minority groups the disabled, women, and other social sectors. Its vision for serenity and humanity strengthened environmentalists, consumer groups and socially responsible movements. Its strategies of peace and nonviolence helped a violent world turn away from the paths of death and destruction. Almost all the nations of the world were influenced by the American Civil Rights Movement. "We Shall Overcome" being sung in the antinuclear movements in Europe, the anti-communist struggles in Tiananmen Square in Beijing and the Berlin Wall in Germany, Eastern Europe, the anti-Apartheid movement struggle in South Africa, and workers struggles in India and Latin America bear testimony to the global impact of the American Civil Rights Movement.

Howard University, with a notable place in history as an institution that helped redefine Africa and the African world as important actors in the past and future of humanity, is featured to underscore global transformations that have been made possible through the multiple ways the institution assisted in cementing the collective efforts leaders and heroic citizens transcending race, ethnicity, religion and narrow identities. In a paraphrased analogy of Edith Wharton's quotation, it accomplished this feat through both ways of spreading light: by serving as the candlelight itself and the mirror of enlightenment and public engagement.

NOTES

1. Quoted in William R. Scott, *The Son's of Sheba's Race: African Americans and the Italo-Ethiopian War, 1935–1941*. Bloomington and Indianapolis, Indiana University Press, 1993: 19.

2. Thomas Borstelmann, *The Cold War and the Color Line: American Race Relations in the Global Arena*. Cambridge, Massachusetts, Harvard University Press, 2001: 41.

3. Ibid, 28.

4. William R. Scott, 1993:50.

5. David L. Reed. "Rayford W. Logan: The Evolution of a Pan-African Protégé, 1921–1927." *Journal of Pan African Studies* 6, no. 8 (2014): 27–53.

6. Charlynn Spencer Pyne, Library of Congress Information Bulletin. http://www
.loc.gov/loc/lcib/94/9403/Woodson.html. Accessed 5-11-2009.

7. William M. Banks, *Black Intellectuals: Race and Responsibility in American Life.* New York, London, W.W. Norton & Company, 1996: 183–89.

8. Paul Tiyambe Zeleza, "The Academic Diaspora and Knowledge Production in and on Africa: What Role for CODESRIA?" in Thandika Mkandawire (ed.), *African Intellectuals: Rethinking Politics, Language, Gender and Development.* London / New York, Zed Books Ltd., 2005: 215–19.

9. Herschelle S. Challenor, "African Studies at Historically Black Colleges and Universities" in Cyril K. Daddieh and Jo Ellen Fail (eds.), *African Issues.* New Brunswick, NJ, African Studies Association Press, 2002: 24–26.

10. John Henrik Clarke, "African American Historians and the Reclaiming of African History" in Molefi Kete Asante and Kariamu Welsh Asante (eds.), *African Culture: The Rhythms of Unity.* Trenton, NJ, African World Press, Inc., 1990: 167.

11. Robert O. Collins and James M. Burns, *A History of Sub-Saharan Africa.* Cambridge, New York, Cambridge University Press, 2007: 378.

12. Edward A. Alpers and Allen F. Roberts, "What is African Studies? Some Reflections" in Cyril K. Daddieh and Jo Ellen Fair (eds.), *African Issues: Identifying New Directions for African Studies*, volume 30/2 Rutgers, New Brunswick, NJ, African Studies Association Press, 2002: 13.

13. Zeleza, in Mkandawire, 2005: 218–19.

REFERENCES

Alpers, Edward A., and Allen F. Roberts, "What is African Studies? Some Reflections" in Cyril K. Daddieh and Jo Ellen Fair (eds.), *African Issues: Identifying New Directions for African Studies*, volume 30/2 Rutgers, New Brunswick, NJ, African Studies Association Press, 2002: 13.

Banks, William M. *Black Intellectuals: Race and Responsibility in American Life.* New York, New York: W.W. Norton, 1996.

Borstelmann, Thomas. *The Cold War and the Color Line: American Race Relations in the Global Arena.* Cambridge, MA: Harvard University Press, 2001.

Challenor, Herschelle S. "African Studies at Historically Black Colleges and Universities" in Cyril K. Daddieh and Jo Ellen Fail (eds.), *African Issues.* New Brunswick, NJ, African Studies Association Press, 2002: 24–26.

Clarke, John Henrik. "African American Historians and the Reclaiming of African History" in Molefi Kete Asante and Kariamu Welsh Asante (eds.), *African Culture: The Rhythms of Unity.* Trenton, NJ, African World Press, Inc., 1990: 167.

Collins, Robert O., and James M. Burns, *A History of Sub-Saharan Africa.* Cambridge, Cambridge University Press, 2007: 378.Pyne, Charlynn Spencer. Library of Congress Information Bulletin. http://www.loc.gov/loc/lcib/94/9403/ Woodson.html. Accessed 5-11-2009.

Reed, David L. "Rayford W. Logan: The Evolution of a Pan-African Protégé, 1921–1927." *Journal of Pan African Studies* 6, no. 8 (2014): 27–53.

Scott, William R. *The Sons of Sheba's Race: African-Americans and the Italo-Ethiopian War, 1935–1941*. Bloomington, Indiana: Indiana University Press, 1993.

Zeleza, Paul Tiyambe. "The Academic Diaspora and Knowledge Production in and on Africa: What Role for CODESRIA?" in Thandika Mkandawire (ed.), *African Intellectuals: Rethinking Politics, Language, Gender and Development*. London / NY, Zed Books Ltd., 2005: 215–19.

Chapter 2

The Creation of a University

Dr. John Manuel Gandy and Virginia State University, 1914–1943

Oscar Williams

The success of Historically Black Colleges and Universities (HBCUs) can be attributed to numerous factors. One of them is the leadership that laid the groundwork for HBCUs to serve their students, faculty, and communities. Established during a time of intense racial segregation in America, the challenge was to provide quality education in a system designed to severely limit African Americans. In response, many leaders were able to guide their faculty and students through these difficult times to meet and exceed expectations. Among them is a lesser-known individual who was able to lead Virginia State University, an institution located twenty-five miles south of Richmond, Virginia, and provide the foundations that would enable it to succeed into the present: Dr. John Manuel Gandy. Coming of age during a difficult period in American history, he overcame odds to become a leader in higher education and set a path of success for Virginia State. In addition to being a college president, he led the following organizations: the Virginia Teachers Association, the National Association of Negro Land Grant Colleges, and the National Association of Teachers in Colored Schools.[1]

Gandy was born the fifth of thirteen children on October 31, 1870, outside Starkville, Mississippi, on Parish Farm in Oktibbeha County. His parents, Horace and Mary, were formerly enslaved African Americans who supported their family via sharecropping on various cotton plantations[2] Despite the circumstances, Gandy recalled that his parents were determined to make the best of their conditions and provide for their children. As a child, he was fascinated by his family's interracial heritage. He later learned of his father being

29

the product of Sarah, an enslaved woman, and Ed Gandy, an Irish slaveholder who migrated to America in the 1830s. Gandy credits his grandmother for being a strong influence in his life with her kindness and attention.[3]

Gandy's recollections reveal the hardships and perils of growing up African American in Mississippi in the late 1800s. He recounts an incident where he escaped being killed by a white man while both were watering their horses at a creek. Sensing danger, he quickly left the creek and rode away while the man was shooting at him. Gandy also acknowledges that his family left Mississippi for Oklahoma in 1890 due to economic hardships tied to sharecropping and protecting their daughters from "illicit relationships between white men and Negro women." The family settled in Sallisaw, Oklahoma where they found other African Americans who migrated for the same reasons.[4]

Despite the challenges, Gandy proceeded to embark on a quest to fulfill his education. Excelling in his academics, he attended Jackson College (now Jackson State University) during the time his family migrated to Oklahoma. After graduation, he reunited with his family and taught grade school while planning his next endeavor. He seriously underwent an effort to go to Liberia with a group from his community. When the group arrived in New York City for their first leg of the trip, funds had disappeared for the project. Gandy then took various odd jobs before resuming his pursuit of education at Oberlin College in 1892.[5] He attended for two years before a lack of funds forced him to consider another institution. He tried to attend Colgate University, but a lack of funds cut the attempt short. Fellow students who came to know the young scholar collected funds to enable him to attend Fisk University in 1894.[6]

During his senior year in 1898, he served as a university representative at a YMCA conference at Shaw University in Raleigh, North Carolina, where he was fortunate to meet James Hugo Johnston, President of Virginia Normal and Collegiate Institute (now Virginia State University). Impressed by Gandy, Johnston offered him a position to become a professor of Latin and Greek. He initially recommended a classmate for the position due to his acceptance of a job offer working at a YMCA in New Haven Connecticut. After his arrival, he began to have second thoughts and decided to contact Johnston again to see if the position was still available. The president replied it was and Gandy eagerly accepted.[7]

At the time of his arrival, Virginia State was in its sixteenth year of existence. Founded in 1882, the institution, despite successfully completing its mission of providing higher education and a teaching force for African Americans, faced opposition from white lawmakers who either wanted the curriculum changed to industrial education or eliminated. One delegate who was promoted to the school board commented in 1885 that "Negro scholars in luxuriously equipped quarters and lecture rooms" learning Latin, Greek, and Chemistry was "nonsense" that needed to stop.[8] Favoring an industrial education curriculum similar to Hampton and Tuskegee Institutes, the Virginia State Legislature in 1902 proposed to establish a new charter to eliminate the collegiate curriculum and rename the school Virginia Normal and Industrial Institute, with the all-white Board of Visitors' approval.[9]

Meanwhile, Gandy settled into his position and became involved with affairs on and off campus. Considered a Professor of Education after the 1902 curriculum change, he immediately put his efforts into improving the school and expanding its services into the community. He became involved in various campus activities, committees, and organizing a night school for the community. In 1907, he and other leaders established the School Improvement League. Recognizing the need for improved education for African Americans in the state, he encouraged President Johnston to head the organization and gained the statewide support of teachers. The league called for improvements in school infrastructure, self-help, support for improved health for African American communities, the Good Roads Movement, and greater access to resources to improve education in Virginia.[10]

Gandy was instrumental in another state organization that was instrumental in improving education for African Americans. In 1903, he became president of the Virginia Teachers Association. Founded in 1887 at Virginia State, the organization was the sole organization for African American teachers before it was integrated during the 1960s. Under his leadership, the organization expanded rapidly, as he launched an ambitious program that promoted the following six points:

1. Organize the counties, cities, and districts into local associations to deal with educational problems peculiar to the special communities.
2. Establish a research bureau to collect and conserve information regarding the Negro in Virginia.
3. Organize and promote a teachers' agency to bring the teacher and the position together.
4. Establish a teacher recruiting week to relieve the teachers' shortage and to direct the attention of more of the best graduates of the high schools to prepare for the field of teaching.
5. Establish a lecture bureau to make available for educational mass meetings and institutes.
6. Promote each year a vocational guidance program to direct the attention of the students of the graduating classes of the high schools to the vocations open to the necessity of making the choice early of the occupations they will enter, and to furnish counsel to those who need it in the selection of a vocation.

Additionally, he recommended the publication of a bulletin for teachers to be informed of the various issues, events, progress, and solutions regarding African American students in Virginia. Under his two terms as president (1903–1906 and 1924–1932), the organization focused on these points and strove to provide the best situation possible for students and teachers. After his last term, the organization showed its gratitude by funding a trip to Europe for Gandy.[11] While keeping busy with his professional career, he took time to develop a life for himself. During his second year at Virginia State, he met Carrie Brown, a teacher who attended the institution's summer school. The two quickly became fond of each other and the friendship bloomed into a relationship. In 1901, Gandy proposed marriage to Brown, and in July, they became husband and wife. The couple had four children, who went on to careers in medicine, education, and administration.[12] In 1914, Gandy's life took a professional turn as he was appointed acting president when the president suffered a heart attack. After his passing on Easter Sunday, the Board of Visitors immediately named Gandy president of Virginia State, beginning a twenty-nine-year tenure in the position.[13] The choice of Gandy also attracted the attention of the NAACP magazine *The Crisis* in its November edition as the Man of the Month. Highlighting his extensive career at the institution and the state, The article concluded with the following statement: "President Gandy's broad formal preparation, extensive experience, full knowledge of educational conditions and needs of Virginia, remarkable constructive ability, and a large following among all classes of people of the state combined to make his selection the fill of the place to which he has been called a happy one."[14]

Settling into the presidency, Gandy immediately set out to improve the institution by acquiring additional funds for expansion. During the first six years of his presidency, there were key developments that would contribute to the school's growth. In 1917, Virginia State gained additional federal funds via the Smith-Hughes Act, which called for more support for schools specializing in vocational education. The school also constructed an athletic field, now known as Rogers Stadium, for football and baseball. The previous year, additional land was purchased from a railroad that passed by the campus, enabling agriculture and mechanics to expand and erect several buildings.[15] The third and most important factor was Virginia State being designated as the land grant college for African Americans in the state. Before this, Hampton University, a private institution, was given the title in 1872. Gandy asserted that because of the Morrill Land Act of 1890, which identified land grant schools for African Americans, the title should be given to the school. To ensure passage, he appealed to the Governor of Virginia and other government officials for assistance. Gaining their support, a bill was presented before the state legislature to award the land grant title to Virginia State. After much debate, the bill passed and in 1920, the institution was officially labeled the land grant college in Virginia for African Americans.[16]

After the land grant title campaign, he turned his attention to the restoration of the college curriculum. Gandy as well as other educators never abandoned the goal of becoming a college again. Now armed with greater access to federal resources and an expanded curriculum, in his report to the Board of Visitors, he cited several factors to support restoration. He noted that several Southern states had restored college curriculums for Negro Land Grant Colleges and that Virginia was the only state that had failed to do so. He additionally stated that because Virginia State did not have a college curriculum, its graduates were denied jobs because of the lack of a college degree. He concluded by stating, "Our state should not deny the Negro people what the times demand and what they so richly deserve. To make ourselves clear, we are asking for a teacher's college not a college of the Arts and Sciences . . . all the normal schools for white girls can carry courses leading to degrees in some phase of education. We feel that this should not be denied to this institution.[17] The following year, a four-year college course was reestablished after a twenty-one-year absence.

To meet the demands of the curriculum, Gandy revived a program called the Reading Circle. Designed to enhance the faculty's knowledge and training, he encouraged them to pursue advanced degrees and attend out-of-state institutions such as Columbia Teachers College, University of Chicago, University of Pennsylvania, Cornell University, University of Michigan, Ohio State University, and other institutions that would accept African Americans for graduate study. Gandy took to heart his own advice and attended Illinois Wesleyan University for a PhD, as well as Columbia, and Cornell for summer school. This yielded distinguished faculty such as Luther P. Jackson, a Professor of History who received his master's and PhD respectively from Columbia and Chicago. He enjoyed a distinguished career as a pioneer scholar of African American History in Virginia.[18]

In the 1930s, Virginia State experienced growth as the campus expanded to a 116-acres campus with several new buildings such as a new gymnasium, dormitories for men and women, a physical plant, a library, an administration building that replaced the first structure built in the 1880s, and cottages for faculty and staff. In 1930, the school's name was changed to Virginia State College for Negroes, and the curriculum was updated to include graduate courses in 1937. Accompanying this expansion was a brief upheaval in the Spring of 1934 when the student body went on strike. In the 1920s, schools such as Howard and Hampton experienced student strikes that targeted practices and rules that seemed out of step with the student body. In the case of Virginia State, the spark that initiated the strike was a rule that stated that if a student returned from Easter break late, their grades would be lowered. In

May, the students drafted a list of demands and refused to attend class until there was a resolution. In response, Gandy sent a memo to the students stating that he would be willing to hear their grievances with the Executive Council if they return to class by a certain day and time. Those who refused would be suspended. The strike ended after four days and students returned to classes, but twenty-eight students were dismissed, and one professor was fired for supporting the students. Some saw the action as heavy-handed, while others supported it. Eventually, there was a compromise between the students and the administration on agreeing that male and female students could socialize on campus at designated places until a certain time.[19]

Gandy found himself at a crossroads in 1940. During his twenty-sixth year as president, he had to take a leave of absence due to declining health. Virginia State's business manager, Luther Foster, served while he was recuperating. Returning to the position after three months, he resumed his position and kept busy with his duties. At age seventy-two, Gandy decided it was time to step down and let younger leadership assume the presidency. In 1943, his retirement was made official and Foster was appointed president, ending a twenty-nine-year tenure, the longest any president has served at Virginia State. He continued to be involved in community and school affairs until his passing in 1947. To recognize his contributions, the Virginia State Legislature ordered all African American schools closed on the day of his service. Six years later, a new academic building was named in honor of him.[20] More than a hundred years after the college curriculum was restored, present-day Virginia State has six colleges, among them exist thirty-six undergraduate degree programs, sixteen graduate degree programs, two doctoral degree programs, and eight certificate programs.[21] Although many can be credited with the university's success, the efforts of Gandy cannot be overlooked. The author hopes that this discussion will generate more interest in the life of this lesser-known but important figure in the history of HBCUs.

NOTES

1. Biography of John Manuel Gandy, from the John Manuel Gandy Papers, Special Collections, Johnston Memorial Library; Petersburg, Virginia.

2. Gandy, John Manuel, *The Life and Times of John Manuel Gandy* (unpublished manuscript), Gandy Papers, 1.

3. Ibid, 2–3.

4. Ibid., 11–12; 17.

5. Ibid, 22–23.

6. Ibid., 40.

7. Ibid., 52–53.

8. Toppin, Edgar A., *Loyal Sons and Daughters, Virginia State University, 1882–1992, A Pictorial History*; Norfolk, Va., Pictorial Heritage Publishers Company, 1992, 53.

9. Ibid., 54–55.

10. Ibid, 91–94; Picott, J. Rupert, *History of the Virginia Teachers Association*; Washington, D.C., National Teachers Association, 1975; 54–55.

11. Picott, 47–48, 90–91.

12. John Manuel Gandy, 92–93.

13. Ibid., 107–108.

14. "A College President," *The Crisis*, November 1914, 12.

15. Gandy, 143; Toppin, 59.

16. Gandy, 149.

17. Toppin, 77.

18. Ibid, 59; Jeffreys, Richard, Dissertation, "A History of Virginia State College for Negroes Ettrick, Virginia," University of Michigan, 1937, 175.

19. "Cossacks Rule Virginia Campus," *Baltimore Afro American*, June 2, 1934; Letter from John M. Gandy to Student Body; Response from Executive Committee to Student Body, Gandy Papers.

20. Two noted Virginia and Carolina Educators Die, Norfolk Journal and Guide, October 11, 1947 (the other was James E Shepard, President, and founder of North Carolina Central University), 1; John Manuel Gandy Hall Dedicated in Petersburg, Norfolk Journal and Guide, June 4, 1953, 7.

21. About VSU, Virginia State University, https://www.vsu.edu/about/index.php.

REFERENCES

"A College President," *The Crisis*, November 1914, 12. https://www.marxists.org/history/usa/workers/civil-rights/crisis/1100-crisis-v09n01-w049.pdf Accessed May 30, 2022

Biography of John Manuel Gandy, from the John Manuel Gandy Papers, Special Collections, Johnston Memorial Library; Petersburg, Virginia.

"Cossacks Rule Virginia Campus," *Baltimore Afro American*, June 2, 1934

Gandy, John Manuel, *The Life and Times of John Manuel Gandy* (unpublished manuscript), Gandy Papers, 1.

Jeffreys, Richard, Dissertation, "A History of Virginia State College for Negroes Ettrick, Virginia," University of Michigan, 1937, 175.

Norfolk Journal and Guide, October 11, 1947.

Norfolk Journal and Guide, June 4, 1953, 7.

Picott, J. Rupert, History of the Virginia Teachers Association; Washington, D.C., National Teachers Association, 1975; 54–55.

Toppin, Edgar A., Loyal Sons and Daughters, Virginia State University, 1882–1992, A Pictorial History; Norfolk, Va., Pictorial Heritage Publishers Company, 1992, pp. 53.

Chapter 3

"The Struggle Staggers Us"

The Institute for the Study of the History, Life, and Culture of Black People at Jackson State, 1968–1979

Rico Devara Chapman and D. Caleb Smith

INTRODUCTION

The mid-sixties began to see a shift from nonviolent direct action to a more aggressive display of resistance. There were countless high-profile murders of civil rights activists in the mid-sixties. Medgar Evers in 1963, Goodman, Chaney, and Schwerner in 1964, Malcolm X in 1965, and Martin Luther King Jr., later in 1968. There were countless others, locally in Mississippi and across the United States. In 1965, Malcolm X, who had become a central figure in calling for self-defense was assassinated in the Audubon Ballroom in Harlem. Less than two months prior, SNCC organizers working in Mississippi had taken some McComb youth to hear him speak. The Meredith March followed in 1966. James Meredith, who enrolled at the University of Mississippi as the first African American student in 1962, started a one-man walk from Memphis to Jackson. He was shot along the way, prompting other civil rights leaders, including Martin Luther KingJr., and Stokely Carmichael to complete the journey. It was during this moment that the slogan "Black Power" began to take center stage. The following year, in 1967, local Jackson youth activist, Benjamin Brown was killed only a few blocks from the JSC campus by police; and Martin Luther King Jr., the most well-known civil rights leader and proponent of nonviolence was assassinated in 1968. His death spurred urban riots throughout major cities in the U.S. and young people were now seriously questioning the practicality of nonviolence. Black college campuses were becoming sites of contestation and expressions of Black assertiveness. Students were wearing Afros, and African dress and exploring ideas of Black self-empowerment. This self-empowerment spirit led Black students to demand that university officials increase the minority population at predominantly white institutions and establish Black studies departments and programs that offered more courses on the Black experience. The establishment of Black studies departments and programs often came as a result of student protests. While students were protesting for Black studies at predominantly white colleges and universities, this was not the case at an HBCU located in the heart of the deep south in Jackson, Mississippi. It was quite the opposite. It was a joint effort by faculty and administration to spearhead one of the first Black studies programs in the country at Jackson State College.

HBCU STUDENT ACTIVISM IN MISSISSIPPI

Student activism at HBCUs has a long history in Mississippi. As early as February 1957 At Mississippi Vocational College, now Mississippi Valley State University, students started a boycott to create a Student Government Association "marking the first large-scale disruptive event at a black college in Mississippi during the mid-twentieth century."[1] The following month Alcorn A & M College students boycotted classes over inflammatory remarks made by the minister and history instructor Clennon King.[2] The 1960s leading up to the founding of the Institute for the Study of the History, Life, and Culture of Black People (Black Studies Institute) at Jackson State College (JSC) was one of the most turbulent eras in US history. The modern civil rights movement was garnering national attention, and white supremacists were ramping up their efforts to thwart the growing momentum of the civil rights movement in Mississippi. The sixties began with college students challenging Jim Crow segregation through nonviolent direct action in Jackson, Mississippi.

Tougaloo College, located just north of the capital city of Jackson, served as a haven for civil rights workers by providing meeting space and housing. The President of Tougaloo, Dr. Adam D. Beittel, was sympathetic to the plight of students and supportive of movement activities. Tougaloo students formed the Tougaloo Movement to confront racist practices and policies head-on. The campus was home to "the most politically involved faculty of any college in Mississippi."[3] On 27 March 1961, nine students from Tougaloo attempted to integrate the whites-only Jackson Municipal Library by staging a read-in. The students were arrested and spent the night in jail. The read-in and their arrests attracted media attention, and the JSC Student Government Association came out in support of the Tougaloo Nine by marching to the city jail. The infamous read-in ultimately resulted in the desegregation of the Jackson Public Library. Jackson State students showed their support by mobilizing hundreds of students on campus in protests. The JSC students were attacked by police with tear gas and dogs, and, for their courage, the SGA was revoked by the Reddix administration. Later, Tougaloo students attempted to desegregate a Woolworth whites-only lunch counter in March 1963, gaining national attention with the symbolic photo of students with bloodied faces along with the added condiments of ketchup, mustard, and salt. Tougaloo's civil rights activity on the part of its progressive student body and supportive faculty and administration was due in part to its standing as a private college.

Campbell College was also a private historically Black college located in close proximity to Jackson State College, literally across the street from the JSC campus. Before being appropriated by the state of Mississippi in 1964, Campbell College hosted civil rights events, posted notices of boycotts on its campus, and like Tougaloo, had a sympathetic administration. Campbell College also invited McComb high school students who were expelled due to a protest march to enroll at Campbell. In 1960, the NAACP Youth Councils, consisting of students from Tougaloo, JSC, Campbell College, and local Black high schools, helped to bring attention to the Easter boycott organized by Medgar Evers and Charles Jones, dean of religion at Campbell College. The boycott did not prevent as many shoppers as hoped for; however, students did get hands-on experience in organizing a nonviolent direct action protest. As a recourse, the clandestine Mississippi Improvement Association of Students (MIAS), was founded consisting of mostly JSC students. The following month Jackson State students who were members of the intercollegiate NAACP chapter staged a bus sit-in on April 19, 1961. Shortly thereafter, Campbell students and NAACP youth members sat in at the Jackson Zoo, where they were promptly arrested for breach of the peace. Campbell College's activism and proximity to JSC and downtown Jackson were the major reasons for its seizure by the state.

Jackson State College, unlike Tougaloo and Campbell, was a public institution, and its president at the time, Jacob L. Reddix, was beholden to the wishes of the paternalistic State College Board, which was itself segregated and had a special committee to deal with the concerns of the "Negro" colleges called the Special Education Committee.[4] JSC students did, however, participate in the movement and made their grievances known. President Reddix had all but abolished student government at Jackson State because it instigated student civil rights demonstrations. During the civil rights struggle, the College Board as well as the governor's office exerted extreme pressure on the presidents of the state colleges to keep down any pro-civil rights demonstrations. At the Black colleges, the presidents knew that if civil rights demonstrations were not quickly suppressed, their jobs would be at stake.[5] Dr. John A. Peoples, a young protégé of Reddix, however, much more progressive and sympathetic to student issues of the day, took the helm at JSC on March 8, 1967. As early as 1948–1950, while John A. Peoples was a student at Jackson State, he had been one of the activists in a secret interracial movement for educational change consisting of college students from Jackson College, Mississippi State University, and the University of Mississippi. They had meetings at Jackson State and Mississippi State and pledged to work in the state for racial justice through education.[6] One of his first moves as the new campus leader was to reestablish the student government association, which had been disbanded by Reddix. In a matter of months, he was faced with increased campus disturbances and violence perpetrated by local police.

In May 1967, the racial tension came to a head when local youth activist Benjamin Brown was killed by police near campus. It happened after two days of unrest, known as the "Riot of 1967," on the campus that culminated in an SNCC-led march. Police came to the campus to break up the march firing live ammunition and tear gas, leading to the death of Brown. The following year students would revolt in frustration over the killing of Dr. Martin Luther King Jr. in April 1968, stoning cars of white passersby going to and fro on John Roy Lynch Street, which ran through the Jackson State campus. The first large student disturbance of People's administration was precipitated by J. R. Lynch Street traffic, which was a contributing factor in all others that occurred during People's tenure at JSU. In April 1969, a conflict between Jackson State male students and corner boys ended with stone-throwing directed at passing white motorists prompting Thompson's Tank to come put down the disturbance.[7] The street bordered Jackson State College to the South and Campbell College to the North. Thus, J. R. Lynch Street became a troublesome bisector of the campus at a time when African-descended peoples were asserting themselves all over the nation, and Black students had become the cutting edge of momentous change.[8] Student unrest would continue as students were becoming more conscious of their role as social change agents.

The location of JSC gave students exposure to activists from SNCC, CORE, SCLC, and the NAACP which was essential in introducing them to the movement. The Council of Federated Organizations (COFO) founded in 1961 by Aaron Henry and Bob Moses served as an umbrella organization for local and national civil rights organizations operating in Mississippi, such as the NAACP, CORE, SNCC, and the SCLC. Its headquarters were located on J. R. Lynch Street, only a few blocks from the JSC campus, and was instrumental in organizing the 1963 Freedom Vote mock election and Freedom Summer in 1964. Medgar Evers, field secretary for the National Association for the Advancement of Colored People (NAACP), whose office sat on the edge of campus on J. R. Lynch Street, often mentored students from Jackson State College as well as Tougaloo. He was killed in front of his home by the white supremacist Citizen Council member Byron de la Beckwith in 1963. Students were harassed and arrested during the mass funeral procession which also started on J. R. Lynch Street.

Mississippi, during the mid-sixties, was a hotbed for civil rights struggles, and the Black college campuses in the state were no exception. The efficacious call for Black Power was made by Willie Ricks a.k.a. Mukasa Dada and Stokely Carmichael a.k.a. Kwame Ture in 1966 in Greenwood, Mississippi. SNCC had been working in Mississippi for over five years by now and had established a generous support network from Black Mississippians. The call came after the one-man "March Against Fear" from Memphis, Tennessee, to Jackson, Mississippi, started by James Meredith. On the second day of the march, Meredith was shot by snipers and had to be taken to the hospital. As Carmichael, Martin Luther King Jr., and others came to Meredith's aid by completing the march, the debate between King and Carmichael over nonviolence as a strategy or principle would take center stage. When the march reached Greenwood, Carmichael was arrested for the twenty-seventh time and upon his release, he made a speech to the crowd in Greenwood calling for Black Power. The speech was exhilarating and the crowd, comprised of mostly young people, was captivated by his message. June 16, 1966, call for Black Power marked a turning point in the movement which subsequently led indirectly to the establishment of Black studies institutes, programs, and departments at predominantly white institutions and HBCUs across the United States. Carmichael spoke to students on the JSC campus in 1965, before the much-publicized call for Black Power in Greenwood, Mississippi. The slogan would come to have a major impact on the civil rights movement that was now taking a more radical turn culminating in the Black Power Movement. Many youths, particularly students, had become frustrated with the strategy of nonviolence and sought now to engage directly with the powers that be. These conditions, along with the hiring of Dr. John A. Peoples as president, helped set the tone for the emergence and founding of the Institute for the Study of the History, Culture, and Life of Black People at Jackson State College.

THE ESTABLISHMENT OF THE INSTITUTE FOR
THE STUDY, HISTORY, LIFE, AND CULTURE
OF BLACK PEOPLE AT JACKSON STATE

At a time when Black studies programs were being established throughout the country as a result of student protests at white colleges and universities,

JSC was unique in that it was a historically Black college with a Black studies program. Historically Black Colleges and Universities (HBCU), which have too often followed a Eurocentric curriculum, have not been leaders in establishing most Black studies programs. The South, with the highest number of Black higher-education institutions and the greatest population of African Americans, has the smallest number of Black studies programs. The founding of the Institute for the Study, History, Life, and Culture of Black People is significant in that it was one of the first Black Studies programs in the country, particularly at an HBCU, established without demand by protesting students, although students did request it.[9] The Black Studies Institute addressed the many issues college students were facing in the 1960s, especially the "widespread ignorance on the part of both black and white youth concerning the history and cultural contributions of black people."[10]

The Black Institute, as it became known, was the vision of both Dr. Margaret Walker Alexander, Professor of English at Jackson State, and Dr. John A. Peoples, the school's president from 1967 to 1984, after receiving multiple requests from Jackson State's students. Dr. Alexander enthusiastically spearheaded the program and thoughtfully developed its curriculum and selected the faculty. She was born July 7, 1915, in Birmingham, Alabama, Margaret Abigail Walker would grow up to become a mother, educator, artist, writer, and internationally honored intellectual.[11] Known to her students and the world of literature as simply Margaret Walker, Margaret Walker Alexander received her BA from Northwestern University (Illinois) and her MA from the University of Iowa in 1940.[12] Despite marriage, having four children between 1943–1954, Alexander received her PhD from the University of Iowa in 1965.[13] Much of Alexander's adult life revolved around literature and her teaching responsibilities at various institutions.[14] Alexander published five books of poetry—*For My People* (1942), *Prophets for a New Day* (1970), *October Journey* (1973), *For Farish Street Green* (1986), and *This Is My Century* (1988).[15] In addition to poetry, she wrote a monumental historical novel titled *Jubilee* (1966), which details the life of her enslaved grandmother.

The Black Studies Institute was founded to initiate a pedagogical approach to enhancing the "self-concept for the Negro student and thus aid in the development of the human personality," and also to aid white students in broadening their perspective of the multiracial world in which they live.[16] From Alexander's perspective, these programs were essential in re-educating the Black students and the surrounding community. The educational structure of the Institute was an "inter-departmental, inter-disciplinary program within the regular college curriculum. Courses were developed under the categories of History, Literature, Art, Music, Physical Education, Sociology, Cultural Anthropology, Physical Anthropology, Psychology, Religion, Philosophy, and Science. Very few HBCUs at the time were offering African American studies courses, yet white colleges were. These institutions were scrutinized and placed under a lot of pressure from students, both Black and white, to establish programs for the study of African American life and history. HBCUs had to react by providing the education that met the standards of a globalizing nation. Jackson State students and professors recognized that "nowhere is this more necessary than on the predominantly Negro College campus."[17]

Dr. Alexander formed the Black Institute in less than one year. She called on fellow Jackson State faculty members from various disciplines to join her in teaching the African and African American centered classes. The committee helped to initiate and teach the courses that began in the Fall semester of 1968. The Institute's advisory committee consisted of both faculty and students. They were:

Dr. Margaret Walker Alexander, Chairman
Mr. Estus Smith
Dr. Samuel Warren
Mr. Lawrence Jones
Dr. Dollye Robinson
Dr. John Uzodinma
Mrs. E. Lipscomb
Mr. Alvin Benson
Dr. John A. Peoples, Ex-Officio
Dean Haskell Bingham
Dean W. Greenfield, Ex-Officio
Miss Lorraine Banks, student
Mr. James Johnson, student[18]

In its beginning stages, the Institute served as a clearinghouse for courses offered in each academic department. Student enrollment was fairly high yet varied from class to class according to the 1969 annual Progress Report. The strength and weaknesses of the programs were closely evaluated through surveys done by the committee and staff members. Feedback from the students was taken very seriously in progressing the Institute's impact. Students also took interest in the development of the program; some even requested a minor in the Institute Curriculum.[19] According to the official memo that established the Institute, it was designed as "an inter-departmental, inter-disciplinary, and inter-cultural program within the regular college curriculum of Jackson State College. The inherent philosophy [being] one of racial inclusion rather than exclusion and the courses designed to enrich the students' general knowledge with specific information concerning the heritage, culture, and life of all

Black people."[20] The courses offered for the first year of the Institute during the 1968–1969 academic year were:

History of Africa-Pre-Colonial Era
Contemporary African History
The Black Man in American History,
The History of Black America From 1915 Until the Present
The Black Man in American Literature From Colonial Days Until the Present
Survey of Literature by Black Authors: Emphasis on Poetry and Drama from Colonial Times to the Present
Survey of Literature by Black Authors
The Musical Culture of Black Americans: Its Roots, Its Development, and Its Influences
The Contribution of Black Americans to Western Music
Folk Music of Black People in the United States
The History and Appreciation of the World Contributions of Black People to Art
Influence of African Sculpture on Modern Art
The Artistic Contributions of Black Americans to Art, and
Relationships of Africa, West Indian, and Black American Art[21]

To administer the courses and other daily functions of the Institute for the 1968–1969 academic year, the Institute consisted of seven teachers, one secretary, one student assistant, and a director. There were three hundred students enrolled in the first six classes during the first quarter, with a slight decline in the winter due to the loss of a basic history course. The report stated that the music courses had not attracted as many students as the other institute courses and the enrollment remained very small throughout the year. A positive is that students began requesting a minor in the Institute curriculum and the report thought that "a major [was] an obvious possibility in the very near future."[22] The report surveyed thirty-eight students about their experience and "all agreed that the program is good and that they have learned much," however, "many felt that the Institute needed broadening to encompass more students and involve them on all levels."[23] Generally, the administration and faculty met requests from the students. A student suggested to Dr. Peoples that Charles Evers, NAACP field secretary, and brother of the late Medgar Evers, speak at the college for Black History week. This turned out to be one of the Institute's first programs. Although Dr. Peoples was uncertain about inviting such a radical activist to the campus, Dr. Alexander supported the student's request.[24]

The report also lauds the success of its cocurricular program of cultural events. It speaks of frequent radio broadcasts and telecasts over local stations with interviews, spot announcements, and newscasts publicized all over Mississippi and the advertisement nationally through brochures and newspaper publicity. During the first year of its founding, there were four public forums with Charles Evers, Juanita Williamson, Dr. Blyden Jackson, and Dr. Lawrence Reddick and three convocation presentations by Dr. John Eubanks, Dean Phillip G. Hubbard, and Dr. Richard Barksdale. Art exhibits and visiting artists included Dr. John Biggers, Mrs. Margaret Burroughs, and Alice Walker was a Writer-in-Residence. Staff members attended five conferences: Summer Workshop at Southern University, August 1968; Southern Historical Association, New Orleans, 6–9 November 1968; 53rd Anniversary Meeting of the Association for the Study of Negro History and Life, New York City, 3–4 Oct 1968; Conference on African & African-American Studies, Atlanta University, 5–7 Dec 1968; and the Human Relations Conference of the National Education Association, Washington, DC, 19–21 February 1969. The report listed recommendations for the 1969–1970 academic year. They were more courses, more teachers in order to involve more students in a greater number of courses and free the director for many more tasks that need doing, more national involvement for exampleA National Evaluative Conference, Black Theatre, offer a Minor in the Institute, beginning of a Regional Museum.[25] The National Evaluative on Black Studies Conference held in 1971 was groundbreaking at the time and included luminaries in the field of Black Studies, such as C. Eric Lincoln, St. Clair Drake, John Henrik Clark, Nikki Giovanni, Alex Haley, Leonard Jeffries, Vincent Harding, and others.[26]

Under Dr. Alexander's direction, the Institute provided frequent quality programs that engaged students and faculty from every learning segment. According to the 1971–1972 Annual Report, they held a student-led program to focus on "the needs and challenges of Blackness, the program was titled 'Relevant Issues in Black Studies,' and conducted by students taking the Institute classes." The topics discussed were, "Black Studies and the College Student," "Black Studies and the College Teacher," "Black Studies and the Public Education," and "Black Studies and the Community."[27] Some of history's greatest luminaries graced the campus of Jackson State thanks to Dr. Margaret Walker Alexander. Artists, writers, scholars, and poets frequented the campus; not only did they lecture at cocurricular programs, but some also spent time in the classrooms working directly with students and professors. Dr. Lawrence Jones, Chair of the Art Department, readily accepted artists such as Margaret Burroughs and John Biggers—who were also college professors, into his classes. Art was a substantial part of the institute's programs. Jackson State also hosted exhibits by master artists such as Jacob Lawrence and Elizabeth Catlett. Dr. Margaret Walker Alexander, in her own right, was a prolific poet and novelist in the Black Arts Movement.

When focusing specifically on the Black Studies Institute at Jackson State, it is evident that Alexander's efforts bred a substantial level of Black consciousness on the campus of Jackson State, but like many Black Studies programs created during the later 1960s and 1970s, financial burdens were evident throughout the process. The Ford Foundation and the National Endowment for the Humanities would prove to be a great assistance for the new Black Studies at JSC. In August of 1970, the Ford Foundation awarded the Black Studies Institute $23,000 to support the 1970–1971 academic school year.[28] After the five-year mark of the institute's establishment, Alexander began to advocate for even more money. In a 1973 letter to Benjamin Payton, director of minority affairs for the Ford Foundation, Alexander asks that the Ford Foundation award $150,000 to carry the Black Studies Institute through the next five years.[29] Within the letter, Alexander explains that the institute has been tentatively promised $10,000 from the National Endowment for the Humanities (NEH) if funds can be found to match. Funding would be a major declining factor in the institute because Jackson State as a whole was not thriving financially. However, various organizations would provide financial assistance in order for Alexander's Institute to survive.

Dr. Alexander's vision for celebrating African American art and culture was highly evident. Annual convocations, such as Dr. Martin Luther King Jr.'s birthday commemoration and the annual Black Arts Festival were highlights on the institution's calendar. Students were actively engaged in plays, musicals, and performances of all kinds. One of Dr. Alexander's most notable events was the Phillis Wheatley Poetry Festival in November of 1973. Twenty well accomplished African American women poets were at Jackson State for four days, engaging in creative performances, recitals, panel discussions and classroom visits. Poets included: Gwendolyn Brooks, Nikki Giovanni, June Jordan, Alice Walker, Audre Lorde, Mari Evans, Sarah Fabio, Margaret Danner, Naomi Madgett, Johari Amini, Marion Alexander, Sonia Sanchez, Julia Peters, Linda Bragg, Malaika Wangara, Carolyn Rodgers, Lucille Clifton, Gloria Oden, Carol Gregory Clemons, and a host of others. Broadway actress Vinie Burrows also put on a one-woman show about the life of Phillis Wheatley. A critical discussion regarding the topic of Wheatley and contemporary poetry was also held during the festival; notable women such as Doris Saunders, Ida Lewis, Paula Giddings, Dorothy B. Porter, and Margaret Burroughs, along with Dr. Alexander, took part in this panel. While under the direction of Dr. Alexander from 1968 to 1979 the institute grew and evolved in many ways to address the cultural and educational needs of an ever-changing American society. In her later years as director, Dr. Alexander brought in colleges and fellow archivists at other HBCUs like Dorothy

Porter Wesley from Howard University, Gean Hutson, Chief Archivist from the Schomburg; Ann Allen Shockley and Jessie Smith, both archivists at Spelman. After she retired in 1979, the Black Institute continued its growth and founding principles to provide high-quality cultural programs, and to archive and celebrate African American history and creativity.

Dr. Alferdteen Brown Harrison was hand-selected by Dr. Alexander to carry the Institute into its next phase—a cultural archive for African American history and literature. Margaret Walker Alexander was an avid note-taker and was encouraged by her father at a young age to save her journals. This she did, and later donated them all to Jackson State. The Black Institute relocated from its one-room office in Dansby Hall, to Ayer Hall, Jackson State's oldest historic building. The Institute's name was changed to the Margaret Walker National Research Center and began focusing on historic preservation and collecting manuscripts. During Harrison's tenure as director of the Institute, Ayer Hall would undergo major efforts to preserve infrastructure. During the 1980s, the Institute would receive more than $200,000 for the preservation of projects from the National Endowment for Humanities and the National Historical Publications and Records Commission.[30] During the 1990s restoration of Ayer Hall became an even higher priority. In 1992, the Mississippi Legislature appropriated $2 million for the restoration of Ayer Hall. Four years later actual restoration began.[31] During Phase I of restoration, an exhibition of Jacob Lawrence was developed. Immense funding would depict the latter portion of the 1990s. From 1995 to 1999, the Margaret Walker National Research Center would receive $600,000 in total aid.[32] In 2000, the personal and literary papers of Margaret Walker Alexander were opened for scholarly use. Within the first five years of the new millennium, the Margaret Walker National Research Center would collect more than $500,000 for the restoration of Ayer Hall.[33] In 2004, Title III funding would add an oral historian position to the research center.[34]

The archival collection includes the manuscripts of Margaret Walker Alexander, photographs, and belongings of the former U.S. Secretary of Education and Interim President of Jackson State University, Roderick Paige. Other manuscripts include Frankye Adams-Johnson's Black Panther Party Collection, Gladys Noel Bate's scrapbook, and the papers of J. R. Chambliss and Rabbi Philip Posner, just to name a few. Other items in the collection include the photography collection of Levi J. Rowan, the first alumnus to become president of Alcorn College, and paintings and photos by Paul Campbell, student of the late Lawrence Jones, chair of Jackson State's art department. Ayer Hall also functions as a museum that exhibits its permanent collections and traveling exhibits.

The Margaret Walker Center (MWC) continues to progress. In 2011 the Center's staff traveled to several colleges, museums, archives, and cultural centers that were similar to MWC to assess the feasibility of a new facility for the MWC. The feasibility study and proposal for a new building were to ensure the "long-term sustainability of the Margaret Walker Personal Papers. Staying in tune with the rhythm Dr. Margaret Walker Alexander set in 1968, the MWC continues to hold several artistic programs, exhibits, and an annual Arts Festival and provides superb academic lectures and events that engage students, faculty, and the greater Jackson community. From 1979 to 2009 the milestones of the Margaret Walker National Research Center were made possible due to the direction of Alferdteen Harrison and sponsorships of various public funding institutions. Robert Luckett, Associate Professor of History, would be appointed director of the research center in 2009. Under Luckett's leadership, the research center has sponsored numerous events on the African American experience; many of which stem from the early years of Margaret Walker Alexander, such as the Martin Luther King Birthday Convocation and the Creative Arts Festival to promote student literacy. The legacy of Margaret Walker Alexander is well preserved on the campus of Jackson State University and will be for years to come.

NOTES

1. Joy Ann Williamson, *Radicalizing the Ebony Tower: Black Colleges and the Black Freedom Struggle in Mississippi* (New York: Teachers College Press, 2008), 39.
2. Ibid., 40.
3. Joyce Ann Joyce, *Black Studies as Human Studies: Critical Essays and Interviews*. (Albany: State University of New York Press, 2005), 64.
4. John A. Peoples, *To Survive and Thrive: The Quest for a True University* (Jackson, MS: Town Square Books, 1995), 45.
5. Ibid., 58.
6. Ibid., 2..
7. John A. Peoples, *To Survive and Thrive*, 164; Corner boys were young boys from the surrounding neighborhoods that did not attend Jackson State but would often come to the campus to socialize. Thompson's Tank was a huge armored truck used by the Jackson Police to put down urban rebellions.
8. Ibid., 59.
9. Minutes, The Committee on History, Life, and Culture of Black People, January 14, 1970.
10. Proposal, An Institute for the Continuing Study of Negro History, Life, and Culture at Jackson State College, April 17, 1968.
11. Joyce Ann Joyce, *Black Studies as Human Studies: Critical Essays and Interviews*. (Albany: State University of New York Press, 2005), 87–88.
12. Ibid.
13. Ibid.

14. Ibid.

15. Ibid.

16. Ibid.

17. Ibid.

18. Memo to President Peoples concerning Institute for the Continuing Study of Negro History, Life, and Culture, July 2, 1968.

19. Progress Report, Jackson State College, Institute for the Study of History, Life and Culture of Black People, March 8, 1969.

20. Institute for the Study of History, Culture, and Life of Black People, Af017, Box 1, Folder 2, Department Budget, October 9, 1968.

21. Ibid.

22. Progress Report, Jackson State College, Institute for the Study of History, Life and Culture of Black People, March 8, 1969.

23. Ibid.

24. Memo, From Margaret Walker Alexander to Haskell Bingham, "Visiting Lecturers to the Institute for the Study of Black Culture, 21 October 1968.

25. Progress Report, Jackson State College, Institute for the Study of History, Life and Culture of Black People, AF017-Institute of General Office, Box 1, Folder 17

26. Correspondence, "National Evaluative Conference." AFO 17 III Box 4 Folder 3. Document Date—Jan 27, 1971

27. Annual Report, Institute for the Study of History, Life, and Culture of Black People, 1971–1972.

28. Margaret Walker Personal Papers [AF012] Series I: Correspondence—Correspondence Box 5 Folder 25, February 26, 1973, Margaret Walker Alexander National Research Center, Jackson State University, P.O. Box 17008, Jackson, Mississippi 39217–0108

29. Ibid.

30. Margaret Walker National Research Center Archives - Subject Files: 2005 Board Retreat. *Milestones*.

31. Ibid.

32. Ibid.

33. Ibid.

34. Ibid.

REFERENCES

Anderson, James D. *The Education of Blacks in the South, 1860–1935*. Chapel Hill, NC: The University of North Carolina Press, 1988.

Biondi, Martha. *The Black Revolution on Campus*. Berkeley, CA: University of California Press, 2012.

Bristow, Nancy K. *Steeped in the Blood of Racism: Black Power, Law and Order, and the 1970 Shootings at Jackson State College*. New York, NY: Oxford University Press, 2020.

Favors, Jelani M. *Shelter in a Time of Storm: How Black Colleges Fostered Generations of Leadership and Activism*. Chapel Hill, NC: University of North Carolina Press, 2019.

Joyce, Joyce Ann. *Black Studies as Human Studies: Critical Essays and Interviews*. Albany: State University of New York Press, 2005.

Lovett, Bobby L. *America's Historically Black Colleges & Universities: A Narrative History, 1837–2009*. Macon, GA: Mercer University Press, 2015.

Myers, Joshua M. *We Are Worth Fighting For: A History of the Howard University Student Protest of 1989*. New York, NY: New York University Press, 2019.

Peoples, John A. *To Survive and Thrive: The Quest for a True University*. Jackson, MS: Town Square Books, 1995.

Rogers, Ibram H. *The Black Campus Movement: Black Students and the Racial Reconstitution of Higher Education, 1965–1972*. New York, NY: Palgrave Macmillan, 2012.

Williams, Joy Ann. *Radicalizing the Ebony Tower: Black Colleges and the Black Freedom Struggle in Mississippi*. New York, NY: Teachers College Press, 2008.

Chapter 4

Art and Activism as HBCU Tradition

Elizabeth Carmel Hamilton

INTRODUCTION

A rich heritage of the arts and activism exists at Historically Black Colleges and Universities (HBCUs). These schools produced world-caliber artists that were not only prepared to create art but also agitate for social change in the lives of Black people in the United States. Some of these artists are Elizabeth Catlett (1915–2012), Benny Andrews (1930–2006), and the artist collective Otabenga Jones and Associates. Their artworks can be described best as agitprop art. Agitprop combines the words agitation and propaganda and describes art that is created to affect social change. HBCUs were founded in the aftermath of slavery to educate a mass of newly freed Black people, who could not be admitted to white colleges and universities because of their race. Although they were forged in the crucible of struggle, HBCUs have thrived throughout generations.

Art departments at HBCUs trained Black artists and raised their social consciousness. Because of their unique founding to educate Black people, their missions were intertwined with the political imperative to improve the lives of Black people. Catlett trained at Howard University (Washington, D.C.), Andrews trained at Fort Valley State University (Fort Valley, Georgia), and Otabenga Jones and Associates trained at Texas Southern University (Houston, Texas). Throughout their careers, these artists devoted their work to subjects that promoted social change, but they were also activists who did not just allow the canvas to speak for them. Catlett advocated for her students when she was head of the art department at Dillard University. Andrews was a cofounder of the Black Emergency Cultural Coalition and they led protests to bring art by people of color into the mainstream. Otabenga Jones and Associates do artwork and performance with Black community outreach at its core.

Through my research, I will demonstrate that artists trained at HBCUs had a unique orientation toward artmaking that allowed them to create works that were not just beautiful, but also significant records of the civil rights movement that promoted social change. I will engage the artwork of Catlett, Andrews, and Otabenga Jones and Associates as primary documents of the civil rights movement that reveal a narrative about the artists' concerns for the well-being of Black people in the United States. Catlett, Andrews, and Otabenga Jones and Associates' time at HBCUs developed the activist stances that they maintained throughout their careers.

Fort Valley State University (FVSU) is a historically Black university located in central Georgia that was founded in 1895. In the middle of the historic quad at Fort Valley State University is Future Fountain. The fountain is round, concrete, and surrounded by shrubs and a bench that allows visitors to sit and contemplate the words etched on its base, which read: "We see today as an opportunity to shape tomorrow." The words came from a former president of FVSU, Luther Burse, in 1983. Although the words are from the twentieth century, they embody the spirit of the nineteenth-century founders. Founders of HBCUs in the aftermath of slavery and dealing with the reality of American apartheid were the epitome of self-determination in that they radically imagined a better future for Black people despite their circumstances. Future Fountain is a reminder of this self-determination and the belief in the future of Black people through education. The radical belief and investment in Black futures are what unites HBCUs across the United States.

ELIZABETH CATLETT

Elizabeth Catlett was born on April 15, 1915, in Washington, D.C., to a mother who had been recently widowed. Both of her parents were educated. Her grandparents had been enslaved, and Catlett recalls hearing their stories in her youth. Even as a youth, she had a social conscience. She protested lynching by standing in front of the Supreme Court with a noose around her neck. Catlett's education at Howard University is essential to understanding her activism and art. Being at an HBCU provided her the opportunity to mature as an artist and activist. Her education provided the race consciousness that so defines her oeuvre. Catlett began her matriculation at Howard University in 1931. She initially wanted to study and was accepted at Carnegie Institute of Technology in Pennsylvania. She performed well on entrance exams; however, when the school found out about her race she was denied admission. Therefore, without the presence of an HBCU, Catlett would not have acquired the initial training to become an artist. At Howard, Lois Mailou Jones taught her design and Catlett was initially a design major, but later decided to focus on painting. This caused a rift between her and Jones. Catlett recalls getting an incomplete grade from Jones that caused her to lose her scholarship.

She took life drawing and painting classes from James Porter and print-making with James Wells, although they did not have a printing press. James Herring was the head of the art department, and he had established it in 1921 as the first art program at an HBCU. I posit that even though she had a fraught relationship with Jones, Catlett was positively affected by seeing another woman artist on the faculty at Howard University. Although Alain Locke was a professor at Howard, Catlett did not have any contact with him because he was an enemy of Herring. Furthermore, Locke was a known misogynist. Therefore, I don't believe his philosophies would have had much effect on Catlett's worldview.

Catlett pledged to Delta Sigma Theta but their abject colorism caused her to withdraw from them socially. The Deltas were reluctant to pledge a dark-skinned friend of Catlett. Once they did accept the dark-skinned pledge, they more readily punished her for infractions. This instance highlights that even at an HBCU, white supremacy can be an issue. Colorism is the belief in the inherent moral goodness and beauty of lighter-skinned Black people, because of their proximity to whiteness. Those with darker complexions are seen as corrupt and ugly. Catlett vehemently rejected colorism and the Deltas as a result. Catlett then became involved with the Liberal Club. She recalls that the "Liberal Club had discussions on the political and social issues of the day."[1] While she was a student at Howard, Catlett was being forged as an activist-artist.

Catlett graduated from Howard cum laude with her Bachelor of Science in Art in 1935. She then accepted a position as a high school art teacher in Durham, North Carolina. She unsuccessfully advocated for Black teachers to receive the same pay as white teachers, with the help of Thurgood Marshall. The low pay and poor working conditions caused her to rethink the teaching position. She wanted to be an artist, so she went to the University of Iowa to work with Grant Wood of the iconic *American Gothic* (1930) fame. The dorms were segregated, and she was not allowed to live on campus. So she shared a room with writer Margaret Walker, who would be a lifelong friend and col-laborator. Since there was not a formal printmaking or sculpture program at Howard University, Catlett honed those skills at the University of Iowa.

After her initial undergraduate training at an HBCU, Catlett remained involved with HBCUs at the beginning of her career. They are part of her trajectory as an activist-artist. After graduating with a Master of Fine Arts from the University of Iowa, Catlett spent a semester teaching at Prairie View College in Texas in 1940. From there, she went on to teach at Dillard University in Louisiana. There her activist stance was fomented. She took her students to see a Picasso exhibition. The museum that held the exhibition was in a segregated park. To get around this gross and inhumane inconvenience, Catlett arranged for her students to be dropped off directly in front of the museum from a bus. At Dillard, Catlett taught studio art and art history. Her use of a live, nude model was controversial. However, what caused her to sever her relationship with Dillard University was the school spreading a ten-month contract over twelve months and requiring professors to teach over the summer without compensation. She left Dillard in 1942. Along with her then-husband, Charles White, Catlett was invited to jury the Atlanta University Exhibition Annuals started by Hale Woodruff as a venue for Black artists to exhibit and earn prizes in the very racist and segregated art world in 1942. With Catlett's help, Woodruff amassed an impressive collection of African American art. In 1943, she worked with art educator Victoria Lowenfeld for six months at the Hampton Institute in Virginia. Not only did Catlett attend an HBCU, but she also trained future Black artists at HBCUs. One of her students, Samella Lewis, is a prominent artist and art historian.

From 1945 through 1946, Catlett received a Rosenwald Grant. With the grant, she traveled to Mexico and completed "The Negro Woman" (later renamed the Black Woman): a series of fifteen linocuts extolling the strength, dignity, and hopes of Black women. The images work with the narrative text to tell a compelling story about Black women's lives in the United States. It reads: "I am the Negro Woman. I have always worked hard in America. In the fields. In other folks' homes. I have given the world my songs. In Sojourner Truth, I fought for the rights of women as well as Negroes. In Harriet Tubman, I helped hundreds to freedom. In Phillis Wheatley, I proved intellectual equality in the midst of slavery. My role has been important in the struggle to organize the unorganized. I have studied in ever-increasing numbers. My reward has been barred between me and the rest of the land. I have special reservations. Special houses. And a special fear for my loved ones. My right is a future of equality with other Americans." The series is graphically appealing and didactic in its visual directness. The first linocut is an image of a Black woman, cropped in closely so that the intense gaze penetrates the viewer. The declaration: "I am the Negro Woman" and the gaze work in tandem to provide a sense of authority and agency often denied to Black women during the period of Jim Crow segregation. Catlett chooses to color the first and last linocuts in the series while leaving the middle linocuts

of the pictorial narrative black and white. It is significant that she uses historical figures, Truth, Tubman, and Wheatley, but also underscores the importance of the plight of ordinary Black women. Catlett highlights the barriers
to Black women's happiness and success, such as segregation, backbreaking
labor, subpar housing, and racist violence against them and their families. But
she also underscores the efforts of Black women through education, activism,
and culture, namely music: "I have given the world my songs." In the con-
cluding linocut, she names the desired future of equality in the United States.
HBCUs encourage race consciousness. Catlett would not have had the tools
to complete this series without her training at an HBCU.

Catlett remarried, had three sons, and remained in Mexico. Due to her
alleged political affiliations with Communists, she was barred from entering
the United States. Despite this, Catlett became a main fixture within the Black
Arts Movement. Due to the popularity of her artwork, she was eventually
allowed back into the United States for an exhibition at the Studio Museum
in Harlem. Although she resided in Mexico, Catlett's art was fueled by the
continued agitation for social justice in the United States. She lamented that
she could not be a part of the fight directly, but through her art, she could
contribute. Her prints and sculptures during the Black Arts Movement are
poignant embodiments of the movement's aims. The works that crystallize
this are *Black Unity* (1968), *Homage to My Young Black Sisters* (1969), and
Target (1970). *Black Unity* is a mahogany sculpture of a fist that is emblem-
atic of the Black Arts Movement. Larry Neal outlines its aims as such:

> The Black Arts Movement is radically opposed to any concept of the artist that
> alienates him from his community. This movement is the aesthetic and spiri-
> tual sister of the Black Power concept. As such, it envisions an art that speaks
> directly to the needs and aspirations of Black America. To perform this task,
> the Black Arts Movement proposes a radical reordering of the western cultural
> aesthetic. It proposes a separate symbolism, mythology, critique, and iconol-
> ogy. The Black Arts and the Black Power concept both relate broadly to the
> Afro-American's desire for self-determination and nationhood. Both concepts
> are nationalistic. One is concerned with the relationship between art and poli-
> tics; the other with the art of politics.[2]

The separate symbolism that Neal calls for is used throughout Catlett's oeuvre, mainly as the fist as a symbol of Black power and protest. Catlett wrote
an article in *The Black Scholar* in 1975 that elucidates the Black Power content in her work and her role as an artist in this vein.[3] She says that the goal
of the Black artist is to get art to Black people that promotes Black liberation.
Target is a bronze sculpture of a Black man's head behind the crosshairs of
a rifle, which functions as a frame. It is referring to police brutality in the

United States: specifically the murders of Fred Hampton and Mark Clark by Chicago Police in December 1969. The rifle's crosshairs place the target directly on the figure's forehead. Looking through the frame implicates the viewer as a witness to the violence and the figure returns the viewer's gaze with a somber expression. It asks: what will you do? This sculpture is still tragically cogent in the twenty-first century. The green patina of the bronze also adds a sense of timelessness.

Homage to My Young Black Sisters is a cedar, full-nude, female figure with a hollow center and upraised fist. The faceless figure is striding forward, which gives the sculpture forward momentum, representing hope for the future. The void at the figure's center is reminiscent of sculptures by Barbara Hepworth. The void indicates that there are possibilities for the woman's life beyond motherhood. It interrogates implicitly: who are you beyond your ability to procreate? The figure has an upraised fist, indicating solidarity with the Black Power Movement. The head reads as upturned, looking toward the sky, and ready to receive. Without facial features, she represents every Black woman.

At the 1968 Summer Olympics in Mexico City, Tommie Smith and John Carlos raised black-gloved fists in the air on the winners' platform as a protest against the continued injustices against Black people in the United States. Catlett, no doubt, saw this protest and used the potent symbol in her sculptures. On the reverse side of the fist in *Black Unity* are male and female faces modeled after African masks - specifically the Baule. With the male and female faces, Catlett is making a statement about unity between the sexes. In other words, unity within the Black community does not look like Black patriarchy that replicates white supremacist structures. Catlett described her husband, Francisco Mora, as a feminist. He took his role as a father and husband very seriously and did not place all of the responsibilities of the household and childrearing on Catlett. As a result, she was able to devote time to being an artist and a teacher outside of the home.

Catlett's oeuvre is replete with images of women. They occupy the majority of her body of work. Therefore, when she chose to depict men, she was making a special statement. She said: "Because I am a woman and I know how a woman feels in body and mind, I sculpt, draw, and print women, generally black women."[4] It was vital that Catlett learned from a woman artist at Howard. Catlett knew she wanted to be an artist, but without Lois Mailou Jones as a model of a successful African American woman artist, I don't think Catlett would have been likely to feel she could do it too.

BENNY ANDREWS

While Catlett's HBCU experience was characterized by an urban experience in Washington, D.C. Benny Andrews's experience was characterized by its rural nature in Georgia. Andrews was born in Plainview, Georgia, on November 13, 1930. Plainview had a segregated one-room schoolhouse for the elementary school. When he was old enough, he went to Burney Street High School in Madison, which was the next town over. He walked the four miles there and back. His parents were sharecroppers on a cotton plantation, and Andrews could only attend school on the days when it rained and the fields were too saturated for work. His father and the plantation's overseer discouraged his education because they felt Andrews's labor was needed on the plantation. However, his mother was very supportive. Sharecropping was an oppressive situation that replicated the same labor exploitation of slavery. In sharecropping, the plantation owner would provide lodging, seed, and equipment in exchange for labor and a share of the crop. It was very rare that the Andrews family was able to earn any money sharecropping although even the children of the family labored, Andrews as young as six years old. The work of farming was difficult and physically taxing. Andrews wanted desperately to escape the oppressive sharecropping system.

In 1948, Andrews became the first person in his family to graduate high school. He then moved to Atlanta and worked as a busboy. While Andrews was in high school he was part of the 4-H Club. This association allowed him to travel to Savannah for competitions and eventually earn a scholarship to attend one of the three public HBCUs in Georgia: Savannah State University, Albany State University, or Fort Valley State University (FVSU). Renowned painter Hale Woodruff was teaching at Clark Atlanta University at that time, but the school was private, more expensive, and out of Andrews's reach. He chose FVSU in rural Fort Valley, Georgia, because an acquaintance in Atlanta had taught there. The 4-H scholarship was $200, and Andrews still owed $405 for tuition, room, and board. He got a part-time job in the art department and his mother took in laundry to earn the rest of the money.

During his freshman year, Andrews was ruthlessly hazed by the upperclassmen. He wanted to quit, but his mother's encouragement caused him to stay. Andrews faced other barriers at FVSU as well. Unlike Howard University, where Catlett attended, FVSU did not have a functioning art department. Although the 1948–1949 bulletin lists several art classes, only one course was offered, and that was Art Appreciation. The course description reads: "This is designed to give students who major in Home Ec a background in art principles such as good taste. Structural and decorative design, balance, proportion, rhythm, emphasis and introduction to color. (One example to be done in block print is required, utilizing as many of the art principles as possible.)"[5] From the course description, the course was not designed with an aspiring artist in mind. Students were taught the practical basics of art. Andrews said: "I wanted to study art, which was impossible. In fact, there was only one course offered in art and that was art appreciation."[6] He was expected to go into agriculture, which he hated because of the oppressive sharecropping. FVSU's educational opportunities were focused on students who wanted to pursue teaching or farming. He did poorly in all his classes except art appreciation. He took the course six times.

His employment in the art studio as the art appreciation instructor was ideal because he had access to art supplies. Andrews spent most of his free time in the studio experimenting with materials that he could have only dreamed of as a child in Plainview. As a child, he would make paintbrushes from animal hair and paint from plants. He said that "The art class was just a minor supplement to majors, and only one or two other students expressed a desire to work in art beyond the one-term basis requirement. I was left alone to work in the art room in anything and in any way that I wanted to, and that is where I spent most of my time."[7] With free rein of the studio, Andrews was able to develop his skills, but he was essentially self-taught.

Unfortunately, there was no future for Andrews as an artist at FVSU. This fact, along with his poor grades, and the scholarship running out, led him to enlist in the newly desegregated Air Force in 1950 at the start of the Korean War. He served for four years and after he was discharged he used his GI Bill to attend the Art Institute of Chicago. The remaining cost was paid by the state of Georgia because they refused to integrate schools. The University of Georgia was not far from his hometown and had an art program, but Andrews would not have been able to attend, because of his race. So, the state would rather pay for Black students to attend schools elsewhere than have racially integrated programs. In Chicago, he visited his first art museum, because museums in the south were segregated. He moved to New York in 1958, after graduating from the Art Institute. Unlike Catlett, he was not involved in any civil rights protests or marches, but he was very much aware of racial inequities. Also being at an HBCU raised his racial consciousness.

In 1968, the Metropolitan Museum of Art planned an exhibition called *Harlem on My Mind*. The curator of the exhibition planned to use photographs instead of works from Black artists. Furthermore, there were no Black curators involved. Andrews and a group of artists tried to negotiate with the museum to right this egregious wrong but to no avail. So, in 1969 they planned to protest. The group of artists met in Andrews's studio on January 9, 1969, and was formally organized as the Black Emergency Cultural Coalition (BECC). They planned a protest outside of the museum for January 12. Carrying placards with messages denouncing the exhibition, they were met with police barricades. They protested again on January 16 and passed out leaflets, which listed their demands. Among the demands were the cancellation of the exhibition, the appointment of Black people as policymakers, and an earnest engagement with the Black community. BECC was successful in getting the museum to withdraw its offensive catalog and issue an apology.

With a success under its belt, Andrews and BECC set their sights on the Whitney Museum in April. They had four demands for the museum: "(1) the Museum should put on an exhibition of Black artists with a Black guest curator, (2) put more Black artists in the Whitney's Annual, (3) hire a Black curatorial staff to coordinate these endeavors and other activities in the future, (4) stage five or more solo exhibitions of Black artists during the year."[8] They agreed to have the exhibition *Contemporary Black Artists in America* but refused to hire a Black curator. As a result, BECC protested the 1971 exhibition. Several of the artists withdrew their work, and they mounted a rebuttal exhibition. Although they were not successful in getting all of their demands met, BECC, led in part by Andrews, was responsible for the increased visibility of Black artists within the Whitney's exhibition programming. With BECC, Andrews continued to advocate for Black artists and eventually shifted gears and developed art education programs within prisons.

Andrew's paintings from this period are filled with political fervor. He often used the flag of the United States to add emphasis to his political message and also as a way to identify the despot of the narrative. This is evident in *Flag Day* (1966), *Did the Bear Sit Under the Tree?* (1969), and *No More Games* (1970). In all three paintings/collages, the flag, and the Black body figure prominently within the narrative. While Catlett, often uses the Black Power fist as a poignant and powerful symbol to discuss social justice, Andrews uses the flag. The imagery of the flag has been used by artists such as Eugene Delacroix as a call to action in the French Revolution and Jasper Johns as a pop icon during the Cold War. The image is highly recognizable and draws from a host of histories. Using the flag is never benign symbolism. Along with it comes the history of the country it stands forthe good and the bad. Andrews's history in the segregated south colored his perceptions and experiences in the United States. While he is critical of that history, he is also a veteran. So the same government that used de facto segregation to keep him and his family in impoverished conditions and substandard schools, also allowed him to earn a GI Bill that enabled him to become an artist. So the flag represents a government that was oppressive in many respects but provided him freedom in another respect. This is the double bind inherent in being a Black American. This is why the Black figures in Andrews's paintings/collages of this period seem at odds with the flags. It is pure conflict.

While Jasper Johns's flags are characterized by their flatness and mimetic quality, Andrews's flags are characterized by their texture and dynamism.

They seem to project from the canvas, partly because of his collage technique. The flags interact with their subjects in a way that makes them a character within the narrative. Within the compositions, they function as something other than an emblem of the United States. In the case of *Flag Day*, the flag becomes a striped prison garment. Moreover, Andrews situated the flag vertically against the picture plane, and the flag's stripes become the man's prison. He seems to struggle to emerge from the field of red and white. However, as the figure's gaze goes toward the stars in the upper-right corner of the composition, it imbues the painting with a sense of hope.

Did the Bear Sit Under the Tree? has an enigmatic title, but its meanings are clear. The flag represents a despot that the Black figure must struggle against. In this collaged painting, the flag is situated horizontally on the left side of the composition, while the figure occupies the right side. The figure's arms are raised and his hands are balled into two fists. His face expresses a scowl. Furthermore, Andrews collages a zipper over his mouth, separating his lips. Andrews's paint application is energetic, which gives the surface a unique texture, especially over the figure's face. There is something indefinite about the way Andrews applied paint around the left arm and right fist. Paint splotches are under the figure's left arm as well. It is as if Andrews was using an action painting technique. The figure's gaze penetrates the flag and his righteous anger and vitriol are directed toward it. Andrews painted *Did the Bear Sit Under the Tree?* during the period when he cofounded BECC. He was fed up with the institutions that pigeonholed and curtailed Black artists' success. As Susan E. Cahan notes in *Mounting Frustration*, the advances of the Civil Rights Movement reached museums later than in the mainstream United States. As a result, "Throughout much of the twentieth century, de facto segregation produced a separate world of African American art centers and museums."[9] In *Did the Bear Sit Under the Tree?* the flag symbolizes racist institutions.

No More Games makes an even bolder statement against racist institutions. The diptych has a figure in each of the two panels. A Black male figure is on the left panel and a white female figure is on the right panel. A flag figures prominently in this composition. It occupies the right panel and spills into the left panel a little bit. The figure on the right is covered by the flag, but her legs are exposed. The figure is seemingly dead. Above the figure is, what looks like, a pedestal with a vine winding up it that the female figure seems to have fallen from. Or perhaps, she has been knocked off. In the left panel, the figure is seated on a box. He wears a T-shirt, jeans, and sneakers. Flowers grow around his box and a hazy sun shines down: it is bright in the center and dark around its edges. As a result, the figure casts a dark shadow. Andrews collaged the large canvases with real fabric. So it serves as a contrast to the painted fabrics in the composition. The conflict between the two figures is evident as well as the apparent victory of the figure on the left. The flag has not been spared in the composition. It has been impaled by the empty pedestal. Although Andrews did not want to be perceived as an activist-artist, his activism with BECC and his paintings caused collectors and curators to ostracize him. Despite this, he was still a highly successful artist whose oeuvre spans decades and it began with his artistic experimentations at FVSU.

OTABENGA JONES AND ASSOCIATES

The members of Otabenga Jones and Associates met at Texas Southern University (TSU) in 1994 and started the collective in 2002. TSU is an HBCU with a rich artistic legacy. The department was founded by the acclaimed artist John Biggers and the imprint of his legacy can be seen throughout the artworks of the members of the collective. They were trained by Harvey Johnson, who was a protege of Biggers. The group was galvanized under Johnson's demanding tutelage. They learned the figure by looking at African sculpture rather than the live model or Western "masterpieces." The members are Dawolu Jabari Anderson (b. 1973), Jamal Cyrus (b. 1973), Kenya Evans (b. 1974), Robert A. Pruitt (b. 1975), and Otabenga Jones. Pruitt's individual artistic practices center on Black women as heroic and aspirational figures. Anderson creates alternate universes for imagining stereotypes anew. Cyrus creates multimedia works of art that interrogate histories. Evan's work is very much steeped in revisionist American histories as a way to critique the current political moment. However, Otabenga Jones is a specter - a figment of the imagination created by the other four members of the collective. Otabenga Jones is an accumulation of African American and diasporic histories from which the members of the group glean. The first name is the name of a real person: Ota Benga (1883–1916). The story of the real Benga was tragic. He was a Mbuti man, born in the Congo region of Africa.[10] Because of his short stature, he was brought to the United States in 1904 for the Louisiana Purchase Exposition (St. Louis World Fair). In 1906, he was exhibited in a cage with primates at the Bronx Zoo. Benga was eventually released, but the trauma of white supremacist exploitation haunted him and he was terribly homesick. He died of a self-inflicted gunshot wound in 1916. The group combined his first and last names into one and added the last name Jones. The collective created timeless mythology for Otabenga Jones. His parents were a part of Marcus Garvey's Universal Negro Improvement Association (UNIA), which was founded in 1914 for racial uplift through economic and educational opportunities, and he was a part of the Black Power/Arts Movement. Because of these associations, he has ancestral wisdom and the collective members seek his guidance concerning their projects.

On their Tumblr site, Otabenga Jones and Associates list their mission statement: "The purpose of this organization is summed up in three simple objectives. (1) To teach the truth to the young Black youth. (2) To extend the parameters of the transatlantic Afro-diasporic aesthetic. (3) To mess wit (sic) whitey."[11] This phrase is taken from the film *The Spook Who Sat by the Door.* The collective also has an organizational diagram that places Otabenga Jones at the top. Arrows point down from him to the other four members, who are displayed at an equal level. Each artist within the collective has his own artistic practice but unites under the collective for performance-based and conceptual projects. Their projects focus on affecting positive change in Black communities. While BECC was focused on change within racist institutions, Otabenga Jones and Associates is focused on dismantling the institutions and building their own. It is indicative of the self-determination inherent in the ethos of the UNIA, Black Power and Arts Movements, and HBCUs.

We Did It for Love (2004) embodies the revolutionary protest spirit of the 1960s and 1970s. It is an installation for an exhibition Amalgama at the Contemporary Arts Museum Houston. It was later shown at the 2006 Whitney Biennial. The installation consists of an overturned police car, which was painted by the group. It is a jarring visual encounter to be confronted with a car that one is accustomed to seeing upright. It leaves the audience to ponder the circumstances that led to its upside-down state. The audience gets some clues with the installation's audio. The car's radio plays police broadcasts from the Watts Rebellion that took place from August 11 until August 16, 1965, in the predominantly Black Watts neighborhood in Los Angeles. It started when police stopped Marquette Frye for reckless driving. An altercation broke out, and witnesses watched the police assault a pregnant woman. The Watts Rebellion resulted in thirty-four deaths, over one thousand injuries, nearly four thousand arrests, and the destruction of property valued at $40 million. The National Guard was deployed to help squelch looting and arson. The Black people of Watts were rebelling against police brutality but also sustained unsatisfactory living conditions in Watts that included substandard housing and unemployment. During the rebellion, cars were overturned in protest. Otabenga Jones and Associates used this method of protest as a continued statement against police brutality and Black suppression. They could have used an unmarked car, but they opted for the overturned police car as a loaded symbol of Black insurrection. In addition to police recordings of the Watts Rebellion on the car radio, the group also added speeches and music.

Africa Is a Continent (2005) is a performance and protest. Two members of the group, Pruitt and Cyrus, marched outside of the Museum of Fine Arts Houston in protest of the exhibition *African Art Now: Masterpieces from the Jean Pigozzi Collection.* The group disagreed with the museum allowing a Swiss collector's aesthetic choices to determine the significance and value of

African Art. Also at issue is the exhibition's false dichotomy between traditional and contemporary African art. Otabenga Jones and Associates also say: "The title does not differentiate between the 55 countries of the continent and seems to suppose that the 33 countries represented by 15 artists (Only two women? Geez!) makes up the whole of Africa."[12] The members of Otabenga Jones and Associates carried signs that read: "Africa Is a Continent" and "My Blacknuss Is Bigger Than Your White Box!" Like BECC before them, the collective was riled by a museum's exhibition practices. However, unlike BECC, Otabenga Jones and Associates has no faith in the institution. They pointedly exclaim that they do not believe in museums. Their focus in *Africa Is a Continent* and their other projects are "less about asking for change within these institutions, and more about Black folks creating their own institutions. I mean real institutions, not Black versions of the White spaces."[13]

They created their own institution with the Otabenga Jones and Associates Academy of Applied Arts, which was launched in 2012. Their educational philosophy states its objectives and aims. The statement is lengthy, but I think it is worth repeating here:

Educational Philosophy

Despite what you've heard, Otabenga Jones & Associates is not a collective of leather jacket wearing, color flying, foul mouthed felons, whose political ideas veer so far left they form a circle. But rather, we are a group of concerned citizens reigning from Alkebulan, Shabazz State, Tubman City. We are about nation building, which posits that instead of begging for entry into the oppressor's republic, you build your own. In the spirit of our predecessors: Mary McLeod Bethune, W.E.B. Dubois and Amiri Baraka, the road to creating this new state is in institutions and education.

As we forecasted from reading the past and present conditions of our communities, education has often served as a means to restrict rather than to encourage black growth. It is in the field of education that we want to act; by initiating a program of empowering instruction whose foundation is harnessing creative expression for social transformation. And so, in the year 2012, our organization's 10th anniversary, we will be opening the Otabenga Jones Academy of Applied Arts and establishing the Ibrahim Sori scholarship fund to provide financial assistance to worthy students. As you will see, this will be a key maneuver in waking the great Cushitic giant.

With the ascension of the first Black president and the appearance of a thorough integration of Blacks and other minorities into the economic, political and cultural sphere; the national dialogue around race and progress has shifted. While we are permitted the benefits of access to these new platforms, it is our organizational consensus that the Black collective consciousness is not at a point where it can build upon this progress. Traditionally, we have mined for source materials from the objectives and strategies of our radical ancestral arts and political movements. Though still potent, these strategies can often seem dated and need alteration to proactively deal with current incarnations of the white supremacist, and capitalist patriarchy. To wit, we have founded this school for the Black lumpen art student.

OJAAA's curriculum of art instruction is engineered to free the colonized mind. Through our six week program of studio work, seminar courses, international residency opportunities ("all ya'll from Africa!!!"), and interactions with vital working artists, students will learn to define, name, speak for themselves, and forge their own collective futures.

These radical programs will include: The Re-versioning of Art His-story; Pan-African Design Principles; 2D and 3D Telekinesis; (painting and drawing), Intergalactic Flight Patterns and Move-meant (Dance and Performance). Pupils will move through the three-tiered levels of artistic development while simultaneously reconnecting to their pineal gland, chakra centers, melanin switches and the collective consciousness.[14]

The People's Plate (2014) combines multiple elements of art and community interaction through a public health program and addresses obesity and food insecurity in Houston. Otabenga Jones and Associates painted a public mural at the Lawndale Art Center in Houston and conceived a series of accompanying programs, for a yearlong project on health education. The collective was inspired by the Black Panther Free Breakfast for School Children Program, which ran from 1969 to the early 1970s, in which the Panthers cooked and served breakfast to impoverished, inner-city children. With *The People's Plate,* Otabenga Jones and Associates wanted to give those at risk for obesity and food insecurity "a set of tools that encourage self-sufficiency and empowerment in maintaining their health through food choices while building community. Programs at Lawndale and other Houston venues will include cooking classes, a foraging workshop, an urban gardening workshop, an instructional cooking video, and a line of mass-produced lunchboxes that will be made available to the public."[15] The mural is based on the graphic art of the Minister of Culture for the Black Panthers, Emory Douglas. The mural covers the entire wall of the building. It features a Black boy who presents a newspaper that reads: "Dare to struggle, eat to win!" The phrase is translated into Spanish, Vietnamese, Hindi, and Arabic on the right side of the mural, acknowledging the solidarity with communities of color within Houston. In the boy's other hand, he holds a bag of groceries. Behind him and off to the right are shotgun houses. The images are anchored in a field of brilliant green. A crown of broccoli emerges from the boy's left shoulder. The boy's mouth is open as if he was caught in a moment of speech, specifically yelling. By using the strategies of the Black Panthers, Otabenga Jones and Associates are calling forth usable pasts and histories to make them relevant to the current political moment.

While Catlett and Andrews were a part of the Black Arts Movement, Otabenga Jones and Associates draw from the movement and its imperatives of Black self-determination and nation-building. Their activism is closely tied to their artistic practices. The collective's HBCU legacy is explicit through its centering on Black political thought. They balance social activism with art-making. They critique art institutions and work to build their own while acknowledging that to remain relevant they must participate in the traditional systems. Robert Pruitt says: "We're artists, so we're interested, very interested, in being a part of that art system, but we still have social politics that we are working on within our community, and that's a different focus."[16]

CONCLUSION

When *Black Panther* debuted in 2018, audiences were awed by the fictional African country of Wakanda and the technological advances that scientist Shuri, the hero T'Challa's sister, was able to achieve with the country's precious metal vibranium. The main source of conflict in *Black Panther* was the villain Killmonger's desire to share that technology with oppressed people around the world and overthrow dominant regimes. T'Challa was against the idea because he thought vibranium would be misused for evil purposes. In the end, Killmonger is defeated, and the technologies of Wakanda remained a secret. What is so fascinating about Wakanda is that it is hidden in plain sight. They are living in a technologically advanced society, but to the outside world, Wakanda looks primitive. Audiences of Black Panther began to seek a real counterpart to the fictional Wakanda. Like Wakanda, HBCUs are an important site of culture, politics, and technology - not just education. HBCUs emerged as the site of Black progress and self-determination for the twenty-first century because they are filled with endless resources for Black people. Their value is often hidden in plain sight because they are often under-resourced. Created as a response to the cruelty and dehumanization of slavery and segregation, HBCUs have educated thousands of Black people for better futures, while being a site of cultural and technological innovations.

All six of the artists, Elizabeth Catlett, Benny Andrews, and Otabenga Jones and Associates, examined here are unified by the fact that they received an HBCU education and use social activism to make a difference in the world. Each artist addresses specific social issues, from museum tokenism to food insecurity. Their artworks become a container for their politics. HBCUs provide unique environments for the raising of social and political consciousnesses. While Howard and TSU had thriving art departments, FVSU did not, and Andrews had to make do. However, all of the artists' unique experiences at HBCUs forged them into activists.

NOTES

1. Camille Billops, *Interview of Elizabeth Catlett* (New York: Hatch Billops Collection, 1991), 17.

2. Larry Neal, "The Black Arts Movement," *Drama Review* 12, no. 4 (Summer 1968): 28.

3. Elizabeth Catlett, "The Role of the Black Artist," *The Black Scholar* 6, no. 9 (1975): 10–14.

4. "Artist in Focus: Elizabeth Catlett." Philadelphia Museum of Art, 2021, accessed 15 November 2020, https://philamuseum.org/calendar/exhibition/artist -focus-elizabeth-catlett.

5. Benny Andrews Papers, Hunt Memorial Library, Fort Valley State University, Georgia. I would like to thank Ms. Wilmetta Jackson, the archivist at Fort Valley State University, for allowing me to access Benny Andrews's archive at Hunt Library and Mr. Ricky Calloway for providing me with archives and correspondence from the artist in the 1990s.

6. Gruber, J. Richard, Benny Andrews, and Morris Museum of Art (Augusta, GA). *American Icons: From Madison to Manhattan, the Art of Benny Andrews, 1948–1997* (Augusta, GA: Morris Museum of Art, 1997): 53.

7. Gruber, 57.

8. Gruber, 144.

9. Susan Cahan, *Mounting Frustration: The Art Museum in the Age of Black Power* (Durham: Duke University Press, 2016): 3.

10. The term used for him in the early twentieth century was Pygmy.

11. Otabenga Jones and Associates, edited by ojandassociates, Tumblr, April 22, 2014, https://ojandassociates.tumblr.com/post/83493730954/early-mission-statement.

12. Jones, Otabenga and Associates. "African Art Now: Masterpieces from the Jean Pigozzi Collection." *Glasstire: Texas Visual Art* (May 2, 2005 May 2, 2005). https://glasstire.com/2005/05/02/african-art-now-masterpieces-from-the-jean -pigozzi-collection/.

13. Otabenga Jones and Associates, Michelle White, and Franklin Sirmans, *Lessons from Below: Otabenga Jones and Associates*, edited by the Menil Collection (Houston: The Menil Collection, 2007).

14. Otabenga Jones and Associates, edited by ojandassociates, Tumblr, April 22, 2014, https://ojacademy.tumblr.com/post/19863320800/oja-academy-of-applied-arts.

15. Jenny Gill, "Otabenga Jones & Associates Launch "The People's Plate" in Houston," *Creative Capital* (February 25, 2014). https://creative-capital.org/2014/02 /25/otabenga-jones-associates-launch-peoples-plate-houston/.

16. Davenport, Bill. "Otabenga Jones & Associates' Provocative Artwork." *The Chronicle* (July 23, 2006). https://www.chron.com/entertainment/article/Otabenga -Jones-Associates-provocative-artwork-1860147.php

REFERENCES

Andrews, Benny. *"On Understanding Black Art."* *New York Times* June 21, 1970.

Berlind, Robert, and Elizabeth Catlett. "Elizabeth Catlett." *Art Journal* 53, no. 1 (1994): 29–30.

Billops, Camille. *Interview of Elizabeth Catlett.* New York: Hatch Billops Collection, 1991.

Cahan, Susan. *Mounting Frustration: The Art Museum in the Age of Black Power.* Durham: Duke University Press, 2016.

Catlett, Elizabeth. "The Role of the Black Artist." *The Black Scholar* 6, no. 9 (1975): 10–14.

Crawford, Margo Natalie. *Black Post-Blackness: The Black Arts Movement and Twenty-First-Century Aesthetics.* Urbana, Illinois: University of Illinois Press, 2017.

Davenport, Bill. "Otabenga Jones & Associates' Provocative Artwork." *The Chronicle* (July 23, 2006).

Dennis, Ryan N. "Art for the People's Sake." *Gulf Coast: A Journal of Literature and Fine Arts* 27, no. 1 (Winter/Spring 2015): 90–104.

GBH Forum Network. "Meet Otabenga Jones and Associates." July 18, 2008.

Gill, Jenny. "Otabenga Jones & Associates Launch 'The People's Plate' in Houston." *Creative Capital* (February 25, 2014). https://creative-capital.org/2014/02/25/ota-benga-jones-associates-launch-peoples-plate-houston/.

Gouma-Peterson, Thalia. "Elizabeth Catlett: The Power of Human Feeling and of Art." *Woman's Art Journal* 4, no. 1 (Spring-Summer 1983): 48–56.

Gruber, J. Richard, Benny Andrews, and Morris Museum of Art (Augusta, GA). *American Icons: From Madison to Manhattan, the Art of Benny Andrews, 1948–1997.* Augusta, GA: Morris Museum of Art, 1997.

Herzog, Melanie. *Elizabeth Catlett: An American Artist in Mexico.* Seattle: University of Washington Press, 2000.

Morrison, Toni. *The Source of Self-Regard: Selected Essays, Speeches, and Meditations.* New York: Alfred A. Knopf, 2019.

Oral History Interview with Benny Andrews. Archives of American Art: Smithsonian Institution, 1968 June 30.

Otabenga Jones and Associates. *Africa Is a Continent* Edited by ojandassociates: Tumblr, April 25, 2014.

———. "African Art Now: Masterpieces from the Jean Pigozzi Collection." *Glasstire: Texas Visual Art* (May 2, 2005). https://glasstire.com/2005/05/02/afri-can-art-now-masterpieces-from-the-jean-pigozzi-collection/.Otabenga Jones and Associates, Michelle White, and Franklin Sirmans. *Lessons from Below: Otabenga Jones and Associates.* Edited by The Menil Collection. Houston: The Menil Collection, 2007.Scruggs, Dalila. "Activism in Exile: Elizabeth Catlett's *Mask for Whites.*" *American Art* 32, no. 3 (Fall 2018): 3–21.

PART II

Enduring and Evolving
Roles of HBCUs

Chapter 5

"Keeping It Real" on the Decline of HBCU Student Enrollment

A Content Analysis on Rhetoric in Practice

Ivon Alcime, Ashla Hill Roseboro,
and Carlos Morrison

HBCUs BACKGROUND

Historically Black Colleges and Universities (HBCUs) are institutions that were established prior to the Civil Rights Act of 1964. Their principal mission has always been to provide higher education for Black people who had previously been enslaved, then subsequently segregated, as well as their descendants. HBCUs were established in two waves. The first wave of schools was established for freed Blacks in the North before the Civil War. Most of these institutions did not survive, "and their successor institutions are no longer connected to their original campuses or historic structures."[1] The second wave of colleges and universities were established for emancipated Blacks and their offspring in the South after the Civil War. The Freedmen's Bureau, abolitionist organizations, religious groups, local community groups, and people who had previously been enslaved have been credited with the establishment of more than five hundred such institutions across the United States.[2] The quest to provide Blacks with access to higher education did not stop with these stakeholders.

The Second Morrill Act of 1890 was significant in establishing additional institutions for Blacks. In the early 1800s, only the affluent and elite white males enjoyed the privilege of higher education. In 1857, this inequality in higher education prompted Senator Justin Smith Morrill to propose land grants to each state to establish public universities. Morrill's proposal would have granted all Americans access to higher education. However, President James Buchanan vetoed Morrill's proposal. In 1862, President Abraham Lincoln approved and signed the Morrill Act, the same year he signed the Emancipation Proclamation which ended slavery.

Nevertheless, Blacks were still denied admission to the land-grant universities created by the Morrill Act of 1862.[3] In 1890, Senator Justin Morrill introduced the Second Morrill Act to address race restrictions. The Second Morrill Act of 1890 required the former Confederate states to establish universities specifically for Blacks. The Second Morrill Act created the 1890 Historically Black Land-Grant Universities. At present, there are nineteen universities within the fifty states that have land-grant status under the Morrill Act of 1890.[4] Furthermore, two additional HBCUs are designated under the Morrill Act of 1862: 1) the University of the District of Columbia and 2) the University of the Virgin Islands.[5]

In the early twentieth century, many institutions were established for Blacks. During the Great Depression of the 1930s, the number of HBCUs started to decline due to mergers, school closures, and consolidation. This decline was the result of diminishing financial support from northern philanthropists and church groups and the increase of accreditation agencies for colleges and universities.

In the 1950s and early 1960s, new HBCUs emerged, followed by more mergers and consolidations.[6] In 2018, the United States had 101 HBCUs,[7] as defined by the federal Higher Education Act of 1965. These HBCUs were located in nineteenth states, the District of Columbia, and the U.S. Virgin Islands. Of the 101 HBCUs, fifty-one were public institutions and fifty were private nonprofit institutions.[8] There are now fewer than one hundred HBCUs.

CURRENT ISSUES

Despite their extraordinary history and an achievable mission, HBCUs are in danger of declining in numbers. Some of the contributing factors for this decline are not the fault of the HBCUs themselves. However, the incompetence of administrators to carry out the mission of HBCUs is an indisputable and relevant factor. The principal mission of HBCUs was just as important in the first wave of schools as it is today. Even so, the ineffective communication of HBCU administrators is obstructing and undermining the mission of

HBCUs and the visions of the Freedmen's Bureau, abolitionist organizations, religious groups, local community groups, enslaved Blacks, the legacy of Senator Justin Smith Morrill, and others who relentlessly fought for the establishment of HBCUs. The result is plummeting HBCU enrollments.

Between 1976 and 2018, the number of Blacks enrolled at HBCUs increased by 17 percent. However, the number of Blacks enrolled at other postsecondary institutions doubled during this same period. Therefore, the percentage of Black students enrolled at HBCUs dropped from 18 percent in the fall of 1976 to 9 percent in the year 2010. No measurable change was recorded between 2010 and 2018 by the National Center for Education Statistics. Since 1976, female enrollment has been higher than male enrollment. For example, in the fall of 2018, females comprised 62 percent of those enrolled at HBCUs, compared to 53 percent in the fall of 1976.[9] While Black enrollment at HBCUs is declining, non-Black enrollment increased more than 17 percent from 2010 to 2017. Approximately one-fourth of HBCUs students are non-Black.[10]

Effective communication is one of the most important skills that could reverse the downward trend of HBCU enrollment. It is not just any type of communication that could serve this purpose, but specifically the set of communication skills that stem from African cultural influences that have fused Blacks into one undeniable race from the time of slavery until the present. Race is a social construct that differentiates people based upon alleged biological differences related to ancestral origins.[11] These genetic differences are often superficially apparent to the human eye, such as hair color, hair texture, skin color, and the size and shape of facial features. However, it should be noted that race alone is not an indicator of individual differences.

COMMUNICATION IN BLACK CULTURE

Within the Black culture, HBCUs, much like religious organizations, were central forces in bringing the race together for shared purposes that ranged from educational, social, spiritual, and economic uplift. The Black press was another unifier in the community that advocated for the race.[12] Culture was defined as "equally the sum total of agreed-upon social etiquettes by a given human society for practices that classify them uniquely."[13] These institutions had a pivotal role in celebrating the communities of people they served through empowerment to work collectively to improve life for all African Americans. Cultural membership in the Black community was intimately linked with music, art, dance, and food people identified closely with others who possessed these similar shared experiences of being Black in America. Consequently, these in-groups connected with others for emotional support, for they could identify with other shared experiences, such as discrimination, wealth disparities, and racial profiling, among other unpleasant conditions in society. Black culture has norms and traditions that were passed down across generations. For example, cultural practices of marriage, religion, technology, and music have evolved. According to Lyle, human communication is the most essential element for a harmonious society.[14] For example, the 1965 Watts riots were an example of a communication breakdown when people in administrative roles did not listen to warnings, and this resulted in an explosion of violence.[15] Alternatively, Afrocentric communication thrives when information is shared openly to create environments of trust that encourage everyone to work together.

Though many co-cultures exist within HBCUs, such as the administration, alumni, Divine Nine fraternities and sororities, bands, athletics departments, student government, publications, and many others, the mission of these institutions influences everyone to work collectively for the greater good. HBCU culture has supported journalism student organizations which served as voices for uniting campuses to work together collectively for the greater good. In 1937, students from Morehouse College founded the Delta Phi Delta Intercollegiate Honorary Journalistic Society.[16] The organization was formed to "stimulate interest in journalism study in Negro colleges, to unite students of journalism, to honor writers who had distinguished themselves, and to evaluate the works of Negro writers."[17] Delta Phi Delta expanded, with chapters soon springing up on other college campuses. Even though the organization dissolved after twenty years, it nevertheless initiated a communications legacy that has continued to the present day. At Lincoln University in Pennsylvania, the Black Student Press Association was organized to prepare members to work in Black newspapers.[18] Howard University students in the School of Communications formed the National Black Communications Society (NBCS) to develop high standards for student participation in campus media. In addition, the NBCS supported employer recruitment efforts, financial aid, and recognition programs in communications.[19]

These evolutionary changes have happened slowly with the discourse that avoided revolutionary chaos or confusion.[20] Hip-hop music influenced culture through media messages that expressed narratives of what was happening in Black neighborhoods, often using slang words. These artists often were HBCU homecoming or athletic game headliners who represented aspects of the culture which merged diverse elements that depicted the struggle and resilience of the race. According to Wilson, Gutierrez, and Chao, "racial, cultural and gender self-esteem is developed during the childhood years."[21] Television was frequently criticized for its conspicuous absence of diversity. Except for a very small number of educational and public broadcasting programs, television of that era offered only extremely limited opportunities to advocate for minority groups.[22] The underrepresentation of diverse cultures in youth television programming had a great impact on the identity formation of college students. In addition, Black actresses, such as Viola Davis, have been criticized for playing the role of a maid. Even in the twenty-first century, minority women in the media are generally assigned only a narrow range of roles, frequently cast as either jezebels or sapphires and depicted as one dimensional stereotypical hypersexualized, hot-tempered characters. These stereotypical portrayals were blamed for damaging the self-esteem of young women who are celebrated only for their physical appearance, instead of for their intellect, emotional intelligence, positive personality traits, and values.[23]

People of non-heterosexual genders constitute another co-culture that has existed on HBCU campuses for a long time. In recent years, the LGBTQIA (lesbian, gay, bisexual, transgender, queer or questioning, intersex, or non-binary, and asexual or aromantic) has given way to examining masculinity and femininity from a broader perspective. Colleges and universities began encouraging people to use pronouns to explicitly tell others how they identify, such as he/him/his, she/her/hers, or they/them/theirs. Transgender and queer individuals are critical of being identified by gender categorizations, such as biological sex or gender adjectives. This is because they feel these categories do not adequately describe who they are. Diversity and inclusion programs at predominately white institutions (PWIs) often address the LGBTQIA as a place of support. HBCUs have delayed addressing the presence of this co-culture, often taking a position of silence and only addressing this group in crisis or in response to grassroots influences. Subsequently, student-led activism at Howard University and Alabama State University has resulted in a university-recognized student organization that has gained administrative support on campus for these students, which has allowed their voices to be heard.

This is an example of how African culture conflicts with Western views of gay and lesbian practices. Many people of the African diaspora feel there is a "cultural invasion" that attempts to force them to accept the LGBTQIA.[24] Furthermore, gender equity is viewed as a hollow slogan when used in Africa, for in most African nations, men have historically held the vast majority of the parliament, judiciary, executive positions, and political appointments.[25] Male dominance is a norm in Africa that privileges heterosexual men.

Collectivistic and individualistic cultures approach communication differently. In collectivist cultures, people "often feel loyalties and obligations to an in-group such as one's extended family, community, or the organization where they work.[26] In contrast, people in individualistic cultures have an emphasis primarily on themselves. Characteristics of collectivism are harmony, less public egotistical behaviors, and openness to seeing the perspectives of others. Qualities that are associated with individualism are tolerance of conflict, a celebration of personal accomplishments, and valuing independence. This is an example of the cognitive dissonance that challenges HBCU culture: It resides in a Western culture that celebrates individualism, but African Americans still are part of the African diaspora that often adopts many collectivistic principles. Afrocentricity reflects a culture of "communication, love, marriage, death, birth, and religion,"[27] but the globalization of media has greatly devalued, marginalized, and suppressed the beliefs, values, customs, and traditions of Black people.

The concept of "power distance" is a way of describing how social groups are classified within society. In low power distance cultures, an egalitarian belief minimizes differences between social classes based upon wealth or education.[28] Low power distance is reflective of equality. Alternatively, high power distance is associated with environments in which it would be seen as rude to treat everyone the same. For example, in some cultures, the elders are served first and given preferential treatment as a rank higher than other people. In Black culture, elders are set apart in many settings, while in other settings they are ignored or seem to be forgotten about. Again, this calls into question the impact of collectivism and individualism. HBCUs are structured institutions that have historically had clearly defined hierarchical reporting structures with numerous layers between students, staff, faculty, and administration. Students ordinarily demonstrated a great deal of respect for faculty, which has shifted as new generations of millennials and Generation Z students enter classrooms in which pupils expect to be treated with the same respect that these learners may or may not give.

Communication can be either verbal or nonverbal Language is one of the main ways humans use symbols and rules to create meaning.[29] Each community uses language differently. "Slang is the language used by a group whose members belong to a similar coculture or other groups."[30] Studies of Black culture have led to the creation of the term "ebonics" to identify ethnic slang. Hip-hop music influenced culture through media messages that expressed narratives about what was happening in Black neighborhoods, often using slang words. These artists were often featured as headliners at HBCU events. These entertainers represented aspects of Black culture that expressed feelings about the struggle and resilience of the race.

Jargon is another term that explains "the specialized vocabulary that functions as a kind of shorthand for people with common backgrounds and experiences.[31] Acronyms are a form of jargon. The practice of using the first letter of each word in the name of a university is a case of such jargon. For example, rather than always writing or saying "Alabama State University," which is the full university name, the school is often referred to as ASU.

With verbal communication, people can make factual statements that are verifiable as true or false, or they can express opinions based on their beliefs.[32]

The emotive language uses words that reflect the attitude of the speaker about a topic. Black culture has been known for expressive communication that can lead to perceptions of having "an attitude," which comes across as what has been labeled "nice-nasty" language. Minorities have often been referred to by ethnic slurs and derogatory nicknames that impact their own views of themselves, as well as devaluing minorities in the eyes of others. "*Ad hominem* arguments attack the source of a persuasive statement without addressing the reasoning on which the statement is based."[33] Blacks have been spoken of negatively in society, including in private and public discourse, such as media, workplaces, in their communities and in homes.

Rhetoric is persuasive communication that uses language to influence people.[34] This study employs rhetorical analysis to examine written media sources, including print and social media. Scholars have argued the benefits of rhetoric cultivated spaces where people could live together peacefully. Whether through speeches or mediated messages, such as newspapers or social media, the Black community has found voices that speak for them. At Black colleges, such discourse can be heard on charter days, graduations, lectures, or campus radio stations with messages being sent and received. The communication process involves challenges that impact how information is encoded, how messages are decoded and the environment a person is in.[35] Communication is a complex process that requires emotional intelligence to be able to convey and receive messages that closely approximate how they were intended to be understood.

Listening is a skill that is often underappreciated in the communication process, though it is a valuable skill to develop. People who are good listeners are hired and promoted more often, and listening ability is viewed as a leadership skill. In a society in which work overload and rapid thought are barriers to effective communication, any additional cultural differences can further decrease the ability to clearly understand what is spoken or written. These environments challenge people to deal with psychological and physical noise. Workers and students may be frustrated, but they must remember that listening is vital to professional success. Hurtful behaviors include pretending to listen, tuning in and out, acting defensively, avoiding an issue, ignoring underlying issues, being self-centered, and talking too much.[36] Task-oriented listening is often performed in the workplace to obtain information needed to complete a job. Strategies for effective listening include listening for key ideas, asking questions, paraphrasing, and taking notes. It is important to know when to switch between an effective listening style and another listening style, such as a relational, supportive, analytical, or critical style.[37]

Nonverbal communication "involves gestures, sounds, facial expressions, touch, clothing, and much more."[38] In Black culture, how someone uses body language and expression carries a great deal of salience or weight. Kinesics are nonverbal behaviors, including facial expressions, body languages such as posture, fidgeting or manipulators, smiling, eye contact, expressions of emotion, tone of voice, and touch or haptics. Although the United States is considered a low-context culture that uses spoken and written communication for expression, Black Americans are also embedded within a high-context culture that makes extensive use of attention to nonverbal behaviors and messages to communicate meanings. Paralanguage describes nonverbal vocal communication. Attitudes can be communicated through paralanguage, including through differences in "tone of voice, speed, pitch, volume, number and length of pauses, and disfluencies (such as stammering, use of uh, um, er, and so on)."[39]

"Physical environments shape the communication that occurs within them."[40] It is no secret that many HBCUs have experienced funding challenges that have weakened their ability to enhance facilities and provide resources. Black college students, as well as faculty and staff, deserve to work in physical environments that will support their intellectual and creative pursuits in academia, including adequate high-speed Internet access, funding for renovations, and improving buildings to ensure safety on campuses. The Economics of capitalism has resulted in social media characterized by discriminatory impacts on people who hold fewer resources.[41] The asymmetrical politics of visibility privilege those who have established reputations, fame, wealth, or power over those without such advantages.[42] For example, sites such as Twitter or Facebook give voice to people. However, the most frequently followed users have affiliations with large institutions or corporations that have amplified their voices far beyond those of most other users on social media. In response, Black users of Twitter developed "Black Twitter," which has professors, media professionals, activists, and others who are concerned with perspectives that impact the Black diaspora. However, even with "Black Twitter," the most prominent voices come from many retweets that occur from large followership or a high-profile user who has a large number of followers choosing to retweet a post.

AFROCENTRIC COMMUNICATION CONCEPTS AND HBCUS

One of the first Afrocentric concepts that are critical to the development of better communication at HBCUs is the ideal of *harmony*. From an Afrocentric perspective, African Americans[43] seek to communicate harmoniously with one another in order to maintain peace, a sense of serenity, and justness in the "African Village," or, for the purposes of our study, at the HBCU. For example, if a Black college student has a dispute over a grade received from his/her professor, it would be incumbent upon the HBCU administrator (the Dean, for example) to seek a harmonious and just outcome by bringing all parties involved together as a "grade dispute committee." This committee would follow the form and manner of a traditional African village gathering whereby all members would be allowed to present their case, i.e., communicate their perspective and present evidence in a fair and just manner. However, the HBCU administrator may not wish to follow this procedure. They might instead have chosen to forego the forming of a "village" in favor of "choosing sides" with either one villager or the other, i.e., either the professor or the student concerning the grade situation. Such an approach to resolving disputes would have created potential *conflict* among the villagers. The concept of conflict undergirds Western notions of communication. Asante posits that:

> Our theoretical view [of communication] must not emphasize the Western conflict view, but the more humanistic voice which is based on harmony. It is not the tradition of African societies to see conflict as a method of progress; in fact, societies are made livable and kept that way by removing and keeping out conflict as much as possible.[44]

Another Afrocentric concept that is critical to the development of better communication at HBCUs is the notion of the "African collective" or "communal consciousness." From an Afrocentric perspective, *healthy communication is communication that places the wishes, desires, and objectives of the "village" or group at the center of the communication interaction and not that of the individual.* Moreover, the individual and the community are viewed as being interdependent. One of the best examples of the "African collective" is the Black communication linguistic practice referred to as *call-response.* Smitherman defines call-response as the "spontaneous verbal interaction between speaker and listener in which all the speaker's statements ('calls') are punctuated by expressions ('responses') from the listener."[45] While there are various examples of call-response among Black college students at HBCUs that could be cited, an example of the HBCU collective that comes immediately to mind is the Black college band. For example, during a football game, members of the Alabama State University (Montgomery, Alabama) Mighty Marching Hornets band may shout, "Yeh, Yeh, Yeh, State!" (the call), and the students and crowd in the stands immediately respond as a group by shouting, "Yeh, Yeh, Yeh, State!" This example suggests that the communication is: (1) holistic as opposed to being individualistic, (2) interdependent, (3) harmonious, (4) balanced, and (5) interactive. Smitherman further suggested that call-response is an "interactive system [that] embodies communality rather than individuality. Emphasis is on group cohesiveness, cooperation, and the collective good."[46]

A final Afrocentric concept that is critical to the development of better communication at HBCUs is the notion of an *Afrocentric Rhetoric*. Rhetoric, from an Afrocentric perspective, is a discourse of resistance to oppression. Black college students at HBCUs are taught via a variety of courses such as history, sociology, and communications about Black historical events and figures such as Marcus Garvey, E. Franklin Frazier, Fannie Lou Hamer, Dr. Martin Luther King, Jr., and Malcolm X. As a result of such education, they are thus taught about the power of their rhetoric. As a further result of this learning, Black student leaders at HBCUs are not only empowered to go out and confront White oppression in their communities, but these student leaders also work to confront "Black oppression" at their respective institutions. One of the best examples is the student protest at Howard University in Washington, DC in 1968. From March 19 to 23, 1968, more than one thousand students took over the administration building, which shut down the university. The Black student leadership made several demands:

> The activists wanted Narbrit's [the president of Howard University] resignation; a judiciary system for student discipline; an emphasis on African-American history and culture in the curriculum, and the dropping of charges against 39 students inspired by the above issues who had made a protest three weeks earlier at Howard's centennial Charter Day celebration.[47]

In the end, the activities of these students successfully achieved two of their demands met before returning to class: (1) the formation of a student judiciary committee, and (2) the infusion of Black history and culture into the curriculum. The Black student activists used two Afrocentric rhetorical devices: (1) lyrical code, and (2) the rhetorical strategy of legitimation. Asante posits that the lyrical code is the use of rhyming, poetics, and narrations as a persuasive form of communication.[48] Thus, for example, the student protesters chanted the phrase "Beep, Beep, Bang, Bang, Ungawa, Black Power."[49] This chant served as both a rhetorical invective levied at the administration as well as a unifying device for the cause of the protesters. Smith claims that the strategy of legitimation is the Black rhetorician's "use of language to answer the opposition, it is a refutative strategy . . . an argumentative rebuttal to an opponent; it is a psychological weapon."[50] During the protest, "a group of students hung a hand-made sign over the 'Howard University' sign on the front of the [administration] building reading 'Black University.'"[51] By placing the "Black University" sign over the "Howard University" sign, the Black protest students were essentially challenging the legitimacy of the institution by saying that Howard University, which to the protesters was code for "White University" was now a *Black University* as a result of the student protest. In the end, the use of Afrocentric rhetoric by Black student protesters at

Howard University and other HBCUs seeks to be "combative, antagonistic, and wholly committed to the propagation of a more humanistic vision of the world."[52] "Charity starts at home." Thus, Black college leaders are called to use the knowledge learned at HBCUs to make them a better place for all.

METHODOLOGY

This qualitative inquiry examined a collection of journal articles, print news, magazines, and social media forums (i.e., Facebook, Twitter, Instagram, etc.) created between the years 2015 and 2020. "A case study is a good approach when the inquirer has identifiable cases with boundaries and seeks to provide an in-depth understanding of the cases or a comparison of several cases."[53] Content analysis used in this study utilized a collective case study approach to examine an issue within multiple bounded systems or institutions.[54] Purposeful sampling was used to select the texts that were chosen through online search engines. An examination of language explored the power that communication messages had on HBCU students. Texts were analyzed for nonverbal, verbal, jargon, paralanguage, and the words associated with the communication. Because of the limited previous scholarship on how discourse at HBCUs has impacted declines in HBCU student enrollments, few previous sources identified this phenomenon.

The data from this study were coded based on *HBCU, sources, online site, social media presence, print news, date, year, gender, student status, communication format, types of messages, power differentials* and *people*. The code *HBCU* denoted the name of the college or university being discussed in the article. In this instance, Clark Atlanta University, Morehouse College, and Spelman College were studied as the HBCUs which are part of the Atlanta University Center. Very few sources could be found on Morris Brown College during exploratory research, and therefore this institution was omitted from the study. *Sources* were defined as the publication or online medium where rhetorical statements were located.

The code *"online site"* was used to designate the name of the website that reviewed student experiences, including Niche, RateMyProfessor, YR Media, Unigo, and None. The code *"social media presence"* identified trademark logos that appeared within the communication, such as Facebook, Twitter, Instagram, LinkedIn, Snapchat, or TikTok. The code *"print news"* was used to represent the name of the campus's official newspaper or publication. For example, the print news publications that were investigated were *Spelman Connection Newsletter, The CAU Panther Newspaper,* and *The Maroon Tiger*. The *date* and *year* that the communication appeared to be published were recorded. The code *"gender"* was selected based upon the name of the person, how they identified their gender, or the name of the institution. The code "*student status*" was used to differentiate between current, prospective, and past students within the alumni category.

The code "*communication format*" was used to assess how the communication was expressed through either paralanguage, nonverbal communication, jargon, text, or verbal. There were two levels of communication: (1) internal, and (2) external. Internal communication was defined as messages of conflict that had shared meanings, such as documented harsh communications in a classroom, department, or institution. External communication could be helpful or hurtful.

The code "*types of messages*" examined statements that were made to students, such as encouraging, disparaging, unknown (unclear), empowerment, indifferent, or absent. The code "*business empowerment*" was suggested by Booker T. Washington's philosophy of how respectability influenced communication. The politics of respectability have traditionally followed Eurocentric norms of elite goals in advocating for young Black students to attend universities to become educated.[55] In Black culture, respect has traditionally been defined within Black institutions, such as HBCUs and African American churches, which embodied Afrocentric perspectives through the everyday lived experiences of Black people. Intellectual empowerment philosophies refer to the philosophies of W. E. B. Du Bois. Students who did not know or who were unaware of something had their comments coded as "*unknown*" or "*unclear*," such as when a statement was unclear to both parties.

The code "*power differentials*" was used to designate messages that were associated with power distance between students and HBCU employees at various levels in the institutions. Cultural differences of power were demonstrated through several means: (1) authoritarian or hierarchical leadership in high power distance relationships, (2) authoritative leadership or low power distance, (3) transformational leadership or equality in power, or (4) no power differential. People identified the roles of individuals named in the statements, including students, professors, parents, support staff, executives, alumni, and external.

RESULTS

Unlike Clark Atlanta University (CAU) which is a coeducational institution, Morehouse College and Spelman College are both single-gender institutions. As of Fall 2020, Clark Atlanta University had 3,776 enrolled students, Spelman College had 2,100 enrolled students, and Morehouse College had 2,200 enrolled students. Through the Atlanta University Center Consortium, these institutions, along with Morehouse School of Medicine, have fostered "a vibrant intellectual community with a long tradition of scholarship, service, and community engagement."[56] The following section describes the verbal, jargon, and nonverbal communication of these universities as perceived by their students.

VERBAL COMMUNICATION

Current, former, and prospective students from all three institutions perceived their institutions to have strong verbal communication. They believed that administrators and faculty established a communication system that was positive and challenging. For instance, students from all three institutions reported that the classrooms provide an environment conducive to constructive communication. One current student at Spelman College stated, "classes provide an open and safe environment for learning and discussions." Similarly, a Morehouse student reported that this institution fostered an atmosphere of "open communication with counselors and the student aid office."

Communication was also perceived as challenging due to miscommunication by administrators, as well as a result of their slow response or non-responsiveness to accusations. One current Spelman College student complained that "the school does have a history of attempting to sweep rape accusations under the rug." Furthermore, a current Clark Atlanta University student said, "Clark Atlanta University needs to reevaluate for the whole student body or they will continue to lose students annually due to the miscommunication."

The students clearly perceived the verbal communication at each of the three institutions as a roller-coaster ride. For instance, financial aid counselors might give good news to one student and bad news to another. Since communication is subject to interpretation, the good news may perhaps be perceived as positive verbal communication and the bad news as negative verbal communication. Overall, students believe that the three institutions strived to foster positive verbal communication with them, but that there still needed to be a sense of urgency for improving all aspects of communication, including nonverbal communication.

NONVERBAL COMMUNICATION

Nonverbal communication within academia can be complex. The paralanguage and body language of administrators and faculty can evoke mixed emotions in students. At Morehouse College, Spelman College, and Clark Atlanta University, the students expressed both comfort and discomfort as well as satisfaction and dissatisfaction with the way administrators spoke to them (i.e., tone of voice, condescending, etc.), as well as with the "reassuring" or "unnerving" body language of administrators. One Morehouse student indicated that "one thing I would change is the school's attitude and the way they look down on everyone else."

The condition of the buildings of the institutions and the quality of living at the schools are part of the nonverbal communication of those institutions with the students. One Spelman college student stated, "Freshman housing does not have air conditioning, and in the Georgia summer heat, this is not ideal." However, the small, intimate classroom size is a positive nonverbal communication for her. She went on to say, "Spelman is a small, private institution, class sizes are equivalent to high school classes. This means that professors know each of their students and work to make sure every student can succeed in his or her class."

The students from these three institutions perceived the nonverbal communication of their institutions to be both constructive and destructive. However, students can interpret nonverbal communication differently if there is not a shared meaning established between the students and the administrators. Verbal and nonverbal communication at these institutions is not the only factor that emerged from the data that could impact enrollment. The jargon used at the institution can be equally detrimental to the survival of the institution.

JARGON

According to the Oxford Learner's Dictionaries, jargon is "words or expressions that are used by a particular profession or group of people and are difficult for others to understand." Oxford Learner's Dictionaries advises people to "try to avoid using too much technical jargon." For any institution, the overuse of certain words or expressions that are not comprehended by its students can have long-term effects on its students, which can impact enrollment.

Several students alluded to university officials using words and expressions with them in bewildering ways. "When I heard, I was super excited," said queer Morehouse sophomore and activist Daniel Galberth. "But when I sat down to read the policy, it really hit me that what Morehouse said is, 'We're gonna accept transgender men, but kick out anyone who doesn't identify as a man.'" Clearly, the Morehouse College's policy on transgender men had some technical legal jargon that caught Daniel by surprise.

On the other hand, the jargon used in these institutions can be considered as the "glue" that binds the students together - which can maintain the current enrollment or even increase it. In the words of a Morehouse College student, "like any school where the experiences are unique to your setting, it is hard to explain to outsiders. When we speak of 'Club Woody' or 'Hump Wednesday' or 'Crown Forum,' others just don't understand."

The objective of this study was to investigate the verbal, nonverbal, and jargon of Morehouse College, Clark Atlanta University, and Spelman College. It was assumed that those communication dynamics would severely impact the enrollment of these institutions. However, data shows that perceptions of the students attending these universities varied. Their dissatisfaction with the negative communication between them and administrators did not alter their decision to stay or leave their universities.

DISCUSSION

The student insights into the communication dynamics of their institutions centered on three themes: (1) encouraging, (2) disparaging, and (3) absent.

"Encouraging" was very common across the board. Communication was perceived as very encouraging and empowering during various interactions between the students, professors, and administrators. Students felt that the institutions worked diligently to ensure that they were involved in bettering the community, graduation rates, and graduating with employment. One Morehouse student stated, "I love the brotherhood Morehouse has. You literally cannot walk past someone without getting a 'what's up?' or 'how are you?' I love how they strive on bringing people up instead of tearing them down."

Schoenaker, Bahlmann and Dinter stated:

> encouragement is everything a person does that makes another person feel better, function more effectively, deal with his or her problems more effectively, have greater self-confidence, and have a greater willingness to contribute to the well-being of others and society in general. These results evolve because that person has the feeling that he or she is good enough, belongs, is accepted by others, and has the feeling of *I can.*[57]

"Disparaging" was another emergent theme concerning students' perception of communication from the administrators. Some students wrote that certain administrators made disparaging remarks to and about them as well as having displayed disparaging behaviors toward them. One Morehouse College student disclosed that "the most biggest controversy on the campus was when MC described and treated me as a common thug that is nobody and is not going to get ahead in life." Furthermore, a Morehouse College transgender woman said, "who I am on this campus, they are trying to kind of like remove me from self-identifying myself."

"Absent" is a sentiment that students of all three institutions shared about the communication from administrators and faculty. Some students believed they were not being heard, and little was done to address their complaints (i.e. robbed at gunpoint on campus, raped, uninhabitable dorms, etc.). Some students saw some professors and administrators as being detached and aloof and perceived them as only caring about themselves. One Clark Atlanta University student alleged that "administration as far as the faculty, most of them only come to collect their checks and do not do a good job of ensuring the students can understand the material." A Spelman student affirmed that her college "Needs better advising and support." Another Clark Atlanta University student declared, "Overall, I would rate Clark with a two-star because they don't fulfill their commitment for our safety or academic growth."

CONCLUSION

Historically Black Colleges and Universities were established to provide higher education for Black people. Now, HBCUs are open to anyone who chooses to attend. It was assumed that the communication of HBCU administrators and faculty with students and prospective students might contribute to the low enrollment at the institutions. However, the findings of the study did not support this claim. As has been the case since the founding of HBCUs, students have displayed resilience in adapting to the evolution of Black culture. HBCUs have elevated the status of the Black community.

Students from Morehouse College, Spelman College, and Clark Atlanta University all recognized the communication dynamics of the administrators and faculty of their institutions. They described the communication from the administrators and faculty to be sometimes encouraging, sometimes disparaging, and sometimes absent. These three institutions need to be mindful that students may prefer the Afrocentric concept of communication, a collectivistic style of communication that has traditionally been practiced and revered within the Black community that focuses on harmony. The challenge for Black institutions within Westernized cultures will be to identify and proactively articulate their values from a holistic perspective that takes into account everyone who is part of the community. This approach will position HBCUs as empowered leaders, rather than seeing these cultural changes as imperialistic forces.

As stated earlier in this chapter, *healthy communication is communication that places the wishes, desires, and objectives of the "village" or group at the center of the interaction rather than the interests of the individual.* When the Afrocentric concept was abandoned at these institutions, this created the potential for disparaging and absent communication. Failure of this sort leaves the institutions in a state of agitation filled with uncertainty about the future of the HBCUs. These students have used their agency on new and traditional media to tell their experiences. Comments posted online may or may not receive a high number of views, but even so, the voices of these students are being heard. With the onset of the COVID-19 pandemic, online instruction has increased at HBCUs, and this method of learning is most likely here to stay. Social media allows everyday people to become citizen journalists or creators of news. This suggests that Black culture should embrace the power of digital media in their communication interactions to collectively advocate for HBCUs, just as the traditional Black press has so effectively done.

Students have always found ways to express themselves by developing media of their own, from the Black press to radio shows and now social media, these students demonstrate their agency. Technology discourse can debate how these tools were created by Western culture, but these Black students have used digital media to form alliances that have stimulated activism. HBCU students from previous generations have known the power of communicating with mass audiences. These student-driven organizations offer a sense of connection within the communication, which stimulates growth, participation, and life readiness skills. From these experiences, alumni of these universities are positioned to become entrepreneurs and to have greater appeal to employers.

Gender equality is a struggle that continues at HBCUs, with a disproportionately higher number of male presidents and senior executives than females in such positions. Black women comprise the majority of student enrollees at HBCUs. This has implications for future alumni endowments and funding, for Black women are one of the lowest wage-earning groups. As college tuition costs continue to soar and single mothers continue to be a significant presence in Black communities, it is imperative to further investigate the economic implications this has on the present and future student enrollments and graduation rates. African values demand a patriarchal family structure with a husband and wife who is his equal. The LGBTQIA community fits into a gender matrix beyond what has traditionally assumed the existence of only two genders. HBCUs have ongoing internal struggles about how to respond to LGBTQIA students whose gender identity has not been broadly accepted. Such students feel unsafe or unsupported revealing their total identity, which has resulted in silencing and suppression.

Media representations have greatly influenced gender and racial stereotypes, making it difficult to raise the self-esteem of minority groups. This study demonstrates the appeal the HBCUs have to attract students of all races to spaces where they feel like they belong and fit into the culture. Despite evident flaws of these institutions, many students have found them to be places of acceptance. Mainstream media images that depict Black women and men as being subordinate have caused HBCUs to be seen as places of refuge for students. These institutions weld great power in the Black community. As the Black church questions the role it has in the future, HBCUs serve as institutions to help students find their places and voices to positively impact the world as community changemakers.

The good news is that the negative communication students have experienced from administrators did not persuade them to leave their institutions. No statement that was analyzed in this study revealed that students left their school because of the way the administrators had spoken to them. Therefore, there was no evidence that ineffective communication from the administrators decreased enrollment at Morehouse College, Spelman College, and Clark Atlanta University. The results reflect a rich history of HBCUs that have done far greater good than harm to the Black communities where they continue to be a vital contributor to economic, intellectual, and social capital. To keep it real, the culture of homecomings, Greek life, and jargon specific to each university and alumni associations continue to make HBCUs appealing in 2021 and continue to attract and retain the best and brightest students.

NOTES

1. Arthur J. Clement and Arthur J. Lidsky, "The Danger of History Slipping Away: The Heritage Campus and HBCUs," *Planning for Higher Education* 39, no. 4 (2011): 149, accessed November 11, 2020, http://web.b.ebscohost.com.libalasu.idm.oclc.org /ehost/pdfviewer/pdfviewer?vid=4&sid=cbc4b3a7-de2c-4123-9b14-0bc142b2bbc1 %40pdc-v-sessmgr02

2. Ibid

3. Bea Wilson, "The Tale of Two Morrill Acts: 1890 Historically Black Land-Grant Universities," AG Daily, October 22, 2020, https://www.agdaily.com/insights/tale-of -two-morrill-acts-1890-historically-black-land-grant-universities/

4. Ibid

5. "Council of 1890s Institutions," Association of Public Land-Grant Universities, accessed November 11, 2020, https://www.aplu.org/members/councils/1890 -universities/council-of-1890s-institutions.html.

6. Arthur J. Clement and Arthur J. Lidsky, "The Danger of History Slipping Away: The Heritage Campus and HBCUs,"

7. "Historically Black Colleges and University," National Center for Education Statistics, accessed November 11, 2020, https://nces.ed.gov/fastfacts/display.asp?id =667.

8. "Digest of Education Statistics," National Center for Education Statistics, accessed November 11, 2020, https://nces.ed.gov/programs/digest/d19/tables/dt19 _313.10.asp

9. "Historically Black Colleges and University," National Center for Education Statistics

10. Richard Vedder, "Is 'Diversity' Destroying The HBCUs," *Forbes*, November 4, 2019, https://www.forbes.com/sites/richardvedder/2019/11/04/is-diversity-destroying -the-hbcus/?sh=49f8a2d64195.

11. Ronald Adler, George Rodman, and Athena du Pre. 2020. *Essential Communication*. Second ed. New York, New York: Oxford University Press, 32.

12. Wilson, Clint C. 2014. *Whither the Black Press?: Glorious Past, Uncertain Future*. Thorofare, NJ: Xlibris LLC, 152.

13. Langmia, Kehbuma. 2016. *Globalization and Cyberculture: An Afrocentric Perspective*. Cham, Switzerland: Palgrave Macmillan, 23.

14. Lyle, Jack, ed. 1968. *The Black American and the Press*. Los Angeles, CA: The Ward Ritchie Press, x.

15. Lyle, 74.

16. Pride, Armistead S., and Clint C. Wilson. 1997. *A History of the Black Press*. Washington, DC: Howard University Press, 203.

17. Pride and Wilson, 203.

18. Pride and Wilson, 203.

19. Pride and Wilson, 203.

20. Langmia, 23

21. Wilson, Clint C., Feliz Gutierrez, and Lena M. Chao. 2013. *Racism, Sexism and the Media: Multicultural Issues into the New Communications Age*. Los Angeles, CA: SAGE, 111.

22. Wilson, Gutierrez, and Chao, 111.

23. Wilson, Gutierrez, and Chao, 115.

24. Langmia, *Globalization and Cyberculture*, 23.

25. Langmia, 90.

26. Adler, Rodman, and duPre, *Essential Communication*, 38.

27. Langmia, *Globalization and Cyberculture*, 23.

28. Adler, Rodman, and duPre, *Essential Communication*, 40.

29. Ibid., 48.

30. Ibid., 54.

31. Ibid.

32. Adler, Rodman, and duPre, 56.

33. Borchers, Timothy A. (2002). *Persuasion in the Media Age*. Boston: McGrawHill.

34. Berger, Arthur A. 2020. *Media and Communication Research Methods: An Introduction to Qualitative and Quantitative Approaches*. Fifth ed. Los Angeles, CA: SAGE, 98.

35. Berger, 106

36. Adler, Rodman, and duPre, *Essential Communication*, 71.

37. Ibid.

38. Ibid., 80.

39. Ibid., 85.

40. Ibid., 87.

41. Fuchs, Christian. 2014. *Social Media: A Critical Introduction*. Thousand Oaks, CA: SAGE, 196.

42. Ibid., 196.

43. The terms "Black" and "African American" are used interchangeably throughout the chapter.

44. Molefi Kete Asante, *Malcolm X as Cultural Hero & Other Afrocentric Essays* (New Jersey: African World Press, Inc., 1993), 184.

45. Geneva Smitherman, *Talkin and Testifyin: The Language of Black America* (Detroit: Wayne State University Press, 1977), 104.

46. Smitherman, 109.

47. Rick Massimo, *"Our demand is an answer-50 year since Howard University Protest,"* WTOP (March 19, 2018). https://wtop.com/dc/2018/03/demand-answer -howard-university-protest-50/.

48. Molefi Kete Asante, *The Afrocentric Idea* (Philadelphia: Temple University Press), 43.

49. Massimo, "Our demand is an answer."

50. Arthur L. Smith, *Rhetoric of Black Revolution* (Boston: Allyn and Bacon, Inc.), 40.

51. Massimo, "Our demand is an answer."

52. Asante, *Afrocentric Idea*, 170.

53. John W. Creswell, *Qualitative inquiry and research design: Choosing among five approaches* (Thousand Oaks: SAGE Publications), 74.

54. Creswell, *Qualitative inquiry and research design*.

55. Ashla Hill Roseboro, *National Association of University Women: Advocacy in The Black Press for an Organization of African American Intellectual Women, 1910–1980*. [Dissertation, 2019], 35.

56. "Mission & Vision." Atlanta University Center Consortium. Accessed February 25, 2021. https://aucenter.edu/about-us/mission-vision/.

57. Renie Bahlmann and Lynda D. Dinter, "Encouraging Self-Encouragement: An Effect Study of the Encouraging-Training Schoenaker-Concept," *The Journal of Individual Psychology* 57, no. 3 (Fall 2001): 273.

REFERENCES

Asante, Molefi Kete. *The Afrocentric Idea*. Philadelphia: Temple University Press, 1987.

Asante, Molefi Kete. *Malcolm X as Cultural Hero & Other Afrocentric Essays.* New Jersey: African World Press, Inc., 1993.

Adler, Ronald B., George Rodman, and Athena du Pre. 2020. *Essential Communication*. Second ed. New York, New York: Oxford University Press.

Bahlmann, Renie, and Lynda D. Dinter. "Encouraging Self-Encouragement: An Effect Study of the Encouraging-Training Schoenaker-Concept." *Journal of Individual Psychology* 57, no. 3 (Fall 2001): 273–288

Berger, Arthur A. 2020. *Media and Communication Research Methods: An Introduction to Qualitative and Quantitative Approaches*. Fifth ed. Los Angeles, CA: SAGE.

Clement, Arthur J., and Arthur J. Lidsky. "The Danger of History Slipping Away: The Heritage Campus and HBCUs." *Planning for Higher Education* 39, no. 4 (2011): 149–158. Accessed November 11, 2020. http://web.b.ebscohost.com.libalasu .idm.oclc.org/ehost/pdfviewer/pdfviewer?vid=4&sid=cbc4b3a7-de2c-4123-9b14 -0bc142b2bbc1%40pdc-v-sessmgr02.

"Council of 1890s Institutions." Association of Public Land-Grant Universities. Accessed November 11, 2020. https://www.aplu.org/members/councils/1890 -universities/council-of-1890s-institutions.html.

"Digest of Education Statistics." National Center for Education Statistics. Accessed November 11, 2020. https://nces.ed.gov/programs/digest/d19/tables/dt19_313.10 .asp

Fuchs, Christian. 2014. *Social Media: A Critical Introduction*. Thousand Oaks, CA: SAGE.

"Historically Black Colleges and University." National Center for Education Statistics. Accessed November 11, 2020. https://nces.ed.gov/fastfacts/display.asp ?id=667.

Langmia, Kehbuma. 2016. *Globalization and Cyberculture: An Afrocentric Perspective*. Cham, Switzerland: Palgrave Macmillan.

Lyle, Jack, ed. 1968. *The Black American and the Press*. Los Angeles, CA: The Ward Ritchie Press.

Massimo, Rick. "Our demand is an answer-50 year since Howard University Protest." (March 19, 2018). https://wtop.com/dc/2018/03/demand-answer-howard -university- protest-50/.

"Mission & Vision." Atlanta University Center Consortium. Accessed February 25, 2021. https://aucenter.edu/about-us/mission-vision/

Pride, Armistead S., and Clint C. Wilson. 1997. *A History of the Black Press*. Washington, DC: Howard University Press.

Smith, Arthur L. *Rhetoric of Black Revolution*. Boston: Allyn and Bacon, Inc., 1969.

Smitherman, Geneva. *Talkin and Testifyin: The Language of Black America*. Detroit: Wayne State University Press, 1977.

Vedder, Richard. "Is 'Diversity' Destroying The HBCUs." Forbes. November 4, 2019. https://www.forbes.com/sites/richardvedder/2019/11/04/is-diversity-destroying -the-hbcus/?sh=49f8a2d64195.

Wilson, Bea. "The Tale of Two Morrill Acts: 1890 Historically Black Land-Grant Universities." AGDaily. October 22, 2020. https://www.agdaily.com/insights/tale -of-two-morrill-acts-1890-historically-black-land-grant-universities/

Wilson, Clint C. 2014. *Whither the Black Press?: Glorious Past, Uncertain Future*. Thorofare, NJ: Xlibris LLC.

Wilson, Clint C., Feliz Gutierrez, and Lena M. Chao. 2013. *Racism, Sexism and the Media: Multicultural Issues into the New Communications Age*. Los Angeles, CA: SAGE.

Chapter 6

Twenty-First-Century HBCU Students

Living in An Era of Oppression

Carla Brown

INTRODUCTION

"Say their name." Many Black individuals have tragically lost their lives at the hands of police or have been a victim of oppression. The Black Lives Matter (BLM) movement, which was created in 2013 as a response to the acquittal of Trayvon Martin's killer, has grown and is a platform that works in hopes to ensure that Blacks are no longer systematically targeted without notice. Sadly, even with protests, marches, and vigils, Blacks are still being unfairly mistreated across the nation. Whenever Blacks are victims of oppression, cities across the United States begin to publicly acknowledge the situation or person by hosting vigils, marches, and protests. As the BLM Movement swept across the nation, historically Black college and university (HBCU) students also became vocal about the prolonged mistreatment of Blacks.

Black people are systematically and institutionally targeted daily. This can be experienced in multiple areas such as employment, academics, and the laws. This is the world that HBCU students are witnessing from inside of their institutions, but this is what they experience once they step off their campus. Unfortunately, outside of their institution, there is a world of prejudiced systems and policies that are not created for them. This causes apprehension and emotional stress on Black HBCU students. The research conducted exposes many truths about the prevalence of Black oppression and how it's affecting

HBCU students. This research uses a qualitative approach to analyze survey and interview data on Black HBCU students' experiences, challenges, and concerns about being a Black student in America. The study actively shows that there is a relationship between HBCU students and oppression, racism, and prejudice.

TWENTY-FIRST-CENTURY PROTESTS

The word "protest" in America has had somewhat of a negative connotation, though many protests have been and still are peaceful. However, there have been protests that have caused havoc and chaos, but all protests shouldn't be anticipated to host violence. The historical protests have left such a bad meaning behind that in the twenty-first century protests have to be identified as "peaceful" protests. The majority of the protests that were held for Black individuals who lost their lives at the hands of officers haven't been violent. However, news stories, city administrators, city officials, and some citizens have been shedding a negative light on protesting, specifically the BLM protests. This then influences negative thoughts about the protests and demonstrations before they begin. The negativity surrounding this movement could be rooted in feelings of hate, fear, or uncertainty. Luckily, cities and towns do not let foul comments stop the community from joining together.

Overall, the approach to fighting social injustices in the twenty-first century is nothing new from what we have seen before. Protest and public demonstrations have been performed before. However, there is a difference in the causes of initiation and who's participating. Living in a world that's supposed to be open to diversity and inclusion has opened the door for individuals to freely gather for any purpose or cause they support. The BLM Movement was created to ensure that Blacks are no longer systematically targeted without notice. Ever since 2013, BLM protests, demonstrations, and marches have been hosted nationwide to draw attention to the injustices Blacks suffer. Within these demonstrations, it is not odd to spot races other than Blacks and African Americans. Other races are starting to publicly support and represent Blacks in the BLM Movement. An HBCU graduate expressed that witnessing other races protesting showed "unity." Especially since there was once a time when other races wouldn't interfere with the issues of Black people, and if they did it was done in private. Today, there are individuals of different races fighting for Black lives.

US vs. THEM: THE EFFECTS

The chapter actively shows the positive correlation between HBCU students and oppression, racism, and prejudice. The study sample consists of ninety-six anonymous women and men who attended an HBCU between 2014 and 2020. Out of the sample size, 83.3 percent of the students witnessed discrimination outside of their HBCU campus. Meaning, that Black students were exposed to seeing other Blacks, outside their HBCU, being mistreated within the community. HBCU student #1 stated, "Honestly, it is so overwhelming that it negatively affects how I function, how I care for my children, and how I live. I am so numb and traumatized that it's depressing."[1] This reveals that HBCU students are affected by the woes of oppression even when it's not directly linked to them. This is due to the underlying factor that seeing the oppression of someone you can identify with can be traumatizing. This is also due to the knowledge of previous experiences that are closely related to what they are seeing others go through, which provides an emotional pathway from themselves to others.

Did you ever witness discrimination outside of your HBCUs campus?
96 responses

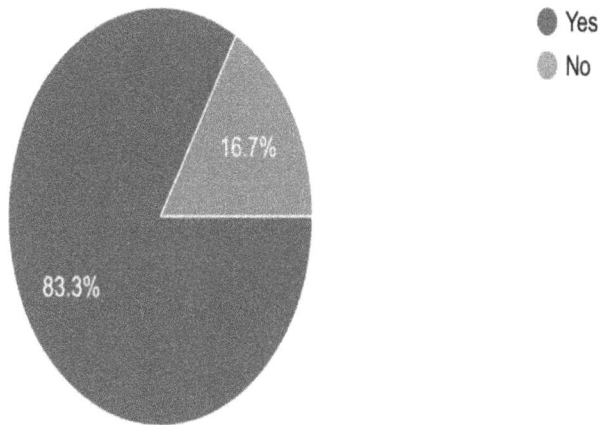

Figure 6.1 HBCU Students Responses To If They Have Witnessed Discrimination Outside Of Their HBCU Campus
Source: Created by Author: Carla Brown, 2021

Out of the sample , 77.1 percent of the students personally experienced racism and/or unfair treatment while outside of their HBCU community. When asked to specify, the majority of the students (53.1 percent) experienced mistreatment in their jobs. Followed by restaurants (50 percent) being the next-highest-ranking location. HBCU student #2 expressed her personal experience of what was said to her while she was working. "When I was working at a retail store during college, I decided one day to wear my hair straight. I usually wear an Afro. When I came in to work that day my manager said to me, 'You look so nice! I can see your face now!' As if she couldn't recognize me with my natural hair."[2] The statement made was a microaggression, which Black people experience quite often. The comments made can be intentional or unintentional, however, they leave an emotional scar.

If you answered "yes" where did you experience the unfair treatment *Check all that apply*
96 responses

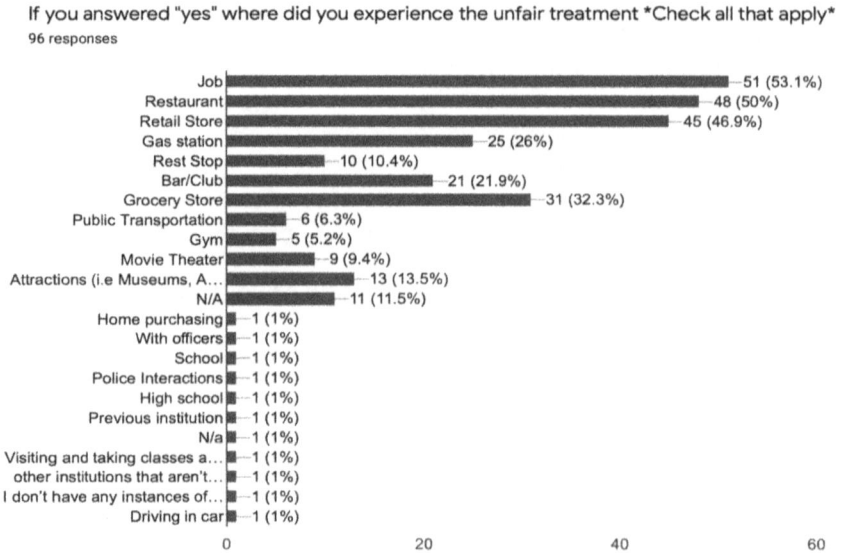

Figure 6.2 HBCU Students Responses To Where They Have Witnessed Discrimination Outside Of Their HBCU Campus
Source: Created by Author: Carla Brown, 2021

Not only are the majority of HBCU students personally experiencing oppression, but they also have friends and classmates who are or have been oppressed as well. This causes additional stressors, as well, for the HBCU students. Out of the survey sample, 84 percent of the HBCU students were emotionally affected, during their academic careers, after discovering news stories about racism, oppression, and mistreatment of Black people. HBCU student #3 stated, "It makes school much harder than it is because my mind is in a million different places. Worrying about my safety and the safety of my family and friends on top of doing work is very stressful for me. I have little to no motivation these days."[3] Therefore, HBCU students aren't only forced to be concerned about their academics, extracurriculars, job searches, and internships, but to also be apprehensive of what may happen to them or a colleague due to being Black. Out of the survey sample, 92.7 percent of the HBCU students questioned their safety due to being Black. Along with being concerned with their own safety, 91.7 percent also question the safety of their Black friends and colleagues. HBCU student #4 mentioned, "The whole year of 2020 has been a deep reflection period of realizing I'll never be truly safe in my black skin even with my HBCU college education as an additive. I'm still at a disadvantage"[4] This highlights the lingering trauma that is attached to oppression. For an HBCU student to be concerned about their safety is an indication that they are living in fear. "I just don't know if today will be the day I die but I know my chances are higher because I'm black,"[5] stated HBCU student #5. This thought process is prevalent among the Black community due to the experiences that Black people have witnessed and endured. This ideology has now trickled down to younger generations and has HBCU students on high alert. This causes anxieties and overwhelming emotions, due to just being Black.

At any moment, have you questioned your safety due to being Black?
96 responses

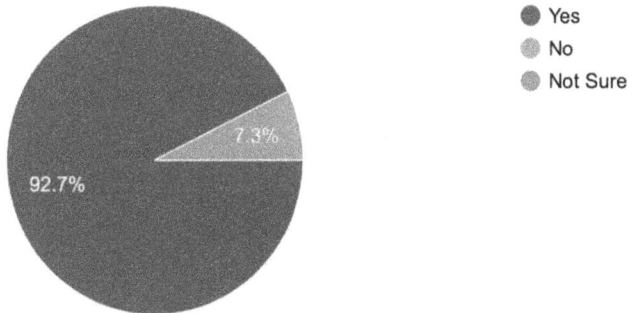

Figure 6.3 HBCU Students Responses Concerning Their Safety Due To Being Black
Source: Created by Author: Carla Brown, 2021

At any moment, have you questioned the safety of friends and colleagues due to them being Black?
96 responses

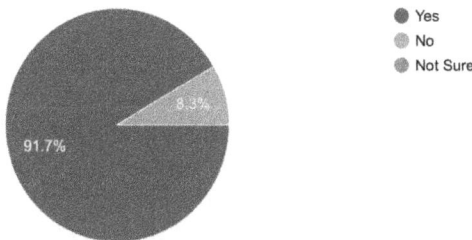

Figure 6.4 HBCU Students Responses Concerning Their Friends and Colleagues Safety Due To Being Black
Source: Created by Author: Carla Brown, 2021

Of the HBCU students, 89.6 percent are concerned about being a victim of systematic and institutionalized racism. Systematic and institutionalized racism dates back to the 1900s. It was to be expected that this form of prejudice would be subject to change due to the Fourteenth and Fifteenth Amendments, affirmative action, and the Civil Rights Act of 1964. However, systems and policies have loopholes where those in power have an opportunity to mistreat Black people.

Today, Blacks are still being systematically and institutionally attacked. HBCU student #6 declared, "I see it widely expressed on a daily basis from microaggressions to systematic and institutional racism, standards used for Whites compared to Black people. It's tiring having to work harder to still not obtain the respect and receive the established wealth of our counterparts. When will there become a time when we are seen as valued contributors to this society?? It's sickening and saddening that I feel like the answer to my question is NEVER! We're oppressed . . . despite all the protesting."[6]

Are you concerned about being a victim of systematic and institutionalized racism?
96 responses

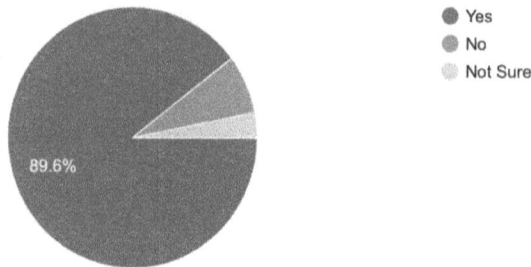

Figure 6.5 HBCU Students Responses Concerning Being A Victim of Systematic and Institutional Racism
Source: Created by Author: Carla Brown, 2021

LESSONS OF CIVIC LIFE AND THE JUSTICE SYSTEM

The injustice against Blacks has been an ongoing issue. Clarence Taylor addressed that "African Americans and the U.S. criminal justice system have had an adversarial relationship for well over a century, and it persists into the 21st century."[7] Black people have been systematically targeted by the justice system for decades. The issues have never truly been fixed, but instead swept under the rug and covered up. Why are Blacks dying at the hands of officers? Why isn't there any justice being served? "America still has a ton of work to do,"[8] stated a 2014 HBCU graduate. This statement serves to be correct after observing the racial climate of America. There hasn't been much change in the thought process of the majority. This is proven through the systematic oppression that Blacks endure. In the twenty-first century, Black people are still encountering and fighting similar issues from generations ago.

Transparency and accuracy are needed in the justice system. On a national level, Lyle and Esmail declared that approximately 50 percent of 14,800 police agencies don't report police-involved homicide to FBI-UCR.[9] Along with failed reports, there is no trust between police and citizens. There is a negative stigma around police, and this is due to the unlawful events that have occurred at the hands of police. Even on a local level, there is an issue of trust. Transparency and communication are the lacking key factors when it comes to policing. This is due to policing being built upon secrecy. If there was more transparency and accuracy within policing, citizens would be more trusting of officers. However, HBCU students are witnessing the secrecy and lack of communication which takes away from the credibility of the justice system.

Transparency and accuracy are expected of government officials and officers, which relies on them following the rules. Due to Black people feeling that rules, laws, and regulations aren't being followed in the justice system it leads to protests for justice. Protests that are held are the product of the absence of proper implementation of the justice system following the law. HBCU students feel that Blacks are unjustly treated by the justice system and officers and that the justice system doesn't attempt to provide justice for Black individuals. An HBCU student made the comment stating, "For me, the ongoing dismissals of cops not being convicted of crimes, as was the case with Mike Brown, Trayvon Martin and as of yesterday Breonna Taylor. It makes me so angry that here we are as college students attempting to make our lives better and hope to leave a legacy for our communities are still being emotionally scarred by our brothers and sisters being slaughtered by the police. Sandra Bland's life is still an awful tragedy. We can't trust the police. We can't trust the justice system. We are gunned down in our own communities and our own homes. This is America. Full of racism and the death of Black bodies. A coalition needs to be had addressing each state where a Black person has been slaughtered by local police departments and then the state legislature and congress need to be pushed to make changes so that police officers are held accountable under the law for their actions."[10]

CONCLUSION

"Say their name." Many Blacks have tragically lost their lives at the hands of police. Not only have Blacks lost their lives, but every day is a struggle for Black people to succeed. Oppression comes in many forms such as police brutality, wrongful arrest, employment discrimination, mass incarceration, and much more. This is the world that HBCU students are witnessing from inside their institutions. Through interview responses, it is found that HBCU students are negatively affected by the oppression of Black people. When HBCU student #5 sadly mentioned at the conclusion of their interview that they know their chances are higher of dying because they are Black, highlighted the thought process that many Black HBCU students have to live with. This is a crippling, yet factual ideology due to the past and current climate of oppression. The desires of HBCU students are transparency, equality, and fairness in the justice system. Once credibility and trust are restored there will be a decrease in the negative stigmas surrounding our justice system. "Say their name" is more than just a chant, it's a long-term cry for justice for Black Americans. Unfortunately, for the cry to be heard the life of another Black person must be stolen or mistreated.

NOTES

1. HBCU student #78 interview response, August 2020.
2. HBCU student #66 interview response, August 2020.
3. HBCU student #77 interview response, August 2020.
4. HBCU student #63 interview response, August 2020.
5. HBCU student #14 interview response, August 2020.
6. HBCU student #70 interview response, August 2020.
7. Clarence Taylor. "Introduction: African Americans, Police Brutality, And The U.S. Criminal Justice System." *Journal of African American History* 98, no. 2 (2013): 200–4.
8. 2014 HBCU graduate, April 2020.
9. Perry Lyle and Ashraf M. Esmail. "Sworn to Protect: Police Brutality—A Dilemma for America's Police." *Race, Gender & Class* 23, no. 3–4 (2016): 155–85.
10. HBCU student #74 interview response, August 2020.

REFERENCES

Clarence Taylor. "Introduction: African Americans, Police Brutality, And The U.S. Criminal Justice System." The Journal of African American History 98, no. 2 (2013): 200–04. Accessed April 12, 2021. doi:10.5323/jafriamerhist.98.2.0200.

Lyle, Perry, and Ashraf M. Esmail. "Sworn to Protect: Police Brutality—A Dilemma for America's Police." Race, Gender & Class 23, no. 3–4 (2016): 155–85. Accessed April 12, 2021. https://www.jstor.org/stable/26529213.

Chapter 7

Historically Black Colleges and Universities

Laboratories for Social and Political Activism

Regina M. Moorer

INTRODUCTION

Historically Black Colleges and Universities (HBCUs) were founded to provide postsecondary educational opportunities for Black Americans. Before their founding, and for many years afterward, traditionally white institutions denied admission to Black students. As a result, HBCUs became the primary means of higher education attainment for Black Americans. Since their founding, Historically Black Colleges and Universities (HBCUs) have served as laboratories for social and political activism. As amended in Title III of the 1965 Higher Education Act, an HBCU is any Historically Black College or University founded and accredited (or on the verge of accreditation) before 1964 and whose primary mission was and continues to be the education of Black Americans.[1] The first HBCUs were established for freed Black Americans who lived in the North before the Civil War. Cheney University, originally called the Institute for Colored Youth, is recognized as the first HBCU; the university was founded in 1837. Miner Normal School (1851) in Washington, D.C., Lincoln University in Pennsylvania (1854), and Wilberforce University in Ohio (1856) were the next three HBCUs to be established.[2] Though the first HBCUs were founded in the North, the next wave of HBCUs were established for recently emancipated enslaved men and women and their children in the South following the Civil War. The majority of HBCUs were founded between 1865–1900, with many founded in 1867, two years after the Emancipation Proclamation. The key actors in the establishment of many HBCUs were philanthropists and free Blacks and faith-based institutions such as the American Missionary Association (AMA) and the African Methodist Episcopal (AME) Church. Though most HBCUs were founded long before President Lyndon B. Johnson signed the Higher Education Act into law, the legislation created a unified federal definition under which HBCUs were to be accounted for and provided direct federal funding. Steeped in legacy and tradition, these institutions are known for providing their students a sense of duty, pride, social and political awareness, and unabashed courage in the face of injustice.

Students at HBCUs played an integral role in the Civil Rights Movement (CRM) during the early 1960s. One of the most impactful civil rights organizations, the Student Nonviolent Coordinating Committee (SNCC), was formed following a three-hundred-student conference at historically Black Shaw University in North Carolina. Ella Baker organized this first meeting of SNCC. After the meeting at Shaw University, the organization went on to organize voter registration drives and the Freedom Rides.[3] Like Shaw University, Claflin University was also a driving force in the fight to end segregation in Orangeburg, South Carolina. Students at South Carolina State University also fought against the evils of Jim Crow and segregation in Orangeburg, South Carolina. One effort to desegregate local bowling alleys culminated in the 1968 Orangeburg Massacre, which resulted in three student protesters' death.[4] Like Shaw and South Carolina State, many HBCU campuses served as incubators for civil rights organizing and activism. HBCU campuses served as meeting spaces and training grounds for nonviolent protest. The Civil Rights Movement happened, in part, because of HBCU students. Not only did HBCUs prepare some of the Civil Rights Movement's most notable leaders, including Fred Gray (Alabama State University), Diane Nash (Fisk University), Stokely Carmichael (Howard University), Ralph Abernathy (Alabama State University), and Martin Luther King Jr. (Morehouse College), Historically Black Colleges and Universities were also indispensable to communities beyond the campus.

This chapter explores how the heritage and traditions of HBCUs helped shape students' social and political activism. This chapter pays particular attention to four HBCUs—Alabama State University, Albany State University, Bennett College, and North Carolina A&T University. This chapter unpacks how these uniquely American institutions instigated and powered the push for racial inequality during the Civil Rights Movement (CRM). The examination of these historically influential institutions will uncover the social climate that enveloped and currently envelop HBCUs and forged them into social progress agents. Though often overlooked in the extant CRM literature, HBCUs acted as significant players on the sociopolitical playing field. Each school played an essential role in its respective state in the fight for civil rights. More specifically, this chapter will analyze the role that Alabama State University played during the Montgomery Bus Boycott; the role that Albany State University played during Albany Movement; and the roles that Bennett College and North Carolina A&T University played during the Greensboro Sit-Ins. This HBCU analysis shows that Historically Black Colleges and Universities made significant contributions to the push for social justice. This chapter highlights how HBCU student-led activism resulted in systemic social change, both in the communities where the schools are located and throughout the country.

ALABAMA STATE UNIVERSITY AND THE MONTGOMERY BUS BOYCOTT

Alabama State University (ASU) was founded on July 18, 1867. Originally called the Lincoln Normal School, the college was established in Marion, Alabama. Nine freed slaves referred to as the Marion Nine, with help from local community members, raised $500 to purchase land for the school. The Marion Nine included Joey P. Pinch, Thomas Speed, Nicholas Dale, James Childs, Thomas Lee, John Freeman, Nathan Levert, David Harris, and Alexander H. Curtis.[5] Though the founders filed the incorporation papers on July 18, 1867, the Lincoln Normal School opened its doors on November 13, 1867, with 113 students.

The Lincoln Normal School relocated to Montgomery, Alabama in 1887. As a descendent of the Lincoln Normal School, ASU is one of the oldest insti- tutions of higher education founded for Black Americans. After relocating to Montgomery, the ASU campus community was involved in several civil rights activities. The students and faculty played a particularly prominent role in the Montgomery Bus Boycott. Mary Fair Burks, the head of ASU's English Department, founded the Montgomery Women's Political Council (WPC) in 1949 to encourage Black Americans to "live above mediocrity, to elevate their thinking . . . and in general to improve their status as a group."[6] The WPC worked to increase the political presence of the Black community by increasing civic participation and voter registration and pressing city leaders to eradicate discriminatory policies. The initial WPC chapter was composed of middle-class professionals, most of whom were educators who taught at ASU or in the Montgomery Public School System. Burks served as the WPC's first president. By the early 1950s, Jo Ann Robinson, also a

faculty member at ASU, succeeded Burks as president. The core membership included at least thirty women, including Thelma Glass, Mary Cross,
Irene West, Euretta Adair, Elizabeth Arrington, and Zoeline Pierce.[7] The
women were either faculty members at ASU, teachers at the local Black
public schools, or wives of local Black professionals. Well before the 1955
Montgomery Bus Boycott, the WPC was working to organize a citywide
boycott of buses. In 1953, the WPC complained to Montgomery City
Commissioners about discriminatory bussing practices, including forcing
Black Americans to board the bus through the back door despite paying their
bus fare at the front entrance. In 1954, Robinson wrote a letter proposing a
city ordinance similar to those already in place in other cities. Under the proposed law, Black passengers would be seated from the back of the bus to the
front, and white passengers would be seated from the front of the bus to the
rear until all seats were full. The WPC's concerns were repeatedly ignored
by city commissioners even after Robinson cautioned that "plans are being
made to ride less, or not at all."[8] After the arrest of Claudette Colvin in March
1955 for refusing to give up her seat on a city bus, Rev. Martin Luther King
Jr., Rufus Lewis, E. D. Nixon, Robinson, Irene West, and Burks met with city
commissioners but made no progress. On December 1, 1955, Rosa Parks
was arrested for refusing to give up her seat on a city bus that the WPC's
planning and organizing paid off. The WPC members assisted in initiating
the Montgomery Bus Boycott. Parks's attorney and ASU alumnus Fred Gray
contacted Robinson and told her about Parks's arrest and solicited the assistance of the WPC. Robinson and the WPC agreed to call for a boycott of city
buses starting Monday, December 5, 1955, the day of Parks's trial. Robinson
and other WPC members met at ASU at midnight to copy 35,000 pamphlets
about the upcoming bus boycott. The following day, Robinson and some of
her students from ASU drove around to the local Black schools to distribute
the pamphlets so the students could take them home to their parents. About
40,000 and 50,000 Black residents of Montgomery, Alabama, participated in
the yearlong boycott of the city buses. Once the Montgomery Bus Boycott
began, the WPC supported the day-to-day operations by assisting with carpools, mass meetings, and other protests. According to Burks, members of
the Women's Political Council were trailblazers for their ability to mobilize
Black middle-class women to effect reform in segregated Montgomery.[9]

The participatory role of individuals connected to ASU, however, had both
positive and unintended consequences. One of the positive results was the
continued activism efforts among members of the ASU campus community.
On February 1, 1960, Black students from North Carolina Agricultural and
Technical College attempted to order coffee at a segregated Woolworth's
lunch counter in Greensboro. Drawing inspiration from the Greensboro sit-
in, protest spread across North Carolina, and Virginia, and by late February,

sit-ins were occurring across the Deep South. In 1960, nine ASU students organized the Montgomery sit-in. On February 25, 1960, thirty-five Black men and women approached the snack bar at the Montgomery County Courthouse and requested service. The white owner of the snack bar acted quickly to put an end to the protest, locking the lunchroom, shutting off the lights, and telling patrons to vacate the establishment. The governor of Alabama in 1960, John Patterson, was concerned that ASU's student leaders would mobilize the campus community for more citywide demonstrations. Due to his fears, Patterson pressured and directed ASU's president to expel any student involved in the demonstration, threatening to withhold the school's public funding if the president did not comply with his demands. Under duress, the ASU President gave in to the governor.

The cost of involvement was also particularly high for WPC members who were also faculty members at ASU, where officials conducted extensive investigations into those participating in the boycott and other student demonstrations. Tensions on campus, especially in the aftermath of the 1960 sit-ins, prompted several activists, including Robinson and Burks, to resign from ASU and seek employment elsewhere. Their resignations resulted in the dispersal of key WPC members around the country.

ALBANY STATE UNIVERSITY AND THE ALBANY MOVEMENT

Albany State University was established in 1903 in Georgia. In 1917, the state of Georgia started supporting the school financially and granted it two-year status. The school added agricultural training and changed its name to Georgia Normal and Agricultural College. Albany State eventually joined the University System of Georgia and, in 1943, was granted four-year status.[10]

Before 1961, small student groups at Albany State led many of Albany's civil rights activism efforts. However, the arrival of SNCC reenergized grassroots activists and organizers. In September 1961, SNCC arrived in Albany to begin voter registration drives and encouraged the students, who had previously led the movement alone, to take on the Albany administration and segregation in general.[11] On November 1, 1961, nine students from Albany State decided to test an Interstate Commerce Commission (ICC) ruling that no bus facility, bus, or driver could deny access to its facilities based on race. The students went to the bus station, and as planned, when the police ordered them out, the students left the station without being arrested and then filed an immediate complaint with the ICC under the new ruling. Following this protest, the Albany Movement was formed with members of the SNCC, the NAACP, the Ministerial Alliance, the Federation of Women's

Clubs, and the Negro Voters League.[12] The Albany Movement sought to abolish all forms of racial segregation in the city, initially by desegregating transportation services, establishing a permanent committee to consider further desegregation, and freeing those imprisoned in segregation-related demonstrations. Through the campaign, Albany protesters utilized various methods of nonviolence, including mass demonstrations, jail-ins, sit-ins, boycotts, and litigation. Notably, besides student activists from Albany State, the campaign involved large numbers of Black adults of varied class backgrounds. The group held mass meetings and organized demonstrations and marches. By mid-December 1961, about five hundred demonstrators were arrested by Albany authorities. At this point, the Albany Movement organizers urged Martin Luther King Jr. to seize the momentum generated by the recent arrests and garner more media attention for the campaign. King and the Southern Christian Leadership Conference (SCLC) temporarily joined the movement, bringing national attention to Albany. King spoke at a mass meeting in December and was arrested the next day during a march in Albany. However, the movement suffered a significant setback when King, believing that Albany officials had agreed to a set of terms, posted bail and was released. However, following his release, he found that the city authorities did not accept any of the Albany Movement's demands. Following this failure, King committed to desegregating Albany and enlisted the Southern Christian Leadership Conference (SCLC) to organize the movement. The campaign faced a significant challenge in Albany Police Chief Laurie Pritchett, who had perfected the art of appearing nonviolent. The police chief preached nonviolence, emphasizing mass arrests over mass beatings, and was very conscious of being nonviolent in front of television cameras and reporters. Pritchett was able to keep up with the massive number of arrests by using jails in neighboring counties. The Albany Movement came to an end in late summer 1962, when mobilization attempts stalled in the face of Pritchett's almost endless capacity to prosecute and imprison all demonstrators the campaign threw at him. The civil rights coalition was forced to concede; however, organizers would apply the tactics and lessons learned to a subsequent victory in Birmingham, Alabama. Singing was perhaps the most unusual nonviolent technique used during the Albany Movement. Singing proved to be a compelling method for rallying and energizing protesters during the mass meetings. After the Albany Movement, SNCC formed the "Freedom Singers" to utilize this powerful tactic in other protests and demonstrations.[13]

NORTH CAROLINA A&T UNIVERSITY
AND THE GREENSBORO SIT-INS

North Carolina Agricultural and Technical University (NC A&T) was established in 1891 with the mission "to teach practical agriculture and mechanic arts and such branches of learning as relating there to, not excluding academic and classical instruction" to the Black citizens of North Carolina.[14] Like most HBCU, NC A&T served as an institution of higher learning and civil rights innovation.

In 1960, most white-owned restaurants in the Deep South required Black patrons to pick up their food at back doors; restaurant owners reserved dine-in seating for white customers. Woolworth's Department Store in Greensboro, North Carolina, was no different. In defiance of such Jim Crow practices, on February 1, 1960, four NC A&T freshmen went to the lunch counter at Woolworth's, sat down, ordered, and refused to move until closing time. By sitting down, Ezell Blair Jr. (now Jibreel Khazan), Franklin McCain, Joseph McNeil, and David Richmond stood up to Jim Crow and ushered in a new era of change in the United States—one that emphasizes the significance importance of HBCUs. Within a day, the NC A&T student sit-in prompted additional protests at Woolworth's and other department stores along Greensboro's main shopping street, Elm Street. The next day, February 2, "twenty-five men and four women students arrived at Woolworth's."[15] Throughout the following days, large crowds of students demonstrated against segregated counters at Woolworth's and the nearby Kress shop. The Woolworth and Kress stores were chosen as a way to draw attention to national companies with southern locations that practice Jim Crow. Additionally, they desired to focus their attention on a few stores in order to avoid spreading protesters too thin. Just 10 percent of Woolworth stores were located in the South at the time, and stores in other areas of the country did not have segregated lunch counter service.[16] By Friday more than three hundred students were taking part in the protest; by that Saturday, "hundreds of students, including the A&T football team, descended on the downtown area."[17]

The Greensboro sit-ins attracted crowds of white teenagers and young men on Saturday evening, February 6, 1960, who hurled racial slurs at the demonstrators in an attempt to threaten and fear them. By that evening, the students had voted to call a halt to protests to allow for talks with city leaders. Not only were the most significant demonstrations held on that day, dubbed "Black Saturday," but there was also a bomb scare. Both Kress and Woolworth's reported that they would close their lunch counters early due to the threat of abuse. As a result, the students decided to cancel their protests. According to the official statement, the demonstrators must "pledge their dreams of serving alongside whites" through "peaceful channels of negotiation." The Mayor's Advisory Committee became the official forum for negotiation. Mayor George Roach named nine residents to the Advisory Committee on Community Relations; one African American and eight white citizens served on the committee. Councilman E. R. Zane, committee chair; Councilman Waldo Falkener; Bland Worley; Councilman David Schenck, Arnold Schiffman, O. L. Fryman, Howard Holderness, James A. Doggett, and W. M. York were appointed to the Mayor's Advisory Committee.[18] The Mayor's Advisory Committee could not resolve the lunch counter controversy, and students renewed their demonstrations. The Committee recommended that establishments designate "an appropriate portion of their seating capacity" for food service to both races and reserve the rest for service to "exclusively white customers."[19] The Black community realized store managers were unwilling to comply with any negotiated terms. Sit-ins resumed, and Greensboro city police began arresting protestors. The Black community, outraged by the arrests, mobilized a boycott of a variety of stores. Finally, faced with sales declines, some managers caved, opening lunch counters at Woolworth's, Kress, and Meyer's department stores. Because of the success of direct action in Greensboro, demonstrators across the state and throughout the South pursued similar strategies over the next few months and into the next year, organizing read-ins at public libraries, kneel-ins at segregated churches, walk-ins at theaters and amusement parks, and wade-ins at segregated pools. "By the end of February, thirty-two cities in North Carolina, South Carolina, Virginia, Tennessee, Florida, Maryland, Kentucky, and Alabama had experienced sit-ins and other demonstrations protesting racial restrictions. By the end of March, another forty-one city had been subject to these demonstrations, and Georgia, Texas, Louisiana, and Arkansas were added to the list of states struck. In April even Mississippi joined."[20]

When protest activity resumed in April after negotiations did not prove fruitful, local law enforcement arrested forty-five students for refusing to leave the Kress lunch counter. Reportedly, Woolworth's and Kress were sensitive to public perception and feared the financial repercussions of desegregated lunch counter service, even if it was on a limited basis. Woolworth's managerial leadership ordered the lunch counter in the Greensboro store closed on April 4, 1960, and Kress soon followed suit. Woolworth's indicated that business practices would yield to the local customs and traditions. Kress's management officials also left lunch counter integrations decisions to the local citizens.[21] On April 22, 1960, several students from both Bennett and NCA&T were arrested. Sin-ins continued over the next few weeks, and protestors achieved desegregation of the lunch counters in Greensboro in July 1960. The July 26, 1960, headline in the *Greensboro Daily News* read: "Two Stores Integrate Counters; Equal Service Starts Quietly." Integration came nearly six months after the four NCA&T students sat down at the Woolworth's counter.[22]

BENNETT COLLEGE AND THE LUNCH COUNTER SIT-INS

While much has been written about the student sit-ins, primarily concentrating on the four students from NCA&T who participated in the February 1, 1960 sit-in, historians and scholars have paid little attention to other participants in the subsequent Greensboro sit-ins. Many of the local media outlets covered the sit-in demonstrations for the first week. They held the second day of sit-ins and occupied seats. By the third day, student participation increased even more, and students were able to occupy sixty-three of the sixty-six lunch counter seats. By the fourth day of sit-ins, the *Greensboro Daily News* first reported that students from Bennett and other colleges were participating in the demonstrations. Black high school students, church members, and members of the greater Greensboro community were all protesters. The presence of the women from historically Black Bennett College was especially noteworthy. At one point during the sit-in protests, local authorities had arrested nearly 40 percent of Bennett College's student body for their participation.[23] Bennett College was founded in 1873 in the basement of the Warnersville Methodist Episcopal Church (now known as St. Matthews United Methodist Church). In 1874, the Freedmen's Aid Society took over the school, and Bennett remained under its auspices for fifty years.[24] The women of Bennett College had a legacy of civil rights advocacy before the 1960 sit-ins. The earliest example of student activism and protest by Bennett's students, as noted by William Chafe, was the picketing of local movie theaters in the 1930s. Bennett's students led protests against Greensboro movie theater owners who censored movies that depicted whites and African Americans as equals.[25] Bennett's students also partnered with the Greensboro Citizens Association in 1951 and "Operation Door Knock" in 1960 to register Greensboro residents to vote.[26] Bennett students consistently participated in organizational meetings to plan, strategize, and mobilize movement participation. Willia Player, the first woman president of Bennett, supported the strategy sessions by making space available on the Bennett College campus for the meetings. In November 1959, many Bennett students proposed staging a sit-in; however, Player opposed the proposal due to the chaos that would result at the end of the semester when several students were preparing to leave Greensboro for the holiday break. By the time the February 1960 sit-ins began, the women from Bennett College served as the foot soldiers for the sit-in movement by "providing pickets, marchers, and canvassers."[27] Following the first week of sit-ins, the Student Executive Committee for Justice (SECJ) was formed; the committee was cochaired by Gloria Brown of Bennett College and Ernest Pitt of NCA&T. This committee was tasked with developing a plan, informing students about the protests, and recruiting new demonstrators. The committee also organized carpools and provided replacement protesters as the sit-ins grew in size.

Player and other Bennett College officials expressed open support for the students' protest participation. Dr. Frederick Patterson, chairman of Bennett's board of trustees, claimed in a February 1960 address that he regretted that the sit-ins "disturbed the peace and tranquility of a community . . . but once an issue has been joined or faced up to, there should be no turning back until the issue has been successfully resolved," because "segregation on the basis of race . . . is morally wrong."[28] Patterson expressed additional support for the students' protest activities in May 1960 when speaking to an audience in Boston, saying that the "demonstrations should be viewed against the background of non-compliance with the law by the South and the total pattern of discrimination."[29] Other civil rights organizers, including Dr. King, connected the Greensboro sit-ins to broader civil rights movement goals. King proclaimed that the Greensboro sit-ins were not just protests against the refusal of service at lunch counters but were protests against such things as limited job opportunities for HBCU college graduates.

Efforts to desegregate other public accommodations in Greensboro lasted through 1963, and Player remained a staunch supporter of the Bennett Belles. When some of Bennett's students were arrested in 1963, Player refused to order them back to campus, opting instead to provide them with course materials and personal needs while in jail. In 1965, nine Bennett and NCA&T students were arrested for organizing a sit-in at the mayor's office. Player did not attempt to change the students' minds or convince them to end the protest. Player said, "they are a part of this protest and as long as they are willing to stand up for their beliefs until the problem is properly resolved, I'm not looking for an exceptional way to get them out of something very difficult, but very important."

CONCLUSION

Historically Black Colleges and Universities played an indispensable role in advancing the causes of civil rights and social justice. These institutions of higher learning served more than just the enrolled students. The Civil Rights Movement was one of the most dramatic times in American history. The fundamental shifts that occurred during this period happened, in part, because of HBCUs. As a refuge for Black thinkers, writers, and revolutionaries—and a pathway to the American dream—HBCUs trained the founders of liberation movements and developed leaders in every area. Thousands of unnamed students met and organized on Historically Black Colleges and Universities campuses and developed the institutional and systemic roadmap for change. Many of the Civil Rights Movement campaigns and organizations grew out of HBCU socialization. The founders of the SCLC and SNCC were products of HBCU campuses. The students, staff, faculty, and local community members risked firings, expulsions, arrests, and even death to fight for change. Each of the historic movements referenced here—the Montgomery Bus Boycott, the Albany Movement, and the Greensboro Sit-Ins—transformed the local communities and shifted the arm of civil rights protections for the entire Black community. They faced racism and Jim Crow with bold resolve. While this chapter highlights the roles of four schools, almost every HBCU campus catalyzed political and social change. Black colleges and universities continue to uphold this legacy today.

NOTES

1. "White House Initiative on Historically Black Colleges and Universities," White House Initiative on Historically Black Colleges and Universities (U.S. Department of Education), accessed February 22, 2021, https://sites.ed.gov/whhbcu/one-hundred-and-five-historically-black-colleges-and-universities/.

2. "HBCU History Timeline," HBCU First, accessed February 22, 2021, https://hbcufirst.com/resources/hbcu-history-timeline.

3. "Birth of SNCC," SNCC Digital Gateway, April 4, 2017, https://snccdigital.org/inside-sncc/the-story-of-sncc/birth-of-sncc/.

4. History.com Editors, "Orangeburg Massacre," History.com (A&E Television Networks, April 6, 2018), https://www.history.com/topics/1960s/orangeburg-massacre.

5. "History & Tradition," History & Tradition | Alabama State University, accessed January 10, 2021, https://www.alasu.edu/about-asu/history-tradition.

6. Robinson, Jo Ann Gibson, *The Montgomery Bus Boycott and the Women Who Started It: The Memoir of Jo Ann Gibson Robinson* (Knoxville: Univ. of Tennessee Press, 1987), 23.

7. David J. Garrow, "The Origins of the Montgomery Bus Boycott," Southern Changes (Lewis H. Beck Center, October 1, 1985), http://southernchanges.digitalscholarship.emory.edu/sc07-5_1204/sc07-5_006/.

8. Robinson, 21.

9. Vicki L. Crawford, *Women in the Civil Rights Movement: Trailblazers and Torchbearers, 1941 - 1965* (Bloomington: Indiana Univ. Press, 1993), 76.

10. "History of Albany State University," Albany State University, accessed February 26, 2021, https://www.asurams.edu/history.php.

11. "Albany Movement Formed," SNCC Digital Gateway, July 14, 2020, https://snccdigital.org/events/albany-movement-formed/.

12. "Albany Movement," The Martin Luther King, Jr., Research and Education Institute, April 5, 2018, https://kinginstitute.stanford.edu/encyclopedia/albany-movement.

13. "Civil Rights Movement History 1961," Civil Rights Movement History & Timeline, 1961, accessed February 26, 2021, https://www.crmvet.org/tim/timhis61.htm#1961albany.

14. "A&T History," North Carolina A&T, accessed February 20, 2021, https://www.ncat.edu/about/history-and-traditions/index.php.

15. William Henry Chafe, *Civilities and Civil Rights: Greensboro, North Carolina, and the Black Struggle for Freedom* (Oxford: Oxford University Press, 1992), 84.

16. Chafe, 120.

17. Chafe, 85.

18. "A&T Students Drop Sit-down Protests; Plan Negotiations," *Greensboro Daily News*, February 21, 1960, Black Saturday edition, sec. A-1.

19. "Text of Report By Advisory Committee to Mayor George Roach of Greensboro," *Greensboro Daily News*, April 2, 1960.

20. Jack M. Bloom and Richard G. Hatcher, *Class, Race, and the Civil Rights Movement* (Bloomington: Indiana University Press, 2019), 216.

21. "Woolworth to Close Counter: Food Sale Ends for Time Being," *Greensboro Daily News*, 5 April 1960, A-1; "Kress Store Again Opens Counter," 6 April 1960, B-1; "Kress Co. To Follow Custom, ibid., 18 May 1960, AS

22. Two Stores Integrate Counters: Equal Service Starts Quietly," *Greensboro Daily News*, 26 July 1960, B-1.

23. Linda Beatrice Brown, *Belles of Liberty: Gender, Bennett College, and the Civil Rights Movement in Greensboro, North Carolina* (Greensboro, NC: Women and Wisdom Press, 2013).

24. "History," Bennett College, July 29, 2019, https://www.bennett.edu/about/history/.

25. Chafe, 20.

26. "A&T Students Drop Sit-down Protests; Plan Negotiations," *Greensboro Daily News*, February 21, 1960, Black Saturday edition, sec. A-1.

27. Chafe, 129.

28. "Sitdowns Are Held Inevitable: Ex-College Head Talks at Bennett," *Greensboro Daily News*, February 15, 1960, sec. B-1.

29. Linda Beatrice Brown, *Belles of Liberty: Gender, Bennett College, and the Civil Rights Movement in Greensboro, North Carolina* (Greensboro, NC: Women and Wisdom Press, 2013).

REFERENCES

"Albany Movement." The Martin Luther King, Jr., Research and Education Institute, April 5, 2018. https://kinginstitute.stanford.edu/encyclopedia/albany-movement.

"Albany Movement Formed." SNCC Digital Gateway, July 14, 2020. https://snccdigital.org/events/albany-movement-formed/.

"A&T Students Drop Sit-down Protests; Plan Negotiations." *Greensboro Daily News.* February 21, 1960, Black Saturday edition, sec. A-1.

"Birth of SNCC." SNCC Digital Gateway, April 4, 2017. https://snccdigital.org/inside-sncc/the-story-of-sncc/birth-of-sncc/.

Bloom, Jack M., and Richard G. Hatcher. *Class, Race, and the Civil Rights Movement.* Bloomington: Indiana University Press, 2019.

Brown, Linda Beatrice. *Belles of Liberty: Gender, Bennett College, and the Civil Rights Movement in Greensboro, North Carolina.* Greensboro, NC: Women and Wisdom Press, 2013.

Chafe, William Henry. *Civilities and Civil Rights: Greensboro, North Carolina, and the Black Struggle for Freedom.* Oxford: Oxford University Press, 1992.

"Civil Rights Movement History 1961." Civil Rights Movement History & Timeline, 1961. Accessed February 26, 2021. https://www.crmvet.org/tim/timhis61.htm#1961albany.

Crawford, Vicki L. *Women in the Civil Rights Movement Trailblazers and Torchbearers, 1941 - 1965.* Bloomington: Indiana Univ. Press, 1993.

"Digest of Education Statistics, 2019." National Center for Education Statistics (NCES) Home Page, a part of the U.S. Department of Education. Accessed April 20, 2021. https://nces.ed.gov/programs/digest/d19/tables/dt19_313.10.asp.

Garrow, David J. "The Origins of the Montgomery Bus Boycott." Southern Changes. Lewis H. Beck Center, October 1, 1985. http://southernchanges.digitalscholarship.emory.edu/sc07-5_1204/sc07-5_006/.

Gibson, Robinson Jo Ann. *The Montgomery Bus Boycott and the Women Who Started It the Memoir of Jo Ann Gibson Robinson.* Knoxville: Univ. of Tennessee Press, 1987.

"HBCU History Timeline." HBCU First. Accessed February 22, 2021. https://hbcufirst.com/resources/hbcu-history-timeline.

"Historically Black Colleges and Universities and Higher Education Desegregation." Home. US Department of Education (ED), January 10, 2020. https://www2.ed.gov/about/offices/list/ocr/docs/hq9511.html.

"History." Bennett College, July 29, 2019. https://www.bennett.edu/about/history/.

"History & Tradition." History & Tradition | Alabama State University. Accessed January 10, 2021. https://www.alasu.edu/about-asu/history-tradition.

"History of Albany State University." Albany State University. Accessed February 26, 2021. https://www.asurams.edu/history.php.

History.com Editors. "Orangeburg Massacre." History.com. A&E Television Networks, April 6, 2018. https://www.history.com/topics/1960s/orangeburg-massacre.

"Sitdowns Are Held Inevitable: Ex-College Head Talks at Bennett." *Greensboro Daily News.* February 15, 1960, sec. B-1.

"Text of Report By Advisory Committee to Mayor George Roach of Greensboro." *Greensboro Daily News*, April 2, 1960.

White House Initiative on Historically Black Colleges and Universities. U.S. Department of Education. Accessed February 22, 2021. https://sites.ed.gov/whhbcu/one-hundred-and-five-historically-black-colleges-and-universities/.

PART III

Paradigm Shift and Expanding Possibilities

Chapter 8

Academic Outbreak

Safety, Psychosocial, Enrollment, and Learning Challenges Facing HBCUs as A Result of COVID-19

Patrice W. Glenn Jones

INTRODUCTION

In December 2019, a cluster of pneumonia cases with unknown etiology was first identified in Wuhan, Hubei Province in China. Shortly thereafter, cases also appeared in other countries. On January 3, 2020, Chinese authorities identified and reported forty-four cases to the World Health Organization (WHO); of the cases, thirty-three patients were stable and eleven were severely ill.[1] Within days, WHO published its first disease outbreak news brief on the severe acute respiratory syndrome coronavirus 2 (SARS-Co V-2); they also issued guidelines on detection, testing, and symptoms of the disease caused by the virus, which became known as coronavirus disease 2019 (COVID-19).[2] On January 12, 2020, the Chinese authorities publicly shared the genetic sequence of COVID-19.[3] On January 21, 2020, the first case of COVID-19 was confirmed in the United States, and on February 3, 2020, the U.S. government declared a public health emergency.[4] An alarm of epidemic resounded across the nation. On March 11, 2020, WHO classified the infection of the SARS-CoV-2 as a pandemic,[5] and by April 21, 2020, 793,669 cases were confirmed in the United States.[6]

The Centers for Disease Control and Prevention (CDC) released a Morbidity and Mortality Weekly Report Early Release on May 1, 2020. The report indicated:

> The acceleration phase of a pandemic is complex and requires multifaceted and rapidly adapting public health response. During a 3-week period from late February to early March, the number of U.S. COVID-19 cases increased more than 1,000-fold. Various community mitigation interventions were implemented with the aim of reducing further spread and controlling the impact on health care capacity. Recognition of factors associated with amplified spread during this early acceleration period will help inform future decisions as locations in the United States scale back some components of mitigation and strengthen systems to detect transmission resurgence.[7]

Since the virus' emergence in the United States and the government's declaration of public emergency, state-level government leaders have made decisions about mitigation strategies based on the increase of cases within their states. Reducing physical contact and wearing masks have been the most widely used approaches to stop the spread of the virus.

IMPACT OF COVID-19

Health and Death

The health and well-being of the citizens and residents of the United States have been paramount, but with no federal mandates, the virus continued to spread. And by April 2021, there had been over 31 million national cases and nearly 561,000 deaths; at the same time, the CDC had forecasted an increase in both cases and deaths, especially as variants emerged.[8] The effects of the disease are not limited to the implications on physical health; unemployment, mental health, and education have also been impacted.

Unemployment

A significant U.S. outcome has been the increase in unemployment; because of the need for social distancing, many people lost their jobs. According to Pew Research Center, in September 2020, 15 percent of adults in the United States reported being laid off because of the COVID-19 outbreak; among lower-income adults, 47 percent of these adults in the United States reported they or someone in their household underwent job loss or pay cuts.[9] Exploring the ability to cope with stressors related to COVID-19, including unemployment, Melissa Chee, Nikita Ly, Hymie Anisman, and Kimberly

Matheson surveyed North Americans and found a negative effect of the pandemic was coping by making unhealthy eating choices,[10] which could lead to health issues.

Mental Health

Likewise, the mental health of Americans has been a grave concern. Changwon Son, Sudeep Hedge, Alec Smith, Xiaomei Wang, and Farzan Sasangohar studied the effects of the COVID-19 pandemic on the mental health of 195 college students and found that 71 percent of the students reported an increase in stress and anxiety; 82 percent of the student participants reported increased concerns on academic performance, and 89 percent reported difficulty concentrating.[11] Sara Pinto, Joana Soares, Alzira Silva, Rosario Curral, and Rui Coelho reviewed existing literature on suicides related to COVID-19 and found that "forced lockdowns, canceled medical appoints, lack of social support, unemployment, and fear for the future make several populations prone to suicide."[12] The aforementioned numbers and findings highlight COVID-19's impact on mental health and well-being, but the pandemic has had a less obvious effect.

Education

As the SARS-Co V-2 virus spread across the nation, most schools closed their physical doors and turned to virtual learning to mitigate contact and further student learning. Emergency Remote Teaching (ERT), which involves a temporary shift to virtual teaching, resulted. Elementary and secondary students, along with teachers, were forced to make this fast change. And while schools and families on all levels had to adjust to the challenges that result from ERT, low-income families, who did not have financial resources or the ability to provide their students with various in-home supports, along with the schools that served them, were impacted most. While it may seem unfathomable in this technological age, some families do not have computers or consistent internet service, and some students do not have support from an in-home family member. Therefore, these struggles were profound for students from some low-income families, like those attending Title I schools. And many of these public school officials had to rally resources, equipment, and even food to provide for students at home.

Like elementary and secondary stakeholders, students and faculty at U.S. colleges and universities also had to adapt to ERT. Some colleges and universities were better poised for the transitions than others. For institutions with well-established online programs that include (a) seasoned cross-functional instructional design teams, content experts, and instructional technology staff;

(b) primary and third-party learning software and technology services; and (c) the institutional infrastructure to systematically design, enhance, and optimize online courses and learning components, urgency was the biggest challenge imposed by COVID-19. However, for institutions with infrastructural and technology limitations, ERT presented many obstacles, confusions, and constraints. While many such institutions had learning management systems in place and technology services staff members whose skills were focused solely on network processes, information technology, and computer services, navigating online learning, even during an emergency, was uncharted waters.

It is important to note that online education and programming differ from ERT. Effective online education and programming is systematic, involves many professionals, and takes time. Likewise, at most institutions, virtual learning teams often work with a small number of faculty at one time. In contrast, ERT is usually temporary, institution-wide, and results from a crisis.

Like students at Title I schools, most learners who attend the nation's one hundred Historically Black Colleges and Universities are from families with low incomes and are among those with limited resources. Situational differences produced further disparities in existing learning opportunities among students from diverse backgrounds. For HBCU students and faculty, ERT and the disruption of face-to-face learning caused and continues to pose many challenges. Regarding HBCUs' responses to the shutdown, a staff writer for the United Negro College Fund asserted:

> The economic impact of the crisis is significant for everyone, including schools that were already underfunded. Many people have lost their jobs or are worried that the situation will greatly affect their future employment and income. Understandably, families are looking for opportunities to save and are inquiring about refunds for a variety of school-related expenses. And HBCUs, just like many other colleges and universities across the country, are working with families to resolve these issues.[13]

Among HBCUs, many of these institutions would fall in the latter category of ERT transition. With underdeveloped online courses and programs, as well as limited staff, many HBCUs were forced to address limitations in their virtual learning infrastructure.

PURPOSE OF CHAPTER

Ultimately, the spread of COVID-19 has posed formidable challenges, and these challenges will probably have long-term effects on education at all levels. For low-income students, the impact poses the most potential for negative outcomes. At the nation's HBCUs, issues with learning gaps, growth, enrollment, and sustainability are imminent. Thus, the purpose of this chapter is to identify challenges that HBCUs face because of the COVID-19 pandemic. Many scholars and practitioners agree that education will never "look" the same, even after the threat of COVID-19 is over. Among other considerations, HBCU leaders will be challenged with (a) promoting faculty, staff, and student safety; (b) addressing psycho-social outcomes; (c) addressing enrollment; (d) sustaining and elevating virtual learning progress made during COVID-19; and (e) providing services to advance student learning and academic success. Based on a review of existing literature that highlights conditions and challenges that existed before COVID-19, as well as the research that emerged during the pandemic, this chapter also identifies potential solutions.

Keeping Faculty, Staff, and Students Safe

Promoting continuous feelings of safety among HBCU stakeholders will prove an understandable challenge even after the threat of the pandemic passes. The CDD regularly updates guidelines for social distancing, general, and on-campus settings for postsecondary institutions. And as institutional leaders address reopening or sustaining in-person measures, the challenges associated with keeping faculty, staff, and students safe, as well as amplifying a commitment to safety, persist. As of Fall 2021, many postsecondary institutions are expected to return to a sense of normalcy. This includes increased in-person classes. With this increase, the potential for a concentration of COVID-19 cases proves possible.

Even with COVID-19 vaccinations on the increase, among Black Americans, the number of vaccinations is still low. As of May 2021, over 116 million people in the United States were fully vaccinated, and among them, the ethnicity for nearly 70,000,000 was provided; only 8.5 percent identified as Black.[14] For historically Black institutions, whose enrollment is mostly Black Americans, this is concerning and leads to a logical question. Is there a larger chance of concentrated outbreaks of COVID-19 cases at HBCUs? How then, can HBCU leaders mitigate risk?

CDC RISK LEVELS

The CDD characterizes institutional risk (i.e., from low to highest risk) based on the response strategies chosen:

Lowest Risk

- Faculty and students engage in virtual-only learning options, activities, and events.

Some Risk

- Students, faculty, and staff follow all steps to protect themselves and others at all times, including proper use of face masks, social distancing, and hand hygiene.
- Hybrid learning model: Some students participate in virtual learning, and in-person learning is limited to courses and laboratory instruction that cannot be delivered remotely.
- Students, faculty, and staff participate in small, in-person classes, activities, and events that allow individuals to remain spaced at least six feet apart (e.g., a lecture room with individual seating spaced six feet apart).
- Students avoid out-of-class social gatherings and events and communications and policies discouraged these activities.
- Apply and support a strict adherence to cohorting, alternating schedules, and staggered schedules in residence halls, dining areas, and recreational areas on campus to create small groups of students and minimize their contact with others (e.g., small cohorts of freshmen who live and learn together).
- Students, faculty, and staff do not share objects (e.g., laboratory, art, or recreational equipment and supplies).
- Regularly scheduled (e.g., at least daily or between uses) cleaning and disinfection of frequently touched areas occur as planned (i.e., on time and consistently).

Medium Risk

- Students, faculty, and staff follow all steps to protect themselves and others such as proper use of face masks, social distancing, and hand hygiene.
- Hybrid learning model: Students participate in a mix of virtual learning and in-person learning for all courses (in-person learning is not limited to specific courses).
- Students, faculty, and staff participate in larger in-person classes, activities, and events that allow people to remain spaced at least six feet apart (e.g., classroom with marked seating or seating removed to encourage sitting six feet apart).

- Apply cohorting, alternating schedules, and staggered schedules with some exceptions in residence halls, dining areas, and recreational areas on campus.
- Students, faculty, and staff participate in limited, small out-of-class social gatherings and events.
- Students, faculty, and staff dine outside whenever possible, or in well-ventilated rooms with social distancing applied.
- Students and faculty are to share objects minimally (e.g., sharing of objects is limited to one person at a time for laboratory, art, or recreational equipment and supplies that cannot be purchased or assigned individually and that are wiped down with disinfectant, as possible, between uses).
- Regularly scheduled cleaning and disinfection of frequently touched areas occur as planned with few exceptions.

Higher Risk

- Students, faculty, and staff follow some steps to protect themselves and others at all times such as proper use of face masks, social distancing, and hand hygiene.
- Students and faculty engage in in-person-only learning, activities, and events.
- Students, faculty, and staff attend several small out-of-class social gatherings and events.
- Students, faculty, and staff dine in indoor dining rooms while maintaining social distancing.
- Students and faculty share some objects (e.g., sharing of objects is limited to one group of students at a time for laboratory, art, or recreational equipment and supplies that cannot be purchased or assigned individually and that are wiped down with disinfectant, as possible, between uses).
- Irregularly scheduled cleaning and disinfection of frequently touched areas.

Highest Risk

- Use of public buses, campus buses/shuttles, or other high-occupancy enclosed vehicles with limited ventilation and/or that require students, faculty, or staff to have sustained close contact with others. CDC's Protect Yourself When Using Transportation provides tips for minimizing your risk when using public transportation.

- Students, faculty, and staff do not/are not required to follow steps such as proper use of face masks, social distancing, and hand hygiene to protect themselves and others.
- Students and faculty regularly engage in in-person learning, activities, and events.
- Students, faculty, and staff attend large out-of-class social gatherings and events.
- Students and faculty freely share objects.
- Students, faculty, and staff dine in indoor dining rooms without social distancing.
- Irregularly scheduled cleaning and disinfection of frequently touched areas.[15]

While domestic strategies for on-campus safety should be based on CDC guidelines, the specific strategies used by institutional leaders vary based on campus specifics. The size of the campus, population, history of cases, number of cases, and facilities are factors that impact the strategies used.

TASK FORCE IMPLEMENTATION

Certainly, institutional plans vary; however, one organizational strategy seems universally necessary. The formation of a task force to monitor and address measures to sustain campus health and mitigate exposure is essential. Likewise, the task force needs to develop an emergency response plan and associated policies for campus-wide implementation. The present conditions have underscored the need for systematic preparation to address potential situations in the future even beyond COVID-19.

Role in Vaccinations

Taking a proactive role in vaccinations is equally important. Some institutions, like Alabama State University, coordinate vaccinations for campus stakeholders and the wider community. At other institutions, students are required to provide proof of full vaccination before they can take on-campus courses or occupy campus housing. Requiring vaccination may be risky. Emily Largent and colleagues assessed national attitudes toward COVID-19 vaccinations and found that Black respondents were significantly less likely than other ethnic groups to obtain the vaccine.[16] Audrey Kearney, Liz Hamel, and Mollyann Brodie found similar hesitation among Black Americans; according to the authors, 41 percent of Black women and 45 percent of Black males expressed a desire to delay vaccinations until they could determine the impact on others.[17]

Hesitancy among Black Americans is even more evident when the need for pro-vaccination messages is made by public figures like President Barack and Michelle Obama. Thus, HBCU leaders, as well as leaders among Black communities, will need to take an active role in stressing the urgency and importance of COVID-19 vaccinations as well. And even beyond the pandemic, the message of student, faculty, and staff safety will be of perennial concern on the one hundred HBCU campuses, which are primarily located in the Southeast. Any potential flare in cases, likewise any spread of symptoms, could spark concern among Black Americans and those who attend HBCUs. Therefore, persistent implementation of safety measures, as well as effective communication, will continue to prove necessary for the years to come.

Culture of Safety

Just as research conveys, Black Americans distrust the system and the process. To maintain stakeholder trust, HBCU leaders need to manage the culture and climate of campus life through transparency and proactive communication. Establishing task forces and emergency management committees, as well as encouraging safety think tanks that include all institutional stakeholders (i.e., faculty, staff, alumni, community, and students) in the discourse are basic proactive strategies. Institutional leaders can also provide continuous professional development to faculty, staff, and students.

Institutional leaders can also provide emotional support groups for stakeholders. Feelings of safety often start in how we perceive situations, and for some who experienced COVID-19-related illness and death among their families and friends, returning to normal may seem daunting. Thus, institutional leaders must be sure to provide support to foster feelings of safety; among new student groups, this need maybe even more significant, as transitioning to the college environment—alone—can be difficult for some.

Addressing Psychosocial Outcomes

The transition to college, with a greater impact on those who live on campus, is often accompanied by various psychosocial stressors. R. P. Auerbach et al. surveyed over thirteen thousand full-time college students from among nineteen colleges in eight countries and determined that one-third of the students screen positive for anxiety, depression, or related disorders.[18] Before R. P. Auerbach et al., C. S. Conley and colleagues identified an increase in anxiety and depression among first-year college students, and the highest degree of psychological distress occurred after the initial period of transition.[19] Positive psychology suggests that the stress of transition is mitigated by positive emotions, and positive emotions help people cope.

Beyond safety, one of the most significant challenges HBCU leaders will encounter is student psychosocial well-being. While exposure to stressors varies by individual, COVID-19 has proven to be a common stressor that many people experienced both in isolation and in tandem. Studies on the psychological impact of COVID-19 were conducted in China[20] and Italy[21]; both studies revealed that the pandemic is a risk factor for psychological disorders. For new students, who may be emerging from the stressors of COVID-19 lockdown and transitioning to campus life for the first time, the amalgamation of these factors has a potential threat to student mental and social well-being.

To a large degree, many first-year students were impacted by disappointment. For some, moving away from families and onto a college campus is a milestone to which they look forward. Considering the restrictions imposed by the pandemic, many students were frustrated that they could not depart their homes for a new setting. While other students were able to attend their institutions of choice and live on campus, the negative emotions associated with the degree of illness and death that engulfed society could cause some first-year college students to develop maladaptive situational coping patterns to mitigate their own emotions.

As society begins to return to "normal," as evidenced by decreased distance measures and fewer people wearing masks, the long-term impact of COVID-19 remains to be seen. Despite the unknown, there will be an evident need for psychological interventions to minimize the negative outcomes of the COVID-19 pandemic. The increased interest in post-traumatic stress syndrome and pandemic-specific specialists will prove important additions among institutional counseling and health staff.

Amplify Mental Health

Likewise, it will be essential for HBCU leaders to curtail the negative stigma that is often associated with mental health services among some people of color. The present body of research suggests that Black Americans, specifically, seek mental health services at much lower rates than white Americans, and among diagnosed mental health conditions, Black Americans generally have higher rates of underuse of mental services than among other groups of Americans.[22] Derek M. Novacek and his colleagues made five COVID-19-related recommendations for mental health treatment among Black Americans: (1) development of national health care programs for those impacted by COVID-19, (2) early detection and intervention for post-COVID-19 trauma and stress, (3) utilization of health interventions by mental health providers, (4) mental health provider consciousness of an extensive history of Black Americans' mistrust of medical providers and officials, and (5) clinician and researchers' attentiveness to the analysis and evaluation of mental health outcomes among Black Americans.[23]

EMERGING FROM THE ENROLLMENT TRENDS

While requiring vaccinations is an option to reduce the spread of the virus, many HBCUs are addressing declines in enrollment related to COVID-19. Further requirements—like vaccinations—that seem to counter the attitudes among some Black Americans may further impact enrollment. At this point, however, nothing is certain.

Each December and May, the National Student Clearinghouse Research Center (NSCRC) publishes the Current Term Enrollment Estimates (CTEE) to provide enrollment estimates for postsecondary institutions. In December 2020, NSCRC identified a 2.5 percent overall decline in enrollment and a 13.1 percent decline among freshman.[24] At the state level, thirty-nine of the US states experienced a negative change in enrollment from the 2019 admission year.[25]

Although some Historically Black Colleges and Universities are struggling to attract potential students, there is a degree of variability. Such has always been the case; while some are doing well, others may struggle. The enrollment at a publicly funded historically Black institution in Alabama, for example, declined by nearly one-third of its normal enrollment because of COVID-19. However, at a public HBCU in Florida, little change in enrollment occurred. Alongside the pandemic, increased racial tension and social unrest ensued in 2020—largely due to George Floyd, Breonna Taylor, and Ahmaud Arbery murders, and as a result, for some HBCUs, enrollment is up.

A significant allure among some students who choose to enroll at HBCUs is the cultural connection. According to Jennifer Johnson, who explored factors that influence students to attend HBCUs, the themes of pride and prejudice (i.e., racial prejudice and the likelihood of facing prejudice in predominately White schools) served as catalysts for student attendance; more specifically, Johnson noted that students desired "to pursue post-secondary education in an environment that reflected the Black culture and Black excellence."[26] Likewise, Janelle Williams and Robert Palmer determined that the desire for the connection and shelter of HBCU culture, for some Black students, was further elevated by increased racial tension and what Walter M. Kimbrough called the "Missouri Effect," which refers to the surge of racial tension among Black and White students at predominately White institutions (PWI).[27]

Connecting with others is social, and with the guidelines for social distancing, COVID-19 has limited the effect of social engagement across the nation's college and university campuses, including HBCUs. While such may be true for some PWIs, for many HBCUs, particularly those with funding challenges, a decline in students' abilities to socialize eliminates one of the dominant reasons that some students choose to attend these historic institutions.

Questions about enrollment for the Fall 2021 semester and beyond will persist. Will decreases in enrollment at some HBCUs due to COVID-19 continue? How will the outcomes of the Derrick Chauvin verdict (i.e., the former police officer found guilty of murdering George Floyd) and related cases impact HBCU enrollment? Will mandatory vaccination deter students? Devoid the social component, will students elect to attend a local community college or institution closer to their homes instead of attending the HBCU they may have planned to attend?

Because most institutions offered a larger percentage of virtual than in-person courses, some college and university students emphasized matriculation and took the courses they needed, irrespective of the institution that offered them. Therefore, some students took virtual courses at their home institutions while others decided to take web-based courses at cheaper institutions like community colleges. This can pose another challenge. Most institutions have clear transient student policies, and while the pandemic may result in a degree of flexibility, these policies regularly require current students to obtain preapproval to take related coursework at other institutions. The disconnect between institutional policies and students who took such courses without preapproval could cause student dissatisfaction if the courses are not accepted. This dissatisfaction could lead the students to other institutions. Likewise, some students were originally enrolled at an HBCU but, when faced with COVID-19 restrictions, chose to enroll in virtual courses at other institutions. These students may have found their new experience favorable and decided to transfer.

Issues with the quality of service that students experience are a regular conversation among HBCU stakeholders. At some institutions, limitations in customer service are associated with limited numbers of staff members to service students. For larger institutions that have operated online for years, the degree of service students receives may provide attractive alternatives for students. For example, many online institutions or large institutions offer their students 24/7 technical support through online and phone-based help desks. However, at many HBCUs, even their online students are limited to receiving technical support during work hours (i.e., traditionally 8 a.m. to 5 p.m.) even though one of the benefits of online courses and programs is flexibility. Faced with the lack of support and void of the social component, the allure of HBCUs may prove less significant.

Emphasize Human Touch

How, then, can HBCU leaders mitigate the negative impact of COVID-19 on enrollment? To work against the potential for a decline in enrollment, HBCUs must do what they do best. They must provide learners with an elevated sense of care by emphasizing the human touch throughout students' experiences. For many HBCU students and alumni, these institutions provide acceptance, safety, cultural connectivity, and even hope. In addition to deliberate touch-points, HBCU leaders must be intentional in promoting the cultural experience for which these institutions are known. For Black American students, it is largely about ethnic group membership and a sense of belonging.

Dina C. Maramba and Patrick Valesquez studied ethnic identity among students of color and determined that learning about the group to which they belong had a considerable impact on a sense of belonging among students of color; they also found that developing their ethnic identities impacted students' commitments and sense of belonging.[28] And while research indicates that Black American students at PWIs often feel isolated, Black American students at HBCUs have a higher sense of belonging and report greater engagement on campus.[29] Thus, to address the potential COVID-19 impact on enrollment, HBCU leaders should consider marketing campaigns to emphasize institutional values and student-centeredness. Emerging stronger and more dedicated to community, care, academic scholarship, and service is an important message for HBCU leaders to amplify now. While each of us had individual experiences, we have shared some commonalities from the pandemic. The move away from the pandemic provides a solid opportunity for HBCU leaders and stakeholders to reassess, refocus, and rebrand. This renaissance should include progress in online education.

ADAPTING COVID-19 RESPONSES FOR THE GROWTH AND SUSTAINABILITY OF VIRTUAL LEARNING

In 2018, Patrice W. Glenn Jones and Elizabeth K. Davenport noted online education and program disparity between HBCUs and PWIs; the authors questioned the causes for this perceived resistance among HBCUs to embrace online learning and rationalized possible reasons for the reluctance to change.[30] These reasons include (a) fear of losing students, (b) inadequate computer access, (c) acceptance of negative stigma about online learning, (d) lack of funding, (e) prevalence of competition, (f) flaws in organizational structure, and (g) faculty opposition.[31] While the authors' observations predated the pandemic, the reasons the authors identified are related to the challenges that have occurred as a result of COVID-19.

How did COVID-19 change online learning at HBCUs? While many leaders at these institutions have stated that they recognize the role online learning plays in reaching a wider audience of students, the leaders have also been forthcoming in indicating that their plans for expanding online learning programs were not immediate. COVID-19, however, accelerated these time lines and forced leaders to move courses and programs online through ERT.

Through ERT migration of courses and programs, institutional leaders had to address limitations in organizational structure. They realized they did not have the professionals to sufficiently adapt courses to foster learning through virtual means and resulting in migrating the content faculty provided through the available bodies to make these emergency transitions happen. Thus, a major element that was left out of the ERT process was instructional design.

Ultimately, design and systematic migration are not a priority for ERT, and during the initial spread of COVID-19, getting content materials in place (i.e., online) was the dominant focus. Leaders and staff members were concerned with making the content available to students, even if it was not accessible, meaningful, or designed with the end-user in mind.

For institutions without instructional design (ISD) staff, the responsibility of moving courses online was given to information technology (IT) professionals. While IT and ISD professionals are connected, IT and ISD professionals do not perform the same jobs nor are their roles interchangeable. IT professionals manage and maintain the network, technological systems, and software that ISD staff, who regularly have backgrounds in education, use to plan, design, and develop online courses. These are the same courses that online content faculty facilitate to foster student learning (see Figure 8.1).

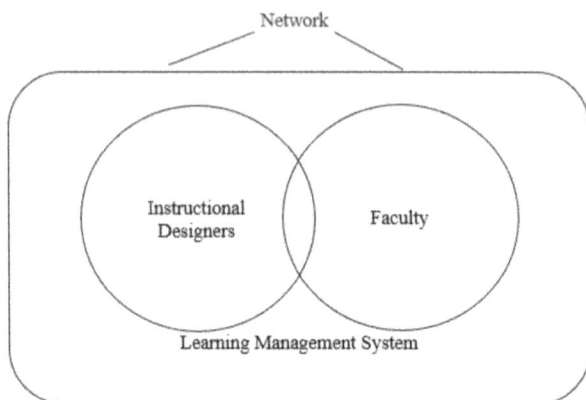

Figure 8.1
Source: Created by Author

As Figure 8.1 shows, the most interconnected relationship is between ISD professionals and faculty. Thus, getting faculty to accept the role ISD and virtual learning specialists play in preparing, designing, and helping to develop online courses can also be tough. For some faculty who are used to "doing things their way," ISD staff involvement can feel like an intrusion and a trampling on their "academic freedom." Thus, institutional leaders must serve as conduits to help faculty understand the role that ISD staff play in supporting the creation of online learning experiences that are accessible, meaningful, didactic, and engaging for all learners.

Through the involvement of ISD staff, particularly for those institutional leaders who identified COVID-response ERT as an opportunity to improve and maintain online courses and programs, these same leaders became aware of ineffective elements of content and implementation. For example, many institutional leaders, at HBCUs and other institutions, realized the significance of accessibility, which remains an elusive concept despite the availability of the Americans with Disability Act and Web Content Accessibility Guidelines that standardize standards to make web content more accessible for all people. These guidelines, for example, indicate that all videos should feature captions and that all audio should be accompanied by a text-based transcript. However, a quick review of online systems, including those featured on institutional websites, will reveal videos without captions and audio without associated transcription.

Likewise, HBCU leaders were confronted with technological limitations among students and faculty. While many eighteen- to twenty-three-year-old college students at HBCUs are digital natives, approximately 72 percent of this same group of students qualify for Pell Grants compared to approximately 38 percent of peer students at other institutions.[32] This disparity reflects limitations in the finances among a large number of undergraduate students who attend HBCUs; thus, even with technological prowess, the regular availability of said technology is less among HBCU students. Monica Anderson and Andrew Perrin of the Pew Research indicated that approximately 15 percent of homes with school-aged children do not have consistent internet connection[33]. Likewise, the *Washington Post* Editorial Board indicated that broadband adoption among Hispanic and Black Americans was less than among White Americans; they also indicated that among households with an income less than $30,000, 44 percent do not have broadband connection.[34] This information thus supports the widely suggested notion that a digital divide exists based on race and socioeconomics. Furthermore, an intersection between those identified by Pew and the *Washington Post* Editorial Board and HBCU-bound students, specifically, is likely.

Therefore, it is logical to conclude that some HBCU students do not have computers or consistent internet access. During the pandemic, some HBCU leaders learned that a large percentage of their students accessed courses using smartphones only. While smartphones are a convenience and better than nothing, composing a research paper or engaging in a breakout group discussion within a learning management system from a smartphone poses a challenge. While there is limited empirical research on the degree to which all HBCU students only use smartphones to access online courses, some HBCUs report that over half of their undergraduate students used smartphones alone to access online courses.

Students were not the only group to face obstacles. Institutional leaders also learned that while their faculty may be content experts, many of them were not comfortable with computer-mediated and online instruction. Moreover, it was determined that faculty too lacked sufficient computer equipment and associated accessories to provide meaningful instruction in the online environment. Even beyond computer access, some faculty were uncomfortable with collaborative platforms like Zoom or functions within a learning management system.

At HBCUs, the cultures are often centered around ethnic group membership, as well as the human touch at multiple student points to promote support services that elevate student success and increase their chances for graduation; thus, online learning can prove challenging. When coupled with some faculty members' limited comfort with computer-mediated instruction and virtual instruction, as well as students whose primary method of internet-based access is a smartphone, the realities and disparities for online learning excellence are heightened.

However, despite these challenges, during the COVID-19 pandemic, some HBCUs made progress with online learning. Some worked to change the climate of the institution in positive ways that help both learners and faculty to recognize and accept the role of online learning in the institutional goals. During the pandemic, some institutions provided faculty and students with training and professional development to address limitations in computer-mediated learning and instruction. Likewise, some HBCUs used the funding to provide students with computers, so they can access their online courses using more effective technology than smartphones alone.

Ultimately, some HBCUs are gaining traction in the online learning space. However, now that COVID-19 is beginning to shift, what will happen to this momentum? Will institutional leaders abandon the progress they have made with virtual learning, or will they continue to optimize the potential for online learning through continued professional development and by adding virtual learning professionals who can build upon the developments that occurred during COVID-19? I hope that HBCUs fall in the latter category.

One characteristic of historically Black institutions is that they were established before 1964.[35] In the 1960s, and certainly before, the United States was far different than it is today. When most HBCUs were established, these institutions were designed to prepare Black students to exist in a racially segregated society and to advocate for equality. Though racism is certainly still an issue, the twenty-first century is fraught with unique challenges and its own opportunities.

The purpose of education should be to prepare students to contribute to the society in which they live. Again, in the twenty-first century, society is largely technological, and it is becoming even more so every day. Thus, a basic objective of twenty-first-century education should be learning that reflects society, as well as technology-centered knowledge production. For the most part, this production involves the Internet. Learning and producing knowledge in the twenty-first century also includes gamification, artificial intelligence, augmented reality, and blockchain technology. Therefore, if HBCU leaders want to maintain the momentum that COVID-19 catalyzed, they need to establish an academic culture that not only considers the learning and producing knowledge in online ecologies but also involves how most people consume information. It is also essential that HBCU stakeholders are actively involved in creating innovation in virtual instruction, adaptive learning software, virtual ecology design, gamification, artificial intelligence, and blockchain technology. While one challenge is that online programming at many HBCUs falls behind some of their counterparts, business and institutional partnerships provide a solid way to build upon existing progress.

CULTURAL CONSCIOUSNESS IN ONLINE COURSES

In a previous section (i.e., Emerging from Enrollment Trends), I recommended that HBCU leaders create cultural experiences with intentionality. While doing such on campus is important, it is also crucial to duplicate such cultural experiences in virtual learning ecologies. Most students who attend HBCUs are looking for a cultural connection. For many Black students, culture includes both racial/ethnic group similarities and the involvement of technology. Learning online does not eliminate the desire for familiarity, as well as a sense of belonging.

Foster a Sense of Belonging

While flexibility is a characteristic associated with online learning, feelings of isolation are regularly reported as inhibitors of online student success while a high sense of community positively affects online student achievement.[36] A sense of belonging, however, is correlated with a social presence, establishing a strong sense of community, and shared experiences. Considering the relationship between cultural experiences and a sense of belonging among Black American students, making advancements in online spaces at HBCUs means incorporating cultural experiences into online courses and online programs. And while social distancing protocols are being lifted, who knows what will happen in the fall of 2021? For that matter, another domestic or global emergency would lead us back to virtual learning.

Providing Services to Address Learning Gaps of Entering Students

When the state of global emergency was confirmed, social distancing measures were put in place, and the pandemic caused many K-12 districts to close school doors and parents to explore alternate methods of learning for students. The unparalleled and spontaneous disruption of educational systems changed the way students learned and teachers taught. Closure-related changes caused many to turn to online and blended (i.e., virtual) instruction as viable alternatives. The primary responsibility for student learning transferred from the school to the home. In some cases, virtual learning proved difficult and unsuitable for some families.

While online learning can be a suitable and even viable solution for education, it is not a good fit for all families and students. Furthermore, the abrupt nature of ERT does not have the same quality as systematic online learning. Most students and families were not prepared for this transition. Limitations in within-home structural support, as well as access to technology were major factors. Likewise, some students lacked organizational skills and motivation; thus, it is logical that interaction between these students and teachers was likely limited. A lack of meaningful interaction may have caused significant variations in overall student success.

Regarding the transition to online learning during COVID-19, Amy J. Catalano, Bruce Torff, and Kevin S. Anderson examined the differences in participation and access among different groups of students and found that nearly 30 percent of the students were not regularly completing their assignments; to some degree, reduced participation resulted from a lack of consistent access to technology.[37] While the abrupt and unplanned transition alone was problematic, the long-term outcomes of learning during COVID-19 could prove even more harmful. Many scholars and practitioners speculate how COVID-19 ERT and emergency transition to virtual and in-home instruction will impact learning measures on a national level. While much remains to be seen, the impact could be most significant among low-income K-12 students of color, like those who will eventually enroll at one of the nation's HBCUs.

Anna Saavedra and colleagues examined the impact of COVID-19 on K-12 students and found significant differences in teacher interaction among students who were working from home.[38] These differences were based on economics; 89 percent of students from high-income households reported interacting regularly with their teachers while that number among low-income households was 57 percent.[39] These differences are concerning if we accept what research suggests about the relationship between student achievement and teacher interaction (i.e., teacher-student interaction is the most significant school variable to promote student achievement). Delaware State Education agency asserted that "This crisis disproportionately affects our most vulnerable students, their physical and mental health as well as their academic outcomes."[40]

During the pandemic, researchers at the Pew Research Center studied concern and satisfaction among parents of K-12 children learning in person and online and determined that parents of children attending school in person were less likely to be concerned and more likely to be satisfied with their children's education.[41] The researchers also examined the degree of online learning experienced by students (i.e., fully online, fully in-person, or a mixture of online and in-person), as well as the level of additional support being provided among in-home adults.[42] They determined that among lower-income parents, children were more likely to receive only online instruction and less likely to be provided with additional instruction.[43]

Family involvement in student learning has been linked to positive learning outcomes. When parents are actively involved in and responsible for student engagement and learning, they can gain a better awareness of students' skills and weaknesses. For example, during the pandemic, I chose to keep my elementary-aged sons at home and enrolled in district-sponsored virtual learning; because I assumed responsibility for their learning, I noted the limitations one of my sons had with multiplying double digits. The younger of the two struggled with certain concepts associated with reading comprehension. To address their weaknesses, I integrated remedial learning tasks to help augment their abilities. I am an educator, and even for me, this was a taxing experience. I even incorporated the assistance of my adult daughter and a virtual tutor into my children's virtual learning experience. For parents who do not have such resources or who cannot recognize their students' underdeveloped skills, the degree of involvement could be more limited, which could directly impact student learning and academic success.

Differentiated Instruction

With consideration of the variability in learning, modality, and degree of satisfaction among parents, once the pandemic has passed, teachers will encounter varied skills, abilities, and weaknesses in the same class, which will call for a greater need for differentiated in-class instruction. While learning variability is not necessarily new and differentiated instruction has been an important strategy even when the matriculation paths for students did not involve ERT, the expectation is that teachers will see an even more significant range in skills, abilities, and weaknesses.

Furthermore, differentiation is not a cure-all. Some teachers express the problematic nature of differentiated instruction, which involves a teacher's use of various strategies tailored to each student's learning needs. While proactive differentiated instruction is considered the most effective, it is also considered more difficult, as it requires extensive planning.[44] Thus, many teachers who do utilize differentiated instruction rely more on a reactive differentiated instruction approach, in which teachers' responses to varied learning among students are after the fact (i.e., after instruction).

This range of COVID-19-related variability will probably persist even as students who are now in elementary enter postsecondary studies and will require appropriate instructional strategies, as well as services to support student learning and academic success. Thus, diversity in learning readiness and the need for remediation among adult students will also continue.

Need for Remediation

At the postsecondary level, Black American students have been enrolled in more remedial courses than White students.[45] Well before the pandemic, the landscape in remediation and developmental education was moving away from more traditional modes of assessing readiness and providing remedial instruction. Instructional reform has included shorter periods of developmental courses, allowing students more autonomy in course selection and their learning pace, and integrating remediation in specific for-credit foundation courses. Ultimately, approaches vary, and among most successful implementations, institutional leaders use data from enrolled or entering student groups to provide research-based measures that are targeted and specific. As groups of students that were impacted by COVID-19 enroll at HBCUs, varied learning abilities, as well as learning deficits, will accompany them. Thus, HBCU leaders will need to take a similar approach, examining student groups to determine where needs exist and providing several that are targeted, meaningful, and student group driven.

Back to Basics

Considering the degree of diversity, meeting student learning needs, which involves varied strategies, is challenging. Some may even ask, '*Where do we begin to address these COVID-19-related limitations?*' One recommendation is to go back to basics. While variation is a major component of differentiation and HBCU leaders should indeed provide targeted services, the national emphasis on high-stakes testing has created a void in practical skills among many students in some states. As an elementary student, I had to know multiplication tables with proficiency. We studied percentages and fractions with practical applications. For that matter, my eldest son's fifth-grade math teacher facilitated math objectives through stocks and gains and losses. In high school, we learned math concepts concerning the budget and fiscal responsibility. Such strategies are not regularly utilized by current teachers because there is a focus on teaching for assessments. However, at minimum, reading, writing, and math concepts should be emphasized through real-life applications. Thus, this strategy is not solely for HBCUs, it lies with all education from the K-20 landscape. Taking a communal approach will yield the best results.

Strengthen Tutoring Services

Another important strategy for HBCU leaders consideration is to provide students with tutoring services and encourage them to take advantage of these services. While most postsecondary institutions provide tutorial services, these services are widely underused by students. Thus, HBCU leaders and faculty must use strategies to promote student utilization. Faculty could make tutoring services a part of student grading (e.g., 10 percent of the student's grade for 4 tutoring sessions). Faculty could also share empirical data associated with the academic or course success among students who utilize tutoring versus those who do not.

CONCLUSION

The COVID-19 pandemic fostered unparalleled disruption in the United States and globally. And even as I pen the conclusion to this chapter, threats of new and emerging variants of SARS-CoV-2 are being monitored. While restrictions have been lifted in many states, the many people who are still in masks, along with many organizations and even institutions with mask mandates still in place, inform the narrative that we are not yet out of the proverbial woods.

COVID-19 has certainly been an obstacle. However, the relationship between obstacle and growth, as well as disappointment and hope, is linked and regularly communicated. Martin Luther King Jr., for example, said, "We must accept finite disappointment but never lose infinite hope," but even positive psychology makes this association. According to positive psychologists, hope is a state of mind that looks optimistically at potential outcomes even during despair. Regarding the COVID-19 pandemic's impact on education, David Jackson, Provost and Vice-Chancellor of Academic Affairs at North Carolina Central University, and former Associate Provost for Graduate Education & Dean School of Graduate Studies & Research at Florida A&M University said that through these obstacles, we have a responsibility to assess and cultivate the opportunities.

The challenges associated with HBCU stakeholder safety, psychosocial outcomes, enrollment, virtual learning, and services to advance student learning and academic success presented herein are by no means meant to be a comprehensive list of challenges. The same is true for the recommendations and discussions; they are not meant to be one-size-fits-all solutions for all our nation's historically Black institutions. Years of research on the impact of COVID-19 are probable. I recommend that this research includes specific challenges, strategies, and outcomes among HBCU stakeholders.

Ultimately, the overarching theme for practice to address the academic outbreak that the pandemic caused is "purposive and proactiveness." While some data suggests that the COVID-19 pandemic is subsiding, the truth is, that we just do not know what the future holds. However, as beacons of opportunity, education, and hope, no matter what happens, HBCUs and the leaders entrusted to guide these institutions have a responsibility to respond with preemptive, service-orientated intentionality to curtail the impact of COVID-19 and associated outcomes.

NOTES

1. "Pneumonia of unknown cause-China," World Health Organization, accessed April 12, 2021, https://www.who.int/csr/don/05-january-2020-pneumonia-of-unkown -cause-china/en/

2. "WHO Timeline COVID-19," World Health Organization, accessed April 14, 2021. https://www.who.int/news/item/27-04-2020-who-timeline---covid-19.

3. See note 2.

4. "A Timeline of COVID-19 Developments in 2020," AJMC, accessed April 14, 2021. https://www.ajmc.com/view/a-timeline-of-covid19-developments-in-2020.

5. See note 4.

6. "Public Health Response to the Initiation and Spread of the Pandemic COVID-19 in the United States, February 24-April 21, 2020," Centers for Disease Control and Prevention, accessed April 14, 2021, https://www.cdc.gov/mmwr/volumes/69/wr/ mm6918e2.htm.

7. See note 6, Discussion section.

8. "United States Forecasting," Centers for Disease Control and Prevention, accessed April 14, 2021, https://covid.cdc.gov/covid-data-tracker/#forecasting_weeklydeaths.

9. "Economic Fallout from COVID-19 Continues to Hit Lower-Income Americans the Hardest," Pew Research Center, accessed April 14, 2021, https://www.pewresearch.org/social-trends/2020/09/24/economic-fallout-from-covid-19-continues-to-hit-lower-income-americans-the-hardest//

10. Chee, Melissa, Nikita Koziel Ly, Hymie Anisman, and Kimberly Matheson. "Piece of Cake: Coping with COVID-19." *Nutrients* 12, no. 12 (December 2020): 3803–22. https://doi.org/10.3390/nu1223803/

11. Son, Changwon, Sudeep Hedge, Alec Smith, Xiaomei Wang, and Farzan Sasangohar. "Effects of COVID-9 on College Students' Mental Health in the United States: Interview Survey Study." *Journal of Medical Internet Research* 22, no. 9 (September 2020). https://www.jmir.org/2020/9/e21279.

12. Pinto, Sara, Joana Soares, Alzira Silva, Rosario Curral, and Rui Coelho. "COVID-19 Suicide Survivors—A Hidden Grieving Population." *Psychiatry* (December 21, 2020). https://www.frontiersin.org/articles/10.3389/fpsyt.2020.626807/full.

13. "How HBCUs are Responding to Shutdowns." United Negro College Fund, accessed April 17, 2021, https://uncf.org/the-latest/how-hbcus-are-responding-to-shutdowns

14. "COVID Data Tracker." Centers for Disease Control and Prevention, accessed May 12, 2021, https://covid.cdc.gov/covid-data-tracker/#vaccination-demographic

15. "Considerations for Institutions of Higher Education." Centers for Disease Control and Prevention, accessed May 10, 2021, https://www.cdc.gov/coronavirus/2019-ncov/community/colleges-universities/considerations.html#PlanPrepare.

16. Largent, Emily, Govid Persad, Samantha Sangenito, Aaron Glickman, Conner Boyle, and Ezekiel Emmanuel. "U.S. Attitudes Toward COVID-19 Mandates." *JAMA* 325, 396. (2020). Retrieved May 12, 2021, from https://www.ncbi.nlm.nih.gov/pmc/articles/PMC7749443/.

17. Kearney, Audrey, Liz Hamel, and Mollyann Brodie. "Attitudes Towards COVID-19 Vaccination Among Black Women and Men." Kaiser Family Foundation. Retrieved May 12, 2021, from https://www.kff.org/coronavirus-covid-19/poll-finding/attitudes-towards-covid-19-vaccination-among-black-women-and-men/.

18. R. P. Auerbach et al. "WHO World Health Surveys International College Student Project: Prevalence and disruption of mental disorders." *Journal of Abnormal Psychology* 127, no. 7 623–38. (2018). Accessed June 15, 2021, 10.1037/abn0000362.

19. C. S. Conley et al. "Negotiating the transition to college: developmental trajectories and gender differences in psychological functioning, cognitive-affective strategies, and social well-being." *Emerging Adulthood* 2, no. 3 195–210. (2014). Accessed June 16, 2021, 10.117/2167696814521808.

20. Muhammad Fakhar-e-Alam Kulyar, Zeesham Ahmad Bhutta, Samina Shabbir, and Muhammad Akhtar. "Psychosocial impact of COVID-29 outbreak on international students living in Hubei province, China." *Travel Med Infectious Disease* 37, no. 101712. (2020). Accessed June 15, 2021, 10.1016/j.tmai.2020.101712.

21. Francesca Favieri, Giuseppe Forte, Renata Tambelli, and Maria Casagrande. "The Italians in the time of Coronavirus: Psychosocial aspects of the unexpected COVID-19 pandemic." *Front Psychiatry* 12, no. 551924. (2021). Accessed June 15, 2021, 10.3389/fpsyt.2021.551924.

22. Thompson, Richard, Barbara L. Dancy, Tisha R. A. Wiley, Cynthia J. Najdowski, Sylvia P. Perry, Jason Wallis, Yara Mekawi, and Kathleen A. Knafl. "African American families' expectations and intentions for mental health services." *Administration and Policy in Mental Health and Mental Health Services Research* 40, no. 5 (2013): 371–83.

23. Novacek, Derek M., Joya N. Hampton-Anderson, Megat T. Ebor, Tamra B. Loeb, and Gail E. Wyatt. "Mental Health Ramifications of the COVID-19 Pandemic for Black Americans: Clinical and Research Recommendations." *Psychological Trauma: Theory, Research, Practice, and Policy.* Accessed June 20, 2020, http://dx .doi.org/10.1037/tra0000796.

24. "Term Enrollment Estimates Fall 2020" National Student Clearinghouse Research Center, accessed May 12, 2021, https://nscresearchcenter.org/wp-content/ uploads/CTEE_Report_Fall_2020.pdf/

25. See Note 24.

26. Johnson, Jennifer Michelle. "Prided or Prejudice: Motivations for Choosing Black Colleges." *Journal of Student Affairs Research and Practice* 56, no. 4 409–22. (2019). https://doi.org/10.1080/19496591.2019.1614936/

27. Williams, Janelle L. and Robert T. Palmer. "A Response to Racism: How HBCU Enrollment Grew in the Face of Hatred." CMSI Research Brief. Accessed April 16, 2021, https://hbcufirst.com/Portals/20/Research/A-Response-to-Racism -How-HBCU-Enrollment-Grew-in-the-Face-of-Hatred.pdf.

28. Maramba, Dina C. and Patrick Valesquez. "Influences of the campus experience on the ethnic identity development of students of color." *Education and Urban Society* 44, no. 3 294–317. (2012). Accessed May 19, 2021, from https://journals.sagepub .com/doi/pdf/10.1177/0013124510393239?casa_token=WCJOGjPdPb0AAAAA: _4i6YamPJzSwnTg3atXvQVXK4V_d4ZRm2AVsSMrZfPROrlchzQ8HAyKaORtL IDF_wxymTRRvKtQW.

29. Pascarella, Ernest T. and Patrick T. Terezini. *How College Affects students: A Third Decade of Research.* San Francisco: Josey-Bass, 2005.

30. Glenn Jones, Patrice. W. and Elizabeth K. Davenport. "Resistance to Change: HBCUs and Online Learning." *Thought & Action* 34, no. 1 59–80. (2018). Accessed April 17, 2021, from http://www.learntechlib.org/p/191795.

31. See Note 30.

32. National Center for Education Statistics. Integrated Postsecondary Education Data System.

33. Monica Anderson and Andrew Perrin. "Nearly one-in-five teens can't always finish their homework because of the digital divide." Pew Research. (2018). Accessed June 12, 2021, https://www.pewresearch.org/fact-tank/2018/10/26/nearly-one-in-five -teens-cant-always-finish-their-homework-because-of-the-digital-divide/.

34. "Coronavirus has made the digital divide more dangerous than ever." *Washington Post.* (2020). Accessed June 11, 2021, https://www.washingtonpost.com

/opinions/coronavirus-has-made-the-digital-divide-more-dangerous-than-ever/2020
/03/29/7ed054e0-706a-11ea-b148-e4ce3fbd85b5_story.html.

35. "Historically Black Colleges and Universities." National Center for Education Statistics, accessed May 19, 2021, https://nces.ed.gov/fastfacts/display.asp?id=667.

36. Shelton, Brett E., Jui-Long Hung, and Patrick R. Lowenthal. "Predicting student success by modeling student interaction in asynchronous online courses." *Distance Education* 38, no. 1, 59–69. (2017). Doi.10.1080/01587919.2017.1299562/

37. Catalano, Amy J., Bruce Torff, and Kevin S. Anderson. "Transitioning to online learning during the COVID-19 pandemic: differences in access and participation among students in disadvantaged school districts." *International Journal of Information and Learning Technology* 38, no. 2, 258–70. (2021). Accessed June 23, 2021. https://doi.org/10.1108/IJILT-06-2020-0111.

38. Saavedra, Anna, Amie Rapaport, Morgan Polikoff, Daniel Silver, Shira Haderlein, and Marshall Garland. "Evidence of COVID-19's Impact on K-12 Education Points to Critical Areas of Intervention." University of Southern California Schaeffer, accessed May 19, 2021, https://healthpolicy.usc.edu/evidence-base/evidence-of-covid-19s-impact-on-k-12-education-points-to-critical-areas-of-intervention/.

39. See note 36.

40. "Supporting Continuity of Learning in Delaware Schools." Delaware Department of Education. (2020). Accessed June 25, 2020, https//www.doe.k12.de.us/cms/lib/DE01922744/Cen-tricity/Domain/599/continuity_of_learning.pdf.

41. Horowitz, Julianna Menasce, and Ruth Igielnik. "Most Parents of K-12 Students Learning Online Worry About Them Falling Behind." Pew Research Center. Accessed June 25, 2020, https://www.pewresearch.org/social-trends/2020/10/29/most-parents-of-k-12-students-learning-online-worry-about-them-falling-behind/.

42. See note 41.

43. Ibid.

44. Janssen, Fred, Hanna Westbroek, Jan van Driel, and Walter Doyle. "How to make innovations practical." *Teachers College Record* 115, no. 7 (2013): 1–42.

45. Aud, Susan, William Hussar, and Grace Kena. "The Condition of Education 2011." National Center for Education Statistics. Access June 28, 2021, https://nces.ed.gov/pubsearch/pubsinfo.asp?pubid=2011033.

REFERENCES

Anderson, Monica, and Andrew Perrin. "Nearly one-in-five teens can't always finish their homework because of the digital divide." Pew Research. (2018). Accessed June 12, 2021, https://www.pewresearch.org/fact-tank/2018/10/26/nearly-one-in-five-teens-cant-always-finish-their-homework-because-of-the-digital-divide/.

Aud, Susan, William Hussar, and Grace Kena. "The Condition of Education 2011." National Center for Education Statistics. Access June 28, 2021, https://nces.ed.gov/pubsearch/pubsinfo.asp?pubid=2011033.

Catalano, Amy J., Bruce Torff, and Kevin S. Anderson. "Transitioning to online learning during the COVID-19 pandemic: differences in access and participation among students in disadvantaged school districts." *International Journal of Information and Learning Technology* 38, no. 2, 258–70. (2021). Accessed June 23, 2021. https://doi.org/10.1108/IJILT-06-2020-0111.

Chee, Melissa, Nikita Koziel Ly, Hymie Anisman, and Kimberly Matheson. "Piece of Cake: Coping with COVID-19." *Nutrients* 12, no. 12 (December 2020): 3803–22. https://doi.org/10.3390/nu1223803.

Conley, C. S., et al. "Negotiating the transition to college: developmental trajectories and gender differences in psychological functioning, cognitive-affective strategies, and social well-being." *Emerging Adulthood* 2, no. 3 195–210. (2014). Accessed June 16, 2021, 10.117/2167696814521808.

"Considerations for Institutions of Higher Education." Centers for Disease Control and Prevention, accessed May 10, 2021, https://www.cdc.gov/coronavirus/2019 -ncov/community/colleges-universities/considerations.html#PlanPrepare.

"Coronavirus has made the digital divide more dangerous than ever." *Washington Post*. (2020). Accessed June 11, 2021, https://www.washingtonpost.com/opinions /coronavirus-has-made-the-digital-divide-more-dangerous-than-ever/2020/03/29 /7ed054e0-706a-11ea-b148-e4ce3fbd85b5_story.html.

"COVID Data Tracker." Centers for Disease Control and Prevention, accessed May 12, 2021, https://covid.cdc.gov/covid-data-tracker/#vaccination-demographic.

"Economic Fallout from COVID-19 Continues to Hit Lower-Income Americans the Hardest," Pew Research Center, accessed April 14, 2021, https://www.pewresearch.org/social-trends/2020/09/24/economic-fallout-from-covid-19-continues-to -hit-lower-income-americans-the-hardest/.

Favieri, Francesca, Giuseppe Forte, Renata Tambelli, and Maria Casagrande. "The Italians in the time of Coronavirus: Psychosocial aspects of the unexpected COVID-19 pandemic." Front Psychiatry, 12, no. 551924. (2021). Accessed June 15, 2021, 10.3389/fpsyt.2021.551924.

"Historically Black Colleges and Universities." National Center for Education Statistics, accessed May 19, 2021, https://nces.ed.gov/fastfacts/display.asp?id=667.

Horowitz, Julianna Menasce, and Ruth Igielnik. "Most Parents of K-12 Students Learning Online Worry About Them Falling Behind." Pew Research Center. Accessed June 25, 2020, https://www.pewresearch.org/social-trends/2020/10/29/ most-parents-of-k-12-students-learning-online-worry-about-them-falling-behind//

"How HBCUs are Responding to Shutdowns." United Negro College Fund, accessed April 17, 2021, https://uncf.org/the-latest/how-hbcus-are-responding-to -shutdowns/

Janssen, Fred, Hanna Westbroek, Jan van Driel, and Walter Doyle. "How to make innovations practical." *Teachers College Record* 115, no. 7 (2013): 1–42.

Johnson, Jennifer Michelle. "Prided or Prejudice: Motivations for Choosing Black Colleges." *Journal of Student Affairs Research and Practice* 56, no. 4 409–22. (2019). https://doi.org/10.1080/19496591.2019.1614936.

Jones, Glenn, Patrice. W. and Elizabeth K. Davenport. "Resistance to Change: HBCUs and Online Learning." *Thought & Action* 34, no. 1 59–80. (2018). Accessed April 17, 2021, from http://www.learntechlib.org/p/191795.

Kearney, Audrey, Liz Hamel, and Mollyann Brodie. "Attitudes Towards COVID-19 Vaccination Among Black Women and Men." Kaiser Family Foundation. Retrieved May 12, 2021, from https://www.kff.org/coronavirus-covid-19/poll-finding/attitudes-towards-covid-19-vaccination-among-black-women-and-men/.

Kulyar, Muhammad Fakhar-e-Alam, Zeesham Ahmad Bhutta, Samina Shabbir, and Muhammad Akhtar. "Psychosocial impact of COVID-29 outbreak on international students living in Hubei province, China." *Travel Med Infectious Disease* 37, no. 101712. (2020). Accesses June 15, 2021, 10.1016/j.tmai.2020.101712.

Largent, Emily, Govid Persad, Samantha Sangenito, Aaron Glickman, Conner Boyle, and Ezekiel Emmanuel. "U.S. Attitudes Toward COVID-19 Mandates." *JAMA*, 325, 396. (2020). Retrieved May 12, 2021, from https://www.ncbi.nlm.nih.gov/pmc/articles/PMC7749443/.

Maramba, Dina C., and Patrick Valesquez. "Influences of the campus experience on the ethnic identity development of students of color." *Education and Urban Society* 44, no. 3 294–317. (2012). Accessed May 19, 2021, from https://journals.sagepub.com/doi/pdf/10.1177/0013124510393239?casa_token=WCJOGjPdPb0AAAAA:_4i6YamPJzSwnTg3atXvQVXK4V_d4ZRm2AVsSMrZfPROrlchzQ8HAyKaORtLIDF_wxymTRRvKtQW.

National Center for Education Statistics. Integrated Postsecondary Education Data System.

Novacek, Derek M., Joya N. Hampton-Anderson, Megat T. Ebor, Tamra B. Loeb, and Gail E. Wyatt. "Mental Health Ramifications of the COVID-19 Pandemic for Black Americans: Clinical and Research Recommendations." *Psychological Trauma: Theory, Research, Practice, and Policy.* Accessed June 20, 2020, http://dx.doi.org/10.1037/tra0000796.

Pascarella, Ernest T., and Patrick T. Terezini. *How College Affects Students: A Third Decade of Research.* San Francisco: Josey-Bass, 2005.

Pinto, Sara, Joana Soares, Alzira Silva, Rosario Curral, and Rui Coelho. "COVID-19 Suicide Survivors—A Hidden Grieving Population." *Psychiatry* (December 21, 2020). https://www.frontiersin.org/articles/10.3389/fpsyt.2020.626807/full.

"Pneumonia of unknown cause-China," World Health Organization, accessed April 12, 2021, https://www.who.int/csr/don/05-january-2020-pneumonia-of-unkown-cause-china/en/.

"Public Health Response to the Initiation and Spread of the Pandemic COVID-19 in the United States, February 24-April 21, 2020," Centers for Disease Control and Prevention, accessed April 14, 2021, https://www.cdc.gov/mmwr/volumes/69/wr/mm6918e2.htm.

R. P. Auerbach et al. "WHO World Health Surveys International College Student Project: Prevalence and disruption of mental disorders." *Journal of Abnormal Psychology* 127, no. 7 623–38. (2018). Accessed June 15, 2021, 10.1037/abn0000362 "United States Forecasting," Centers for Disease Control and Prevention, accessed April 14, 2021, https://covid.cdc.gov/covid-data-tracker/#forecasting_weeklydeaths.

Saavedra, Anna, Amie Rapaport, Morgan Polikoff, Daniel Silver, Shira Haderlein, and Marshall Garland. "Evidence of COVID-19's Impact on K-12 Education Points to

Critical Areas of Intervention." University of Southern California Schaeffer, accessed May 19, 2021, https://healthpolicy.usc.edu/evidence-base/evidence-of-covid-19s-impact-on-k-12-education-points-to-critical-areas-of-intervention/.

Shelton, Brett E., Jui-Long Hung, and Patrick R. Lowenthal. "Predicting student success by modeling student interaction in asynchronous online courses." *Distance Education* 38, no. 1, 59–69. (2017). Doi.10.1080/01587919.2017.1299562

Son, Changwon, Sudeep Hedge, Alec Smith, Xiaomei Wang, and Farzan Sasangohar. "Effects of COVID-9 on College Students' Mental Health in the United States: Interview Survey Study." *Journal of Medical Internet Research* 22, no. 9 (September 2020). https://www.jmir.org/2020/9/e21279.

"Supporting Continuity of Learning in Delaware Schools." Delaware Department of Education. (2020). Accessed June 25, 2020, https//www.doe.k12.de.us/cms/lib/DE01922744/Cen-tricity/Domain/599/continuityoflearning.pdf.

"Term Enrollment Estimates Fall 2020" National Student Clearinghouse Research Center, accessed May 12, 2021, https://nscresearchcenter.org/wp-content/uploads/CTEE_Report_Fall_2020.pdf.

Thompson, Richard, Barbara L. Dancy, Tisha RA Wiley, Cynthia J. Najdowski, Sylvia P. Perry, Jason Wallis, Yara Mekawi, and Kathleen A. Knafl. "African American families' expectations and intentions for mental health services." *Administration and Policy in Mental Health and Mental Health Services Research* 40, no. 5 (2013): 371–83.

"A Timeline of COVID-19 Developments in 2020," AJMC, accessed April 14, 2021 https://www.ajmc.com/view/a-timeline-of-covid19-developments-in-2020.

"WHO Timeline COVID-19," World Health Organization, accessed April 14, 2021 https://www.who.int/news/item/27-04-2020-who-timeline---covid-19

Williams, Janelle L. and Robert T. Palmer. "A Response to Racism: How HBCU Enrollment Grew in the Face of Hatred." CMSI Research Brief. Accessed April 16, 2021, https://hbcufirst.com/Portals/20/Research/A-Response-to-Racism-How-HBCU-Enrollment-Grew-in-the-Face-of-Hatred.pdf

Chapter 9

HBCU Medical Programs in a Globalizing World

Tabitha S. M. Morton, Tamika Baldwin-Clark, and Tiffany Thomas

INTRODUCTION

While the United States claims to be a color-blind society, little has changed for African Americans. From the very beginning, enslaved Africans in the American colonies faced discrimination. They were dehumanized and denied educational and career opportunities and access to quality healthcare regardless of their status in society. To overcome race-based hurdles, African Americans established Historically Black Colleges and Universities (HBCU). HBCUs offer more than educational pathways. They are training grounds for reversing the race-based inferiority myths created and perpetuated by White institutions and preparing future Black leaders and professionals.[1] The oldest Historically Black Colleges and University (HBCU) was established in 1837 by Richard Humphreys. The African Institute, which would later be named Cheyney University, taught African Americans the skills necessary to gain employment.[2] 1865–1900 saw the establishment of many of the HBCUs today, and when combined with the number of Primarily Black Institutions (PBI schools created after 1964), there are 101 institutions founded to educate African American students specifically - four currently with medical schools in operation: Charles R. Drew University of Medicine and Science, Howard University College of Medicine, Meharry Medical College, and Morehouse School of Medicine

Today's HBCUs and PBIs have changed to keep up with the evolving world around them, with many HBCUs witnessing an increase in non-Black student enrollment.[3] Institutions can be "public, private, denominational, liberal arts, land-grant, independent university systems, single-gender serving, research-based, [and] large and small," thus providing African American and non-African Americans students the option to choose the university best suited for them.[4] HBCUs may also be religious and nonsectarian and offer two-year and four-year programs providing flexibility for all students.[5]

From basic skills in 1837 to medical degrees in 2021, HBCUs and HBCU medical programs continue to provide African Americans the educational and career opportunities they need to be successful. These medical programs are necessary to advance African Americans in medicine because, despite civil rights legislation, race-based hurdles in medicine remain. While there are more African American doctors today than there were in 1837, one fact remains the same. African Americans still have limited access to Primarily White Institutions' (PWI) medical schools, and African American communities continue to receive subpar healthcare and experience healthcare racism more than Whites.[6]

For example, from 2020 to 2021, the COVID-19-related African American deaths rate was significantly higher than Whites, and fears and hesitance to get COVID-19 vaccines within the Black community were prevalent due to the historical distrust of U.S. healthcare.[7] Add in the generally poorer health of African Americans, lack of quality clinics, and the racially charged political and social climate stemming from police brutality, and something became extremely clear. The world may be evolving, but racial discrimination, preventative care, and treatment disparities in healthcare remain.[8] There is a desperate need for medical professionals who do not harbor implicit racial bias when treating African American patients. They should provide quality and equal treatment and gain African American patients' trust.[9] The solution scholars recommend; more African American doctors and medical professionals. Given the ever-present legacy of slavery, Jim Crow, and general racial strife, HBCU medical programs still produce the majority of African American doctors.[10]

While African Americans have equal access to PWIs and many medical programs claim to be equal and have anti-discrimination policies, HBCUs produce 70–80% of African American doctors in the United States.[11] Like African Americans pre-1865, African Americans attending PWIs in 2020 continue to report mistreatment, bullying, harassment, and hazing at higher rates than Whites.[12] Likewise, African Americans still report discrimination against them during the admission process to PWI medical schools despite the affirmative action policies established in the late 1960s. The colorblind, holistic admission processes that followed still rely on the MCAT, further discriminating against African Americans.[13] They also report discrimination and mistreatment while attending medical school and practicing medicine. The behavior is unofficially endorsed because the harassers, students, program staff, and faculty are rarely punished.[14] The prevalence of racism, both explicit and implicit, makes HBCU medical programs popular, attractive, and critical for African Americans wishing to continue their education.

EVOLUTION

Today's programs have come a long way. Despite the race-based stereotypes some still harbor against HBCU medical schools, their medical programs today meet the national standards and produce graduates that have made notable contributions to medicine ethically. For example, Dr. John Angelo Lester, a graduate of Meharry Medical College, helped create free clinics offering medical services to those who required surgery but could not afford to pay for it. Dr. Daniel Hale Williams, a graduate of Howard's medical program, became the first doctor to perform open-heart surgery successfully.

Historically, White medical programs, colleges, and professional organizations such as the American Medical Association (AMA) denied most African Americans admission. Systemically, the AMA created consistent barriers for African American men practicing medicine, for example, by placing a "C" next to their name denoting colored. Even those who were able to obtain a medical degree, such as James McCune Smith (the University of Glasgow in Scotland in 1837), the first African American to earn a medical degree, and Rebecca Lee Crumpler (New England Female Medical College in 1864), the first African American female to earn a medical degree, experienced severe racism during their practice.

HBCU medical programs provided African Americans actual opportunities to practice medicine, unlike PWIs, where they could at most observe.[15] Howard University established the first medical program for African Americans in 1868 and the National Medical Association to provide them education and careers in medicine. By directly increasing the number of trained and culturally aware African American practitioners, HBCU medical programs rejected the claims that African American doctors were inferior and highlighted their contributions to the medical sciences.[16] The first graduate from Howard University was James T. Wormley in 1870. Other colleges followed suit, and by the end of the nineteenth century, about fourteen medical schools for African Americans were established.[17] However, several of these schools were for-profit. They did not provide the facilities, faculty, and funds to provide a quality medical program. Graduates were unprepared to practice medicine by the American Medical Association and the Association of Medical Colleges' standards.

Due to these questionable practices, the Flexner Report was commissioned in 1910 by The Carnegie Foundation, and it provided guidelines for who should qualify as a physician.[18] Abraham Flexner's report is an essential document for creating professionalism standards within the medical community despite his lack of formal training. Flexner's recommendations and strong opinions proved harmful to African American training schools and led to many African American medical schools' closure. Using Johns Hopkins Medical school as an example, Flexner concluded that many African American medical schools did not meet standards, resulting in many programs' closure.[19]

The report results prevented many African Americans from obtaining medical degrees during a time in which White doctors still denied African Americans quality healthcare. The White medical community benefited from the "greater good" of the medical trauma placed upon the African American community while absorbing none of the pain or risks. An African American woman named Henrietta Lacks, for example, paid the ultimate price, without consent, for the advancement of medicine. Physicians from John Hopkins, the same school Flexner considered the gold standard, voluntarily abandoned their ethical responsibilities and stole cultured cells from a malignant tumor in her cervix. At the same time, she underwent treatment for cervical cancer. At the expense of a Black female patient, Dr. George Otto Grey, a white doctor, used her cells, referred to as HeLa cells, to revolutionize medical research. Today, HeLa cells have contributed to medical breakthroughs in science, the polio vaccine, the AIDS virus, and cancer research worldwide, yet her family could not determine who could use the cells for research until 2013.[20] Instances like these still contribute to the cultural memory of medical mistrust and fear between White healthcare practitioners and institutions and African Americans today.

White medical programs continued to ignore ethics and use medical programs to practice eugenics by controlling African American women's reproductive roles without their consent.[21] Fannie Lou Hamer is best known for her bold and unapologetic stances regarding the political activities of African Americans. However, her "Mississippi appendectomy" motivated and shaped her political involvement.[22] White doctors would tell African American women they needed their appendix removed. Instead, doctors performed hysterectomies. In 1961, during a routine uterine fibroid tumor removal surgery, Hamer's uterus was removed from her body - without consent and without her knowledge. She was a victim of a social movement to discourage the reproduction by people deemed "undesirable," i.e., African Americans, and deceit by a medical professional. Patient-doctor relationships and equitable treatment have always been critical to quality care. From enslavement to modern times, African Americans have experienced horrors at the hands of White doctors and unequal medical care.[23]

The continued racial disparities and discrimination in medicine demonstrate an increasing need for African American medical professionals and others that do not practice medicine based on explicit and implicit racial bias. Based on self-reports, African Americans only make up 5–6 percent of doctors in the United States, and 70–80 percent of those came from four HBCUs.[24] In recent years there has been a steady increase in the number of African Americans enrolled in medical programs nationwide and abroad. In fact, the 2019 American Association of Medical Colleges (AAMC) reports an increase of 1,417 over five academic years. Since only four HBCUs offer complete medical programs, more and more African American students enroll in PWIs.[25] However, while PWIs may preach diversity today, they often do not have the procedures to implement them successfully, and systemic racism continues to perpetuate racial inequality. The AAMC reports for the 2019–2020 school year, African Americans are still accepted at lower rates than whites (38 percent and 45 percent), respectively, and still enrolled at lower rates than White (37 percent and 43 percent). Implicit and explicit bias and racism still play, and consequently, African American students attending PWIs report lower satisfaction and a less sense of belonging.[26] HBCU medical programs continue to provide opportunities unmatched by PWIs, such as a more welcoming campus climate that promotes students' feelings of self-efficacy, health, sense of belonging, academic performance, and motivation.[27] HBCUs offer students of all races opportunities to engage with African American students and faculty and the surrounding community in ways that are not available at PWIs in and out of the classroom. Despite the legal access to PWIs, HBCU medical programs are still an attractive and viable option for many students 150 years later.

CURRENT ROLES OF HBCUs

Student Population

In 1991 a report, *The State of Blacks in Higher Education*, showed progress and hope, but nearly twenty years later, a study finds racial disparities remain.[28] Waymer and Street (2016) explain that African Americans' lower acceptance and graduation rates at PWIs may not be due to ability or potential. Instead, factors like systemic racism have a profound effect on African Americans' ability to be admitted to medical schools.[29] For example, 50 percent of African American families report yearly incomes of $32,000, while only 16% of White families report the same income. Systemic racism and its effects continue to create an environment that places African American students at a disadvantage at every step of the process, beginning with the MCAT, the medical school entrance exam.[30] The higher scores of White, middle-class students may be attributed tomore access to technology, the ability to pay for test tutoring, and other institutional factors that benefit Whites in the United States.[31]

Even if African Americans can overcome roadblocks such as the MCAT, de facto segregation, the prejudicial attitudes of their white counterparts, and the prevalence of race-related incidents highlight the structural racism still ingrained in the United States and, by default, PWI medical programs.[32] Thus, HBCU medical programs have continued to survive despite the roadblocks the schools face themselves. HBCU medical programs still provide African Americans a safe, positive, and nurturing environment in a world that remains discriminatory in every aspect. HBCUs' greatest strengths remain their ability to implement their institutionalized student support systems and empower African American faculty, staff, and students to have a career in medicine despite the discrimination still prevalent in the field, something PWIs have yet to match.[33] Howard University and Meharry Medical College lead initiatives to increase the number of African American physicians and medical professionals and private HBCUs, like the Xavier University of Louisiana, now produce a significant number of high-quality medical students.[34] HBCU administrators, faculty, and colleagues remain committed to the school's original mission. Creating schools that mimic HBCUs' missions has been suggested to increase the number of African American medical professionals.[35] The value of these medical programs is immense and understood. The medical programs still maintain effective policies and practices that cater to students with less academic preparation and provide resources such as remediation programs and culturally relevant pedagogical approaches to foster students' academic success.[36]

Reducing Discrimination and Health Disparities

As previously mentioned, African Americans constitute 13 percent of the U.S. population, yet only 5 percent of doctors. The lack of representation contributes to the disconnect between those in the medical field and the African American community and perpetuates their long-standing history of mistrust in the health care system.[37] Despite the suspicion, Black communities value African American medical professionals. African American medical professionals' life experiences give them unique perspectives. Their involvement in researching medical conditions that disproportionately affect communities of color can help develop treatments more beneficial for African Americans and build the trust and patient-doctor relationships required for quality care.[38]

For example, quality preventative care could reduce the effects of diseases, injury, disability, and death disproportionately affecting African American women (CDC 2005). Yet, the lack of trust prevents them from doing so, and if they do seek medical attention, they are more likely to be over- or underdiagnosed.[39] The higher rates of COVID-19-related deaths in the African American community in 2020–2021 reinforce the fact that healthcare disparities still exist.[40] Eliminating systemic racism, stereotypes, and prejudices is not a realistic option to provide better healthcare for minorities; however, improving patient-doctor relationships is. By demonstrating and educating cultural competency and cultural sensitivity for African American people within the healthcare system, African American medical professionals' presence in hospitals and clinics can promote equity in their fields.[41] Filut and Carnes (2020) sum up the argument perfectly, "the COVID-19 pandemic must make academic health centers and health care systems recognize Black physicians as the precious resource they are and protect and reward them accordingly."

The benefits of more African American doctors go beyond physical care but also mental health. In 2019 "16% of African Americans reported having a mental illness in the past year."[42] African Americans are often underdiagnosed even though they are more likely to suffer from depression and are prescribed medication and therapy at lower rates than non-African Americans.[43] Instead, they are often diagnosed as schizophrenic even when they have the same symptoms as White patients. Once again, trust plays a role, and African American patients are more willing to express their emotions, thoughts, and feelings to someone they believe has lived similar life experiences and share a culture.[44] As the discussion about mental health continues, African American doctors fill a position that other racial/ethnic groups cannot. Their presence is significant since people of color will be the majority in the United States by 2055.[45]

Even though systemic racism is prevalent, it does not have to result in poor health outcomes for African Americans. The lack of patient-doctor relationships, trust, and unequal treatment often stem from implicit or unconscious bias.[46] By understanding and acknowledging their bias, non-African American doctors can provide "more enlightened leadership, better patient care, more relevant research, and a lower rate of situations that can lead to medical malpractice lawsuits."[47] Training and education are common ways to reduce bias. Working in more diverse settings and meeting people who counter the stereotype associated with their race, ethnicity, or gender groups also help mitigate bias.[48] Attending an HBCU medical school is the perfect environment to reduce bias, and today non-African American students have chosen to do so.

Thus, all HBCU medical program graduates are positioned to have a direct impact on shaping the health status of patients, not only in communities of color within the country but also globally, due to a growing aging population, unfavorable work environments, increasing complexity of health care delivery, and international workforce migration.[49]

Challenges for HBCU Medical Programs

HBCU medical programs face several challenges that threaten their survival in a globalizing world, and popular discourse often questions the quality of education their programs provide.[50] Throughout the literature, declining enrollment, and increasing attrition rates, and lack of funding and support all tie into the question of their relevance.[51]

LOW ENROLLMENT AND HIGH ATTRITION RATES

Lower enrollment and graduation rates at HBCUs and their medical programs, especially among African American males on campus, are cited as a constant struggle, with much room for growth.[52] Those who advocate for their closure claim these rates are due to HBCUs and ineffective medical programs.[53] HBCUs contribute to the mobility of African American medical students through partnerships with various medical organizations and high-impact retention strategies that are culturally relevant and community-based.[54] When HBCU and PWI medical programs create partnerships, PWIs may include HBCUs in grant proposals for projects just to meet grant requirements.[55] Those PWIs benefit greatly from pipeline programs that diversify their programs, yet they tend to give little back to the HBCUs supplying their medical students.[56] As they work to increase their programs' diversity, PWIs entice more and more African American students with promises of scholarships explicitly created for minorities. With their financial resources and pipeline and mentorship programs, PWIs appeal to African American students seeking to increase their medical school readiness.

THE QUESTION OF RELEVANCE

Since their inception, HBCUs' relevance has long been questioned by pundits and detractors, despite their value within the African American community and their place in producing African American medical professionals.[57] They describe them as "second-hand universities that are poorly managed, outdated and are a drain on the economy."[58] Although African Americans have experienced a litany of wrongs thrust upon them under the legal regime of apartheid in the United States, beginning with their involuntary arrival through slavery, Black Codes, and Jim Crow, they now exist in what is considered a "post-racial society."[59] HBCUs and their medical programs continue to battle this myth, which states that racism is a thing of the past. America has transcended its racial divides. There is no need for separate higher education institutions for African Americans to exist since racism no longer exists.[60] This flawed ideology adds to their struggles to secure adequate public funding to provide different opportunities to their African American students.[61]

LACK OF FUNDING AND SUPPORT

Although HBCUs are the primary source of African Americans in academic medicine, their medical programs often face cutbacks in resources and support.[62] Overall support for HBCUs is at an all-time low. Many local, state, and federal governments often fail to see the need to continue supporting these institutions and try to find ways to close them, citing funding shortfalls.[63] Funding disparities, which arise from years of minimal support and the filing of lawsuits aimed at correcting historical inequities, make it increasingly difficult for them to compete with larger PWIs.[64]

Funding from alumni and the community is not enough. Federal and state funding is vital to correcting such disparities after decades of minimal allocations and lower endowments. They heavily depend upon federal resources to meet the distinctive needs of their African American students.[65] One particular initiative, The HBCU Center for Excellence in Behavioral Health (HBCU-CFE) within the Morehouse School of Medicine, offers mini-grants, webinars, and fellowships, among other services, for HBCUs exclusively. Also, the Substance and Mental Health Services Administration (SAMHSA), U.S. Department of Health and Human Services, provides funding to Morehouse to provide essential funding and guidance to HBCUs on various issues, including physical and mental health.

In response to Houston native George Floyd's death, philanthropies and corporations were eager to discuss social inequities and how they have been possibly complicit. They were also willing to support programs and institutions positively affecting African Americans financially. For many HBCUs, this watershed moment was an opportunity for philanthropy to undue the complicit behavior, noted Flexner report. Amid the coronavirus pandemic in 2020, Michael R. Bloomberg donated $100 million to benefit students studying to become doctors at four HBCUs. Bloomberg created the initiative in response to the harmful "stop and frisk" policy he made while mayor that disproportionately impacted Blacks and Latino New Yorkers.[66]

THE FUTURE

Will there be HBCU medical programs in 2050? That is difficult to predict, but the past and present suggest that as long as systemic racism is in place, there will always be a need for them. In 2020 the number of first-year African American students attending medical school increased by 10.5 percent, with most of this growth still occurring at HBCU medical schools.[67] However, Campbell et al. (2020) suggest that if five of the African American medical schools closed because the 1910 Flexner Report had remained open, there would have been a 29 percent increase in the number of African Americans graduating in 2019 alone.[68] A single report still shapes the destiny of many African Americans. The calls to adequately fund and protect HBCU medical schools are very much warranted.[69]

Regardless of their best efforts, racial bias, discriminatory behavior, and the unwillingness to create more inclusive environments continue to plague PWIs. White Coats 4 Black Lives is an organization established in 2014 in response to Eric Gardner and Michael Brown's deaths and the lack of punishment for the officers who murdered them. Its mission is "to dismantle racism in medicine and promote the health, well-being, and self-determination of people of color."[70] The group allows students to rate their schools on fourteen indicators such as representation, discrimination reporting, and marginalized patient protection and creates a yearly Racial Justice Report Card. In 2019 Harvard earned a C+. While the school has an office and resources dedicated to minority students, students are given more freedom and have less supervision when working in the free clinics, which are the clinics that tend to have more minority patients.[71] John Hopkins, the model school from the Flexner Report, also earned a C+. Only twenty-five of the 1,118 students in the 2018 class and 8 percent of faculty were from underrepresented minority groups.[72]

Even with the policies in place today to reduce racial discrimination in higher education, disparities exist. Much like Howard University in 1868, HBCU medical schools continue to provide African Americans education and teaching and administrative careers that are still not readily available to people of color at PWIs in 2021.[73] As African American enrollment in medical schools increases, one can only wonder if PWI medical programs will restructure their programs to embrace diversity in their faculty, students, and content. However, these statistics paint a gloomy picture and suggest the need for HBCU medical schools.

It is possible that the future of HBCUs may also not be in the form of what is traditionally and legally considered an HBCU. The increasing diversity of HBCU medical students and faculty may be to its benefit rather than a detriment. Their missions and culture have so many benefits and have yet to be re-created. HBCUs produce competent doctors that have a better sense of how to treat and care for African American patients. They also produce graduates who have spent years working alongside people of color forcing them to acknowledge their biases and providing them opportunities to form strategies to overcome them. These students will have an advantage over those who attended schools with more homogenous populations and have little experience working with people of color. When PWIs do decide to embrace diversity, they will need to house the systems, beliefs, and values that make HBCUs so special if they want to be successful. So even if HBCU medical programs are not physically present in 2050, their spirit will continue to live on.

NOTES

1. Jelani M. Favors, *Shelter in a Time of Storm: How Black Colleges Fostered Generations of Leadership and Activism* (University of North Carolina Press, 2019).

2. "The First of Its Kind," Cheyney University of Pennsylvania, accessed March 15, 2021, https://cheyney.edu/who-we-are/the first%20hbcu/#:~:text=On%20 February%2025% 2C%201837%2C%20Cheyney,College% 20and%20%20%20 University%20(HBCU).

3. Richard Vedder, "Is 'Diversity' Destroying The HBCUs?" *Forbes,* November 4, 2019.

4. "History of HBCUs," Thurgood Marshall Fund, last modified 2019, https://www .tmcf.org/history-of- hbcus/.

5. Amanda Washington Lockett, Marybeth Gasman, and Thai-Huy Nguyen, "Senior Level Administrators and HBCUs: The Role of Support for Black Women's Success in STEM," *Education Sciences* 8, no. 48 (2018): 1–12, https//doi.org//10 .3390/educsci8020048.

6. Mathieo Rees, "Racism in Healthcare: What You Need to Know," *Medical News Today,* September 16, 2020, https://www.medicalnewstoday.com/articles/ racism -in-healthcare.

7. "COVID-19 Racial and Ethnic Health Disparities," CDC, last modified December 10, 2020, https://www.cdc.gov/coronavirus/2019-ncov/community/health-equity /racial-ethnic-disparities/disparities-deaths.html. See also Saundra Young, "Black Vaccine Hesitancy Rooted in Mistrust, Doubts," WebMD, last modified February 21, 2020, https://www.webmd.com/vaccines/covid-19-vaccine /news/ 20210202/ black-vaccine-hesitancy-rooted-in-mistrust-doubts.

8. Jamila Taylor, "Racism, Inequality, and Health Care for African Americans," The Century Foundation, last modified December 19, 2020, https://tcf.org/content/report/racism-inequalit y-health-care-african-americans/?agreed=1.

9. Douglas Belkin, "Why We Need More Black Doctors - and How to Get There," *Wall Street Journal*, September 8, 2020, https://www.wsj.com/articles /why-we-need-more-black-doctorsand-how-to-get-there-11599597158.

10. Kendall Campbell, Irma Corral, and Jhojana Infante Linares, "Projected Estimates of African American Medical Graduates of Closed Historically Black Medical Schools," *JAMA Network Open* 3, no.8 (2020), https//doi.org//10.1001/jamanetworkopen.2020.15220.

11. Campbell, Corral, and Linares, "Projected Estimates." See also Curtis Bunn, "Enrollment Declines Threaten Future of HBCUs, Disheartening Alumni," NBC News, March 23, 2020, https://www.nbcnews.com/news/nbcblk/enrollment -declines- threaten-future-hbcus-disheartening-alumni-n1158191.

12. Katherine Hill, Elizabeth A Samuels, and Cary P Gross, "Assessment of the Prevalence of Medical Student Mistreatment by Sex, Race/Ethnicity, and Sexual Orientation," *JAMA Intern Med* 180, no. 5 (2020): 653–65, https//doi.org//10.1001/jamainternmed.2020.0030.

13. Valerie Montgomery, "Diversity in Medical Schools: A Much-Needed New Beginning," Morehouse School of Medicine: JAMA Network, accessed April 12, 2021, https://www.msm.edu/RSSFeedArticles/2021/January /jamainterview.php.

14. Hill, Samuels, and Gross, "Assessment," 653–665. See also Damion Waymer and Joshua Street, "Second-Class, Cash Strapped, Antiquated Institutions: Unbalanced Media Depictions of Historically Black Colleges and Universities in the Chronicle of Higher Education," *Journal for Multicultural Education* 10, no. 4 (2016), 489–506, http//doi.org// 10.1108/JME-02–2015–0004.

15. James McKeen Cattel, "Families of American Men of Science," *Science* (1913): 504–15.

16. Ibid.

17. Earl H. Harley, "The Forgotten History of Defunct Black Medical Schools in the 19th Century and the Impact of the Flexner Report," *Journal of the National Medical Association* 98, no. 9 (2006).

18. Harley, "The Forgotten History."

19. Ibid."

20. Malcolm Ritter, "Feds, Family Reach Deal on Use of DNA Information," *Seattle Times*, August 7, 2013.

21. Edwin Black, *War Against the Weak: Eugenics and America's Campaign to Create a Master Race* (New York: Four Walls Eight Windows, 2003).

22. Fannie Lou Hamer, *To Praise My Bridges: An Autobiography* (Jackson, Mississippi: Greenwood Publishing Group, 1967).

23. Adolfo Gabriel Cuevas, "Exploring Four Barriers Experienced by African Americans in Healthcare: Perceived Discrimination, Medical Mistrust, Race Discordance, and Poor Communication" (PhD diss., Portland University, 2013), https://doi.org/10.15760/etd.615. See also Lisa Meredith et al., "Are Better Ratings of the Patient-Provider Relationship Associated with Higher Quality Care for Depression?,"

National Library of Medicine 34, no.4 (2001): 349–360,https://pubmed.ncbi.nlm. nih. gov/11329522/.

24. "Diversity in Medicine: Facts and Figures 2019," Association of American Medical Colleges, last modified 2019, https://www.aamc.org/data-reports/workforce/ interactive-data/figure-18-percentage-all-active-physicians-race/ethnicity-2018.

25. Harley, "The Forgotten History."

26. Waymer and Street, "Second-Class," 489–506. See also Xumei Fan, Kathryn Luchok, and John Dozier, "College Students' Satisfaction and sense of Belonging: Differences between Underrepresented Groups and the Majority Group," *S.N. Social Sciences* 1, no. 1 (2020): 22, https//doi.org// 10.1007/s43545-020–00026–0.

27. Fan, Luchok, and Dozier, "College Students."

28. Kristen E. Broady, Curtis, L. Todd, and Darlene Booth-Bell, "Dreaming and Doing at Georgia HBCUs: Continued Relevancy in 'Post-Racial' America," *The Review of Black Political Economy* 44, no. 1–2 (2017): 37–54, https//doi .og// 10.1007/s12114-017–9243–3.

29. Waymer and Street, "Second-Class," 489–506.

30. Catherine Reinis Lucey and Aaron Saguil, "The Consequences of Structural Racism on MCAT Scores and Medical School Admissions: The Past Is Prologue," *Academic Medicine: Journal of the Association of American Medical Colleges* 95, no. 3 (2020): 351–356, https//doi.org//10.1097/ACM.0000000000002939.

31. Waymer and Street, "Second-Class," 489–506. See also Lucey and Saguil, "The Consequences," 351–356.

32. Waymer and Street, "Second-Class," 489–506.

33. Lockett, "Senior Level."

34. Emily Mader et al., "Status of Underrepresented Minority and Female Faculty at Medical Schools Located Within Historically BlackColleges and in Puerto Rico," *Medical Education Online* 21, no. 1 (2016): 1–7, https//doi.org//10.3402/meo.v21 .29535. See also Broady, Todd, and Booth-Bell, "Dreaming," 37–54.

35. Brendan Murphy, "How to Get Up to 3,000 More Black People in Physician Pipeline," American Medical Association, last modified January 29, 2021, https://www.ama-assn.org /education/ medical-school-diversity/ how-get-3000- more-black-people-physician-pipeline.

36. Lockett, "Senior Level." See also Ivory A. Toldson, "Why Historically Black Colleges and Universities are Successful with Graduating Black Baccalaureate Students Who Subsequently Earn Doctorates in STEM (Editor's Commentary)," *The Journal of Negro Education* 87, no. 2 (2018): 95–98, https//.do.org//10.7709/ jnegroeducation.87.2.0095.

37. Theresa Williamson, "The Goals of Carels There a (Black) Doctor in the House?," *New England Journal of Medicine* 383, no. 6 (2020): e43(1)-e43(2), https// doi.org// 10.1056/NEJMpv2024338.

38. Cuevas, "Exploring Four." See also Meredith et al., "Are Better Ratings," 349–60.

39. Rees, "Racism in Healthcare."

40. CDC, "COVID-19."

41. Maya Corneille, Anna Lee, Sherrice Allen, Jessica Cannady, and Alexia Guess, "Barriers to the Advancement of Women of Color Faculty in STEM: The Need for Promoting Equity Using an Intersectional Framework," *Equality, Diversity and Inclusion: An International Journal* 38, no. 3 (2019): 328–348, https//doi.org//10.1108/EDI-09-2017-0199.

42. "Black and African American Communities and Mental Health," Mental Health America, last modified 2021, https://www.mhanational.org/issues/black-and-african-american-communities-and-mental-health.

43. "Mental Health Disparities: African Americans," American Psychiatric Association, last modified 2017. https://www.psychiatry.org/File percent20Library/Psychiatrists/Cultural-Competency/Mental-Health-Disparities/Mental-Health-Facts-for-African-Americans.pdf. See also Rees, "Racism in Healthcare."

44. "Demographic Characteristics of APA Members by Membership Characteristics," American Psychological Association, last modified 2017 https://www.apa.org/workforce/publications/17-member-profiles/table-1.pdf.

45. Gasman et al., "Contributions of Historically Black Colleges and Universities to the Production of Black Nurses," *Journal of Nursing Education* 59, no. 2 (2019): 76–82, https//doi.org// 10.3928/01484834–20200122–04.

46. Darcy Lewis and Emily Paulsen, "Proceedings of the Diversity and Inclusion Innovation Forum: Unconscious Bias in Academic Medicine How the Prejudices We Don't Know We Have Affect Medical Education, Medical Careers, and Patient Health," Association of American Medical Colleges and The Kirwan Institute for the Study of Race and Ethnicity, 2017.

47. Lewis and Paulsen, "Proceedings," 71.

48. Lewis and Paulsen, "Proceedings," 72.

49. Costellia Talley, Henry Talley, and Janice Collins-McNeil, "The Continuing Quest for Parity: HBCU Nursing Students' Perspectives on Nursing and Nursing Education," *Journal of Best Practices in Health Professions Diversity* 9, no. 2 (2016): 1247–1262, https//doi.org// 10.1016/j.nedt.2016.04.006.

50. Ramon B Goings, "Investigating the Experiences of Two High-Achieving Black Male HBCU Graduates: An Exploratory Study," *The Negro Educational Review* 67, no. 1–4 (2016): 54–75.

51. Waymer and Street, "Second-Class," 489–506. See also Broady, Todd, and Booth-Bell, "Dreaming," 37–54 and Toldson, "Why Historically," 95–98.

52. Michael Anderson, Antwon D. Woods, and Ronald Walker, "The Linkage of Ethics and Leadership to the Decision Making Process of HBCU College Presidents," *Academy of Educational Leadership Journal* 23, no. 1 (2019): 1–11. See also Goings, "Investigating," 54–75 and Toldson, "Why Historically," 95–98.

53. Broady, Todd, and Booth-Bell, "Dreaming," 37–54.

54. Gasman et al., "Contributions," 76–82.

55. Ibid.

56. Ibid.

57. Broady, Todd, and Booth-Bell, "Dreaming," 37–54. See also Shari E. Watkins, and Felicia Moore Mensah, "Peer Support and STEM Success for One African

American Female Engineer," *Journal of Negro Education* 88, no. 2 (2019): 181–93, doi: 10.7709/jnegroeducation.88.2.0181.

58. Waymer and Street, "Second-Class," 489–506.

59. Broady, Todd, and Booth-Bell, "Dreaming," 37–54.

60. Waymer and Street, "Second-Class," 489–506.

61. Ibid.

62. Toldson, "Why Historically," 95–98.

63. Anderson, Woods and Walker, "The Linkage," 1–11.

64. Larry J. Walker, "We Are Family: How Othermothering and Support Systems Can Improve Mental Health Outcomes among African American Males at HBCUs," *Spectrum: A Journal on Black Men* 7, no. 1 (2018): 1–16, https//doi.or//10.2979/spectrum.7.1.01.

65. Broady, Todd, and Booth-Bell, "Dreaming," 37–54.

66. Michael J. de la Merced and Andrew Ross Sorkin, "Michael Bloomberg to Give $100 Million to Historically Black Medical Schools," *New York Times,* September 3, 2020.

67. "Total U.S. Medical School Enrollment by Race/Ethnicity (Alone) and Sex, 2016–2017 through 2020–2021," American Association of Medical Colleges, last modified November 3, 2020. https://www.aamc.org/media/ 6116/download, November 3.

68. Campbell, Corral, and Linares, "Projected Estimates."

69. Broady, Todd, and Booth-Bell, "Dreaming," 37–54.

70. White Coats 4 Black Lives, "Mission"

71. "Racial Justice Report Card," White Coats 4 Black Lives, last modified 2019, https://docs.google.com/ document/d/1 AViDRDASmb_0Qq64bNVVSqrlYOzL9q gCy_UzBZs30D8/edit.

72. White Coats 4 Black Lives, "Racial Justice Report Card."

73. Jose E Rodriguez et al., "The Role of Historically Black College and University Medical Schools in Academic Medicine," *Journal of Health Care for the Poor and Underserved* 28, no. 1 (2017): 266–278, https//doi.org/10.1353/hpu. 2017.0022.

REFERENCES

American Psychiatric Association. "Mental Health Disparities: African Americans." Last modified 2017. https://www.psychiatry.org/Filepercent20Library /Psychiatrists/ Cultural-Competency/Mental-Health-Disparities/Mental-Health-Facts-for-African-Americans.pdf

American Psychological Association. "Demographic Characteristics of APA Members by Membership Characteristics." Last modified 2017. https://www.apa.org/work-force/publications/17-member-profiles/table-1.pdf.

Anderson, Michael, Antwon D. Woods, and Ronald Walker. "The Linkage of Ethics and Leadership to the Decision Making Process of HBCU College Presidents." *Academy of Educational Leadership Journal* 23, no. 1 (2019): 1–11.

Association of American Medical Colleges. "Diversity in Medicine: Facts and Figures 2019." Last modified 2019. https://www.aamc.org/data-reports/workforce /interactive-data/figure-18-percentage-all-active-physicians-race/ethnicity-2018.

Association of American Medical Colleges. "Total U.S. Medical School Enrollment by Race/Ethnicity (Alone) and Sex, 2016–2017 through 2020–2021." Last modified November 3, 2020. https://www.aamc.org/media/6116/download, November 3.

Belkin, Douglas. "Why We Need More Black Doctors - and How to Get There." *Wall Street Journal*, September 8, 2020. https://www.wsj.com/articles/ why-we-need-more -black-doctorsand-how-to-get-there-11599597158.

Black, Edwin. *War Against the Weak: Eugenics and America's Campaign to Create a Master Race.* New York: Four Walls Eight Windows, 2003.

Broady, Kristen E., Curtis, L. Todd, and Darlene Booth-Bell. "Dreaming and Doing at Georgia HBCUs: Continued Relevancy in 'Post-Racial' America." *The Review of Black Political Economy* 44, no. 1–2 (2017): 37–54. https://doi.og// 10.1007/s12114-017-9243-3.

Bunn, Curtis. "Enrollment Declines Threaten Future of HBCUs, Disheartening Alumni." NBC News. March 23, 2020. https://www.nbcnews.com/news/nbcblk/ enrollment-declines- threaten-future-hbcus-disheartening-alumni-n1158191.

Campbell, Kendall, Irma Corral, and Jhojana Infante Linares. "Projected Estimates of African American Medical Graduates of Closed Historically Black Medical Schools." *JAMA Network Open* 3, no.8 (2020). https://doi.org//10.1001 /jamanet-workopen. 2020.15220.

Cattel, James McKeen. "Families of American Men of Science." *Science* (1913): 504–15.

CDC. "COVID-19 Racial and Ethnic Health Disparities." Last modified December 10, 2020. https://www.cdc.gov/coronavirus/2019-ncov/community/health-equity/ racial-ethnic-disparities/disparities-deaths.html.

Corneille, Maya, Anna Lee, Sherrice Allen, Jessica Cannady, and Alexia Guess. "Barriers to the Advancement of Women of Color Faculty in STEM: The Need for Promoting Equity Using an Intersectional Framework." *Equality, Diversity and Inclusion: An International Journal* 38, no. 3 (2019): 328–48. https://doi.org//10 .1108/EDI-09-2017-0199.

Cuevas, Adolfo Gabriel. "Exploring Four Barriers Experienced by African Americans in Healthcare: Perceived Discrimination, Medical Mistrust, Race Discordance, and Poor Communication." PhD diss., Portland University, 2013. https://doi.org/10 .15760/etd.615

de la Merced, Michael J., and Andrew Ross Sorkin. "Michael Bloomberg to Give $100 Million to Historically Black Medical Schools." *New York Times,* September 3, 2020.

Fan, Xumei, Kathryn Luchok, and John Dozier. "College Students' Satisfaction and Sense of Belonging: Differences between Underrepresented Groups and the Majority Group." *S.N. Social Sciences* 1, no. 1 (2020): 22. https://doi.org// 10.1007/s43545-020–00026-0.

Favors, Jelani M. *Shelter in a Time of Storm: How Black Colleges Fostered Generations of Leadership and Activism.* University of North Carolina Press, 2019.

Filut, Amarette, and Molly Carnes. "Will Losing Black Physicians Be a Consequence of the COVID-19 Pandemic?." *Academic Medicine: Journal of the Association of American Medical Colleges* 95, no. 12 (December 2020): 1796–98. https//doi.org// 10.1097/ACM.0000000000003651.

"The First of Its Kind." Cheyney University of Pennsylvania. Accessed March 15, 2021. https://cheyney.edu/who-we-are/the-first%20hbcu/#:~:text=On %20February%2 025%2C%201837%2C%20Cheyney,College%20and%20%20 %20University%20(HBCU).

Gasman, Marybeth, Alejandra Regla-Vargas, Carol Sandoval, Andres Castro Samayoa, and Thai-Huy Nguyen. "Contributions of Historically Black Colleges and Universities to the Production of Black Nurses." *Journal of Nursing Education* 59, no. 2 (2019): 76–82. https//doi.org// 10.3928/01484834–20200122–04.

Hamer, Fannie Lou. *To Praise My Bridges: An Autobiography.* Jackson, Mississippi: Greenwood Publishing Group, 1967.

Harley, Earl H. "The Forgotten History of Defunct Black Medical Schools in the 19th Century and the Impact of the Flexner Report." *Journal of the National Medical Association* 98, no. 9 (2006).

Hill, Katherine, Elizabeth A Samuels, and Cary P Gross. "Assessment of the Prevalence of Medical Student Mistreatment by Sex, Race/Ethnicity, and Sexual Orientation." *JAMA Intern Med* 180, no. 5 (2020): 653–65. https://doi.org//10.1001 /jamainternmed.2020.0030.

Lewis, Darcy and Emily Paulsen. "Proceedings of the Diversity and Inclusion Innovation Forum: Unconscious Bias in Academic Medicine How the Prejudices We Don't Know We Have Affect Medical Education, Medical Careers, and Patient Health." Association of American Medical Colleges and The Kirwan Institute for the Study of Race and Ethnicity, 2017.

Lockett, Amanda Washington, Marybeth Gasman, and Thai-Huy Nguyen. "Senior Level Administrators and HBCUs: The Role of Support for Black Women's Success in STEM." *Education Sciences* 8, no. 48 (2018): 1–12. https://doi.org//10 .3390/educsci8020048.

Lucey, Catherine Reinis, and Aaron Saguil. "The Consequences of Structural Racism on MCAT Scores and Medical School Admissions: The Past Is Prologue." *Academic Medicine: Journal of the Association of American Medical Colleges* 95, no. 3 (2020): 351–356. https://doi.org//10.1097/ACM.0000000000002939.

Mader, Emily M., Jose E. Rodriguez, Kendall M. Campbell, Timothy Smilnak, Andrew W. Bazemore, Stephen Petterson, and Christopher P. Morley. "Status of Underrepresented Minority and Female Faculty at Medical Schools Located Within Historically Black Colleges and in Puerto Rico." *Medical Education Online* 21, no. 1 (2016): 1–7. https://doi.org//10.3402/meo.v21.29535.

Mental Health America. "Black and African American Communities and Mental Health." Last modified 2021. https://www.mhanational.org/issues/black-and -african-american-communities-and-mental-health.

Meredith, Lisa S., Maria Orlando, Nicole Humphrey, Patti Camp, and Cathy D. Sherbourne. "Are Better Ratings of the Patient-Provider Relationship Associated with Higher Quality Care for Depression?." *National Library of Medicine* 34, no.4 (2001): 349–60. https://pubmed.ncbi.nlm.nih.gov/11329522/.

"Mission." White Coats 4 Black Lives. Last modified 2021. https://whitecoats4black-lives.org/.

Montgomery, Valerie. "Diversity in Medical Schools A Much-Needed New Beginning." Morehouse School of Medicine: JAMA Network. Accessed April 12, 2021. Https://www.msm.edu/RSSFeedArticles/2021/January/jamainterview.php.

Murphy, Brendan. "How to Get Up to 3,000 More Black People in Physician Pipeline." American Medical Association. Last modified January 29, 2021. https://www.ama-assn.org /education/ medical-school-diversity/how-get-3000- more-black-people-physician-pipeline.

Rees, Mathieu. "Racism in Healthcare: What You Need to Know." *Medical News Today,* September 16, 2020, https://www.medicalnewstoday.com/articles/racism -in-healthcare.

Ritter, Malcolm. "Feds, Family Reach Deal on Use of DNA Information." *Seattle Times*. August 7, 2013.

Rodriguez, Jose E., Ivette A. Lopez, Kendall M. Campbell, and Matthew Dutton. "The Role of Historically Black College and University Medical Schools in Academic Medicine." *Journal of Health Care for the Poor and Underserved* 28, no. 1 (2017): 266–278. https://doi.org/10.1353/hpu. 2017.0022.

Talley, Costellia, Henry Talley, and Janice Collins-McNeil. "The Continuing Quest for Parity: HBCU Nursing Students' Perspectives on Nursing and Nursing Education." *Journal of Best Practices in Health Professions Diversity* 9, no. 2 (2016): 1247–1262. https://doi.org// 10.1016/j.nedt.2016.04.006.

Taylor, Jamila. "Racism, Inequality, and Health Care for African Americans." The Century Foundation. Last modified December 19, 2020. https://tcf.org/content/ report/racism-inequalit y-health-care-african-americans/?agreed=1.

Thurgood Marshall College Fund. "History of HBCUs." Last modified 2019. https:// www.tmcf.org/history-of- hbcus/.

Toldson, Ivory A. "Why Historically Black Colleges and Universities are Successful with Graduating Black Baccalaureate Students Who Subsequently Earn Doctorates in STEM (Editor's Commentary)." *Journal of Negro Education* 87, no. 2 (2018): 95–98. https://doi.org// 10.7709/jnegroeducation.87.2.0095.

Vedder, Richard. "Is 'Diversity' Destroying The HBCUs?." *FORBES,* November 4, 2019.

Young, Saundra. "Black Vaccine Hesitancy Rooted in Mistrust, Doubts." WebMD. Last modified February 21, 2020. https://www.webmd.com/vaccines/covid-19 -vaccine /news/ 20210202/black-vaccine-hesitancy-rooted-in-mistrust-doubts.

Walker, Larry J. "We Are Family: How Othermothering and Support Systems Can Improve Mental Health Outcomes among African American Males at HBCUs." *Spectrum: A Journal on Black Men* 7, no. 1 (2018): 1–16. https://doi.org//10.2979 /spectrum.7.1.01.

Watkins, Shari E., and Felicia Moore Mensah. "Peer Support and STEM Success for One African American Female Engineer." *Journal of Negro Education* 88, no. 2 (2019):181–193. https://doi.org//10.7709/jnegroeducation.88.2.0181

Waymer, Damion, and Joshua Street. "Second-Class, Cash Strapped, Antiquated Institutions: Unbalanced Media Depictions of Historically Black Colleges and Universities in the Chronicle of Higher Education." *Journal for Multicultural Education* 10, no. 4 (2016): 489–506. https://doi.org//10.1108/JME-02-2015-0004.

White Coats 4 Black Lives. "Racial Justice Report Card." Last modified 2019. https://docs.google.com/document/d/1AViDRDASmb_0Qq64bNVVSqrlYOzL9qgCy_UzBZs30D8/edit.

Williamson, Theresa. "The Goals of Care - Is There a (Black) Doctor in the House?" *New England Journal of Medicine* 383, no. 6 (2020): e43(1)-e43(2). https://doi.org// 10.1056/NEJMpv2024338.

Chapter 10

Black College Renaissance

My Decision to Create the First HBCU History Course and 2020 Proposal for Interdisciplinary HBCU Studies Curricula, En-Masse

Cheryl E. Mango

A THEORETICAL INTRODUCTION TO HBCU STUDIES

In 2020, my efforts to promote a philosophical basis for a Black College Renaissance were strengthened by the humbling, yet nationally welcomed response to creating and offering the first curriculumized Historically Black College and University (HBCU) History course, known as "HIST 349" at Virginia State University. More importantly, I was further appreciative that my following statements were widely circulated on media platforms like *HBCU Digest* and *Journal of Blacks in Higher Education*: "HBCUs, though lauded for their contributions, are no exception when it comes to the need for serious academic study of their historical trajectories. . . . In light of the battle for scholarly confirmation, I believe that HBCU History and HBCU Studies classes are the next frontier for Black colleges."[1] Not only do I advocate for the establishment of courses that critically analyze HBCU realisms as centralized subjects like HIST 349 at VSU. The aforementioned quote also reflects the purpose of this writing—a proposition for interdisciplinary HBCU Studies curriculums as degree programs en masse, particularly at Black colleges. From my viewpoint, Black colleges are comparable to other marginalized groups requiring much-needed comprehensive scholarly treatment of their experience and contributions. Similar to my HBCU History course and proposed HBCU Studies curriculum—African History and African Studies, African-American History and African-American Studies, Black Church History and Black Church Studies, Black Women's History and Black Women's Studies, LGBTQ History and LGBTQ Studies, Latinx History and Latinx Studies—were all created by people like me, who understood the importance of their subject's production in the face of discriminatory barriers to academic and societal legitimation.[2] More vitally, these types of disciplines not only assist with data collection and research analysis. Ultimately, their conclusions help to shape educational and public policy, while providing systematic methods for institutionalizing and improving their subjects' development.[3] In all, serious academic study of subjugated groups and institutions like HBCUs help their agents define, secure, collectivize, and sensitize the general public to their ultimate needs and goals. HIST 349, the newly created Virginia State University HBCU History course, is just the beginning of what I hope will transform into similarly robust HBCU History and HBCU Studies curriculums at all American educational institutions. Simply put, Black colleges deserve inner-directed, scholarly treatment, reflective of their own experience.

In this chapter I endeavor to justify my position, beginning with section 1: "A Theoretical Introduction to HBCU Studies." In the first section, I provide a contextually grounded introduction supporting the development of HBCU Studies as an academic discipline. The following section, "The Scholarly Conversation and HBCU Studies Canonical Positioning," is dedicated to placing HBCU Studies within the scholarly conversation on Black college curriculums that extends back to the 1800s. Section 3 addresses the topic, "Blueprint and Directional Contemplations Concerning HBCU Studies," which evaluates the field's philosophical antecedents while modeling a potential HBCU Studies minor. Section 4, "Creating the Nation's First HBCU History Course, HIST 349 At Virginia State University," documents my decision to design and offer America's first class on HBCU history. Finally, the conclusion reiterates my call for HBCU Studies as the next Black college frontier. Be that as it may, the case for a Black College Renaissance, through the lens of a systematized, well-orchestrated, ground-up, HBCU Studies curriculum, is constructed upon the posterity, regeneration, and understanding of Black college history and production to intensify the institutions' acclaim within a growingly diverse and competitive educational landscape.

My decision to create the first HBCU history course, and proposal for a Black College Renaissance by way of an interdisciplinary HBCU Studies academic curriculum, represent a deliberately inward, self-concerning, and self-promoting shift toward an HBCU-Centered education system. Black college students spend millions of dollars and numerous credit hours learning about human and scientific contributions to the world.[4] It is equally important that an HBCU-Centric system exists that fortifies the same in-depth, methodical analysis of their own educational institutions. The same vacuum exists for HBCU leadership, faculty, and staff members; they also need strong HBCU Studies curriculums to anchor systematic research that explains and advantages Black college developments. HBCUs, though physically separated geographically and administratively, have shared experiences, values, mores, worldviews, cultures, theories, challenges, and triumphs. Yet, without formalized mechanisms to examine these HBCU realities from the ground up, Black colleges are forgoing critical indicators that assist with increasing, measuring, and leveraging the schools' net worth, individually and collectively. Currently, HBCUs are cheered on as if they are some type of marginal vanity or albatross project oftentimes by their supporters and the larger public.[5] Though seasoned scholars from W. E. B. Du Bois and Carter G. Woodson to Marybeth Gasman, Ivory Toldson, Bobby L. Lovett, and Jelani Favors have engaged in istudies of Black colleges, the top-down approach to understanding HBCU phenomena needs an inverse, data-retrieving revitalization. I fear the oversimplification of Black colleges' complexities will continue until the schools are systematically, institutionally, and calculatedly examined from a forensic, investigational level. Doing so will rightfully bring HBCUs to the center of the African-American, American, and educational point of observation. Thus my proposal for a Black College Renaissance, through the medium of HBCU Studies, explains why the democratization of Black college scholarship at the K-12, undergraduate, and graduate levels at HBCUs, Predominately White Institutions (PWIs), and fellow Minority Serving Institutions (MSIs) will provide the intellectual inquiry and societal shifts that HBCUs justly warrant.

HBCUs are both training facilities and sociocultural marvels in need of schematizing. Without HBCU Studies courses, curriculums, and degree programs, Black colleges will continue to operate within the hampered confines of an externally driven academic pursuit, when internally the schools have untapped, undefined, scholarly formulae that lead to trend-worthy professional actualizations. Different from the highly regarded, highly selective, well-funded, majority white, elite, Ivy League institutions, HBCUs epitomize what perseverance, triumph, and success looks like for average Americans, irrespective of race.[6] As such, Black colleges should exist as modes of critical study within education and society at large, beginning with HBCU Studies curriculums at Black colleges. Though I recognize the importance of Black college students immersing themselves in the prevailing academic disciplines and vocations of the era, it is imperative that HBCUs become a modality of investigation that reshapes humanity in a way that privileges Black colleges and their products first. HBCUs deserve the modeling and adoration because of their resourceful history and boundless potential exemplifying progress in an intensely competitive, high-functioning, yet imperfect nation like America. Black colleges serve as potent examples for living, working, and innovating in an arduous, multicultural, globalized society. For the historic racial, sociopolitical, and economic discrimination that Black colleges and their constituents have continually faced did not prevent the institutions from creating the Black middle and upper class, which helped to stabilize the shattered, post-Civil War America.[7] Consequently, Black colleges are expert engines of production with limited resources and socially disadvantaged patrons that mostly everyone can learn and benefit from, which is why HBCU Studies are paramount for the schools and the greater society. The institutions are also portable as investigational apparatuses, with an ability to provide transferable skills and a knowledge base useful for all career paths. In sum, Black colleges are a silhouette worth dissecting, emulating, and improving; thereby, positioning HBCU Studies as a viable academic discipline with cross-demographic, cross-educational, cross-university, cross-profession, and cross-employee appeal.

Although I am explaining what HBCU Studies can do for the country, the establishment of HBCU Studies is also about what the country can provide to HBCUs. With this axiom in mind, my theoretical framework for an HBCU Studies resurrection is purposed exclusively to "wholly" meet the needs of, (1) Black colleges first, (2) the African-American community second, (3) the African diaspora third, then finally, (4) the nation and all others. Arguably, Black colleges have already purposed the meet the needs of the aforementioned groups.[8] Conversely, the key theme is "wholly," meaning addressing their needs "thoroughly," "comprehensively," and "in every respect," to which I argue the schools have not.[9] Due to the constant strives to stay afloat amid pervasive financial inequities, a vulnerable student population, and meeting the demands of largely white accrediting bodies, financers, and policymakers, I believe HBCUs have historically operated on the defense and not from positions of power.[10] Examples of Black college attempts to battle their challenges include: securing their right to provide more than a vocational education during the great Booker T. Washington and W. E. B. Du Bois debates; fighting to hire African-American leaders and faculty, which extended to United Negro College Fund (UNCF) directors; defending their relevance and right to adequate federal resources in post-segregation America to President Jimmy Carter, which led to the 1980 creation of the White House Initiative of HBCUs.[11] More eminently, Black colleges carry the daunting task of educating the formerly enslaved and their offspring. The peculiarity of safeguarding the futures of the United States' formerly enslaved population makes HBCUs distinctive and preeminent. The task, however, has come at quite a high cost resulting from Black colleges enduring a variety of unjust, racially discriminatory consequences.[12] In the like manner, the racial angst witnessed in the year 2020 has led many institutions, companies, universities, and people to reevaluate their awareness and treatment of African-American particularisms comparable to those that HBCUs face.[13] The videoed killings of unarmed African Americans and the racially intensive presidency of Donald Trump have sparked a 1960s type of movement for change on behalf of Blacks.[14] Amid the confusion, HBCUs have rightly emerged as the African-American victors in the over-four-hundred-year battle for racial transformation. From my vantage point, the heightened HBCU celebrity is due to the institutions' statuses as one of the last major autonomously Black epicenters that have yet to dissipate under the auspices of integration and Senator Kamala Harris, an HBCU graduate who is the first African-American female vice president.[15]

Still, the current environment precipitates the question, as HBCU leaders, do we just bask in notoriety or act boldly and reshape society in our image? I know the question is daring; however, most cutting-edge endeavors are. In response, my position is that Black colleges have already proved their capacity to excel and serve as a moral conscience of this nation. The schools have records of production, political capital, and an enduring model. Actually, HBCUs are one of the few covenants with the African-American community that the United States has actually kept and gotten right. With the national recognition Black colleges are now receiving in the media, on major corporate donor lists, and on presidential platforms—now is time to collectively remake education and the nation in the likeness of HBCUs.

As a historian of the African-American experience, I am aware of the lack of stimulus Blacks have received to determine and define the standards for people and institutions. I believe that cultivation should be endemic, curricularized, and primed to drive both scholarly and community processes, hence the purposes of this writing. With the mentioned considerations in mind, HBCUs are not immune to the need for introspective change based on the racial realities of this nation. Fortunately, the institutions have paid their dues. HBCUs even have their own White House office. For these reasons, now is the time for transformative HBCU action en masse. Now is the time for an institutional change of the entire nation through a Black College Renaissance. Now is the time for systematic study and adherence to the HBCU standard. Now is the time to demarcate the societal custom beginning with the rollout of vibrant HBCU Studies courses, curriculums, and degree programs at all of our schools and, thereafter, all educational institutions. On these grounds, I urge Black college leadership to enthusiastically embrace and propel HBCU Studies because HBCU Studies equals HBCU power, coupled with a more advanced society.

THE SCHOLARLY CONVERSATION AND HBCU
STUDIES CANONICAL POSITIONING

Situating this manifestoesque proposition for a Black College Renaissance—
through a new, HBCU-Centered academic discipline—within the rich
scholarly conversation on the institutions is key to understanding the HBCU
Studies proposal's canonical positioning. Thus my HBCU Studies idea is a
part of a long discussion that asks what is the value and purpose of Black, and
more specifically HBCU education?[16] The aforesaid question has troubled
both white and Black leaders since Africans forced migration across the
Atlantic Ocean. Several scholars have addressed HBCU education over the
decades and their arguments display an evolutionary context for a contemporary infusion of targeted Black college treatments within various K-12 and
higher education curriculums. For example, in 1900, W. E. B. Du Bois, the
famed African American academician, examined the HBCU graduate in *The
College-Bred Negro American*. Though Du Bois was delighted to report that
throughout the schools' fifty-year record, "the Negro college . . . has been carried forward . . . with remarkable results," he defended Black colleges from
accusations of curriculum inadequacy.[17] Similar to my argument for HBCUs
serving as a research laboratory to drive innovation in curriculum development and academic discipline offerings, Du Bois supported Black colleges
that provide remedial and high school courses for their education majors to
train in-house.[18] From Du Bois's point of view, HBCUs offered critical education and other services to the Black community, which the government and
other institutions did not meet. His comprehensive study of Black colleges
demonstrated that he believed HBCUs were capable of leading and defining
educational issues for transformational purposes.

   The 1926 creation of what is now known as Black History Month and
scholarship on Black education or "miseducation" by Carter G. Woodson,
also drove the conversations regarding the academic purposes and curriculum
offerings at HBCUs.[19] In Woodson's seminal 1933 work, *The Miseducation
of the Negro*, he expressed his discontent with the course offerings in what
he argued were educationally deficient Negro Colleges. He begins his book
by lamenting, "The 'educated Negroes' have the attitude of contempt toward
their own people because in their own as well as in their mixed schools
Negroes are taught to admire the Hebrew, the Greek, the Latin and the
Teuton and to despise the African."[20] Woodson statements correctly criticized the reality of the time. Due to pervasive and undeserved Eurocentric
hegemony, serious studies on the African and African-American experience
were omitted, even at Black colleges. Du Bois, Woodson, and other scholars
of their era battled for Black legitimacy within HBCU and other academic

arenas. Among them was Kelly Miller, who in 1933 expressed concern in "The Past, Present, and Future of the Negro College," that "the Negro college plays the role of the mimic, whose chief concern is to imitate the white model and prototype . . . the Negro college is not an exact duplicate of the corresponding white institution of learning, and any attempt to do so results in absurd and ridiculous misfit."[21] Miller's position was in line with Carter G. Woodson's calls for a more Afrocentric and HBCU-Centric educational ethos at HBCUs. However, this study's call for HBCU Studies curriculums rooted in Black colleges is situated within Kelly Miller's 1933 ultimate conclusion, that Black colleges desperately need to deviate from following the paths laid by PWIs and instead like "Catholic [Colleges] . . . Women's [Colleges] . . . and Hebrew [Colleges] . . . wisely and justly adapt matter and method to the peculiar needs of its field " and own Black people.[22] My HBCU Studies goal is to realize Miller's 1933 idea of Black colleges establishing HBCU-specific curriculums. As Thomas L. Dabney affirms in his 1934 article, "The Study of the Negro," "Considerable confusion has existed in some Negro colleges and universities with respect to the relative value of courses on the Negro . . . some teachers have expressed approval of such course and some disapproval."[23] While today it seems obvious that HBCUs would offer courses on African and African American history, Dabney's statements reflect the long and hard fight for Black agency in Black college curriculums. Ironically, conventional wisdom would also indicate that Black colleges would have courses that extensively study Black colleges, yet in 2020, that is just not the case.

Horace Mann Bond, a prominent HBCU leader, thinker, and historian examined the politicization of Black agency within academic curriculums in his 1935 publication "The Curriculum of the Negro Child." Bond insists "Negros interested in curriculum building should seek definitions of the social forces . . . in terms of fact, and not of platitude."[24] Weary of the radical Black and White nationalists, Communist, and Fascist political movements of the era, Bond concluded that school curriculums were overly influenced by the external social allegiances and biases, which he believed diminished rational thought. Bond's position was that "Negroes, of all people, can least afford to labor for curriculum revision with no understanding of the real sources of their toil, or the ultimate direction of their efforts."[25] Like Bond, I believe the omission of systematic HBCU Studies curriculums is an intellectually dangerous place for Black colleges and their constituents because the current model leaves Black colleges and their output without formal, unmitigated, HBCU-Centered gauges. Instead, currently, Black college curriculums continue to overly concern themselves with standards set by White institutions. While much progress has been made in creating African and African- American courses at Black colleges, HBCU curriculums and degree programs do not reflect the HBCU experience, which is tragic.

Evident in post-*Miseducation of the Negro* writings, Carter G. Woodson's 1926 crusade for Black scholarly agency, coupled with the Civil Rights and Black Power Movements, reflected a more radical turn in HBCU literature. Black college scholars were largely concerned with matters of racial discrimination, political activism, African-American educational representation, and desegregation's effects on HBCUs. Due to the racially polarizing political environment, many twentieth-century writers understood the power of calibrating HBCU curriculums to meet the needs of the schools and the Black community. Benjamin Quarles lauded Black college scholar, discussed the quandary in his 1943 article, "One Shortcoming in Negro Colleges" in addition to Walter G. Daniel and Robert P. Daniel's 1946 "The Curriculum of the Negro College."[26] Wm. F. Brazziel's treated the same issues regarding HBCU curriculums in his 1960 article, "Curriculum Choice in the Negro College," while Robert D. Reid analyzed Black college course catalogs and sent questionnaire surveys on matters of curriculum to the institutions administrators forming the basis of his 1967 publication, "Curricular Changes in Colleges and Universities for Negroes."[27]

Due to the gains of the Civil Rights and Black Studies Movement, and the changing face of post-*Brown* higher education, scholars were concerned about HBCUs' futures and commitment to Black liberation. Nathan Hare was one of the most provocative. An HBCU graduate, known as the "Father of Black Studies" because of his 1968 creation of the first Black studies degree program, which was housed at San Francisco State University. Hare offered a prolific case for a Black College Renaissance in his 1978 writing, "War on Black Colleges." Hare stipulated, "If Black colleges have a special meaning or a particular mission which distinguishes them from white colleges, it's time they act that way."[28] Notably, Hare's frustrations were in line with the litany of writers who criticized Black colleges for modeling PWIs and failing to create a cyclical, regenerative, Afrocentric educational standard. This study's position directly intersects with and furthers Hare's 1978 position that "Black colleges must become the carriers, the builders, the guardians of Afro-American culture, but simultaneously the architects and catalysts of new social change, which will correct and, in the process humanize the world so not only to save Black colleges and Black culture but also, if the earth is lucky, the whole human existence."[29] My Black College Renaissance thesis echoes Hare's position; I also believe with the right social consciousness, courage, and effort, HBCUs can transform the world.

This 2020 proposal for a Black College Renaissance through an HBCU Studies institutional medium is rooted in and an extension of Hare's 1968 to the present Black Studies and Afrocentric education canonical positioning. HBCU Studies will help Black colleges come to terms with issues like Hare's creditable suggestion that "we need a massive tidal wave of name-changing of Black colleges . . . in memory of a Black person. . . . Where is the Du Bois University? Let along the Nat Turner University or the Marcus Garvey College."[30] Hare's difficulties with the current names of HBCUs is warranted because only three of the approximately 107 schools are named after Black people—Langston University, Bethune-Cookman University, and the now-defunct Morris Brown College.[31] While the majorly white men that Black colleges are named after did good for the schools, it is quite bizarre that HBCU namesakes, mascots, and curriculums are standard-bearers for white cultural domination. The Washington Redskins, along with other institutions have realized the sociocultural damage and psychological dislocation symbols and relics rooted in white supremacy have on societal progress, particularly for African Americans.[32] Accordingly, these issues, along with the catalog of others that past, present, and future HBCU theorists and stakeholders raise, justify the need for a systematic study of Black colleges en masse. I propose erecting a system in the form of an HBCU-specific academic discipline. I ask, without HBCU studies, how can HBCU administrators, faculty, staff, students, and alums familiarize and functionalize these longstanding debates, along with other complexities in a coalesced, operational, exhaustive, methodical manner? Hence, a new way of understanding, classifying, and purposing Black college history and culture is needed for the schools to reach their full, Black liberationist potential. My Black liberationist position means HBCUs' ability to psychologically and culturally unshackle, unchain, emancipate, and deliver themselves and their communities from the infiltrating force of Eurocentric dominion, rooted in the façade of inevitable truth.

Yet, ironically, the more recent and closest study to my 2020 HBCU Studies proposition is—Marybeth Gasman, a White, applauded Black college scholar and Andrew T. Arroyo, a White, HBCU educational advocate, 2014 publication—"An HBCU-Based Educational Approach for Black College Student Success: Toward a Framework with Implications for All Institutions."[33] Similar to my HBCU Studies philosophical context, Gasman and Arroyo commence their writing by establishing "This conceptual study builds an institution-focused, non-Eurocentric, theoretical framework of Black college student success . . . [by synthesizing] the relevant empirical research on the contributions . . . (HBCUs) have made for Black student success . . . leading to an original model that all institutions can adapt."[34] Comparable to my HBCU Studies theoretical framework, Arroyo and Gasman present what they term "An HBCU-Based Educational Approach," which sets out to create an educational method specifically for Black colleges that like my HBCU Studies plan, particularizes the Black college experience. There are a number of added connections between the two authors' positions and my proposal. Among them are the belief that: (1) HBCUs have a history and tradition viable enough to create their own institutional education models (2) HBCUs are well-positioned to create societal change (3) HBCUs help African-American students realize issues that may concern identity formation, leadership roles, and nurturing self-esteem.[35]

Even with a shared vision for an HBCU-Centered educational framework, my HBCU Studies proposal has a number of distinct differences. For starters, Arroyo and Gasman's writing is heavy on the theory and justification for what they term "An HBCU-Based Educational Approach," but shallow on offering a concise, practical, and cultural method for making their model a reality. Contrarily, my HBCU Studies proposal is focused on creating a new field of study, that offers courses and degrees in an HBCU-specific discipline. Moreover, Arroyo and Gasman situate their research within scholarly debates regarding the creation of theoretical academic models, while my HBCU Studies proposal rests on historiographical trends geared towards university curriculum models. Ultimately, the two authors' idea is primarily concerned with the admirable goal of fomenting student success at HBCUs, whereas my HBCU Studies proposal is focused on HBCUs having competitive, cutting-edge, Afrocentric, mechanisms purposed to systematize their history, production, and culture to transform (1) Black colleges first, (2) the African-American community second, (3) the African diaspora third, (4) then finally the nation and all others.

In total, the scholarly conversation on the unfulfilled potential of an HBCU educational method and curriculum extends beyond the days of W. E. B. Du Bois and Carter G. Woodson's early 1900s dismay with Negro Colleges modeling white institutions to Nathan Hare, the "Father of Black Studies" 1970s scathing critique of Black colleges' failures to exchange their Eurocentric orientations for an Afrocentric paradigm. Hence the Black Studies and Afrocentric theoretical frameworks denote the canonical position of my 2020 HBCU Studies proposition. Evident in the listing of writers noted in the literature review, my calls for a Black College Renaissance that is intent on transforming the psychological, cultural, economic, educational, and sociopolitical reality of the Black community are not new. Many writers have recognized the revolutionary potential of Black colleges but fell short in identifying a viable apparatus for engendering the desired change. With this in mind, HBCU Studies as a field of scholarship should serve as a welcomed solution to cultivating the internal and societal remodeling that I and other similar-minded HBCU scholars insist is long overdue.

BLUEPRINT AND DIRECTIONAL
CONTEMPLATIONS CONCERNING THE
HBCU STUDIES DEGREE PROGRAM

Concerning the creation of a critical study, Afrocentric, Black college-centered, educational field, my 2020 interdisciplinary HBCU Studies blueprint moves the centuries-long conceptualization phase of an intentionally racial, social, self-powered, Black College Renaissance to the implementation stage. With this in mind, it is important to note the infancy of this proposal. As such, I invite intense debate, critique, and recommendations with regard to this 2020 HBCU Studies blueprint. Pontificating on HBCU research and other prevailing Black college issues is productive, but often inharmonious and infirm. Thus, substantial innovation is needed, with the capacity for replication and analyzation cross-academy and cross-university that leads to HBCU-led transformation in all sectors, including but not limited to, employment, entrepreneurship, social matters, and most importantly, Black college sustainability. For these reasons, HBCU Studies as an academic discipline are proposed to permit the continuous circulation of in-depth, Black college systems analysis to further the schools and their constituents, in hopes of advancing society in totality.

As previously mentioned, HBCU Studies are an extension of Black Studies and Afrocentricity, in addition to the debates and goals enshrined in the two fields. Both philosophical traditions emerge out of the 1960s and 1970s Civil Rights and Black Power Movements' strides for African American self-determination, self-actualization, and global legitimization.[36] It is estimated that after Nathan Hare, the HBCU graduate "Father of Black Studies, led the first Black Studies program in 1968, by 1971, approximately 160 Black Studies programs existed.[37] The outcome of African Americans fighting to have their experience acknowledged and taught within academic circles resulted in a new academic field known interchangeably as Black Studies or African-American Studies. Black Studies is largely interdisciplinary and focuses on the critical study of the entire Black experience, including history, politics, economics, resistance, gender, and education.[38] To safeguard HBCUs' interests, it is my sincere hope that after the first HBCU Studies academic program is established, the field will grow at the same rates, particularly at Black colleges.

Similarly, Molefi Kete Asante—the acclaimed progenitor of the Afrocentric philosophy, as noted in his 1980 book *Afrocentricity: The Theory of Social Change*—experienced the same successes after creating the first doctoral program in African-American Studies at Temple University in 1987.[39] Afrocentricity calls for the centralization of African culture and realities when analyzing African agents, including the African-American experience.[40] HBCUs and the turbulent transformation of their constituents from enslaved Africans to African Americans emerge out of a 200,000-year African history and four-hundred-year African-American history measured by the Gregorian Calendar.[41] As a result, HBCU Studies must concern themselves with the African world before white supremacy, to create a future African world beyond white supremacy. Afrocentricity provides the theoretical framework that HBCU Studies need to achieve their full power. Many prestigious institutions like Brown, Cornell, Rutgers, and Yale have followed Asante's lead and established doctoral programs in African-American Studies that debate the merits and functionality of Afrocentricity. Noticeably missing from the universities with doctoral programs in African-American Studies are Black colleges. Correspondingly, only one HBCU offers a master's degree in the field—Morgan State University.[42] I believe that this disturbing educational mishap is a result of the limited freedom HBCUs have experienced to determine their own identities and futures. HBCU Studies as a branch of African-American or Black Studies can remedy this vacuum by providing Black colleges with their own critical theory and pedagogical specialization—housed in their own academic space—rooted in Critical, Social, and Cultural Studies in Education.

Fundamentally, in an ideal HBCU Studies bachelor's degree program, every major course would concern themselves with the said Black Studies, Afrocentricity, and Critical, Social, and Cultural Educational Studies philosophical frameworks. The Critical, Social, and Cultural Educational focus would offer the in-depth, epistemological milieu that HBCUs Studies need to unlock their problems and possibilities.[43] Intentionally teetering between Black colleges' problems and possibilities is where HBCU Studies should initially dwell to access and stay ahead of the institutions' challenges while propelling their constituents to a new stage of development. HBCUs have many top Black scholars that deal specifically with African-American, African Diasporic, American, and global issues. Our society would greatly benefit from routinely hearing their voices as they transform at-risk African-American students into high-achieving citizens at elevated rates. HBCU Studies would depend on these brilliant Black college faculty, administrative, staff, student, and alumni voices to move the discipline into its most efficient calibration for reviewing and advancing HBCUs and their interests groups. Furthermore, I envision HBCU Studies courses as solution-based classes. In Western education, supposed objectivity and emotional detachment from your subjects is standard.[44] HBCU Studies does not have to follow the Western standard. Considering the atrocities committed against and attempted spread of coerced African historical and cultural tradition and memory, I welcome an awoke, attached, expressive, vibrant, concerned, solution-oriented approach to studying HBCU realities. I would be more than pleased if the circadian rhythm of HBCU Studies ripples across the academic, professional, and introspective worlds allegorically like a Black college showband. Here, I am referring to the unique Afro-syncretic bravado that HBCUs carry, culturally merging, all while distinguishing the schools from their non-Black college counterparts.[45]

Hence, HBCU Studies should represent all that Black colleges project, even their most pressing quest, in my opinion, total liberation from the burden of Black respectability politics.[46] From my perspective, HBCU leaders are overly concerned with presenting themselves as the "perfect Blacks," in a Cosby Show-like valance, while suppressing the Muhammad Ali-like malaise that keeps the HBCU-Socratic-mind acquiescent.[47] My conclusions descend from my extensive HBCU preparation. In my traverse across the Black college landscape, I have encountered and attempted to resist the flippant plague that Du Bois referred to as "veiled, double-consciousness," Carter G. Woodson diagnosed as "Miseducated Negros," Frantz Fanon, noted as "Black Skin in White Mask," and E. Franklin Frazier termed "Black Bourgeoise," and what Molefi Kete Asante called "African Psychological Dislocation."[48] Despite the term, all of the men were attempting to define what they discovered and considered, the psychologically compromising and ethnically cannibalizing effects of Black respectability politics on the African-American community. I simply call the phenomenon "the African Dark Ages," meaning a time of cultural, and thus, practical absence of unapologetic, unmitigated, African-centeredness. I argue that a gap between African and African-American cultural thought, sociopolitical orientation, and racial allegiance exists, which in turn serves as an impediment to a truly liberating African progress across the Diaspora and in particular at HBCUs. This form of deleterious incrementalism, guided by a desire to benevolently assimilate within the White power structure's guard rails, has shielded HBCUs from the type of self-obsessed education that I propose. Therefore, I recognize the future of HBCU Studies is subject to the negotiation between the pressures that Black college leaders face to ensure their agendas are not perceived as "too Black" or "too revolutionary," in the radical context. Be that as it may, my position is that until HBCU training involves a preoccupation with critiquing, organizing, and altering the African and African-American experience in radically transformational directions than the current trajectory, Black Americans will not be made whole. As a solution to this pressing problem of African-American and HBCU suffering, I offer the described combinations of philosophical frameworks for HBCU Studies to analyze, streamline, systematize, functionalize, direct, leverage, and most importantly, distribute Black college history, culture, and assets into equation-like formulas from K-12 systems up.

Doing so is necessary because the institutions' remarkable contributions are not entirely understood, promoted, or reimbursed.

I present HBCU Studies as the platform for what I call, "systemizing the HBCU system" to provide institutional answers to the institutional challenges that in an Ibram X. Kendi framework, stamped Black colleges from the beginning.[49] For the purpose of this study, I will present a brief overview of a potential HBCU Studies minor model within the current curricula structures found at most American universities. First, theoretically, the minor would have an eighteen (18) credit interdisciplinary curriculum, rooted in the one, flagship HBCU Studies course requirement that each University degree program must create. The flagship HBCU Studies course would have adjustable rigor through a flexible scheduling and credit-level medium. For example, in the History Departments at Black colleges, they develop a flagship or defining course titled "Functionalizing HBCU History and Culture" that can be offered at the freshman, sophomore, junior, senior, and even graduate levels. The same would apply to any degree program like Computer Engineering for example; such a program's flagship HBCU Studies course may carry the hypothetical active-voice title, "Improving Computer Engineering Systems At HBCUs." Sports Management departments may opt for "Managing and Leveraging HBCU Sports Culture," while Political Science may make their disciplinary focus, "Assessing Public Policy's Effect on HBCU Outcomes." More importantly, each of the flagship HBCU Studies course rigor adjustments would cross-coordinate with the credit level at the flagship HBCU Studies course is offered at. i.e., freshman, sophomore, junior, senior, or graduate.

The point here is that the possibilities are enormously consequential and entirely interdisciplinary with regard to HBCU Studies. Every area of the University, whether, STEM, Liberal Arts, Humanities, Social Sciences, or the Professionalized fields, can develop a critical research and analysis, intentionally solution-based course to elevate HBCUs and their interests. Each college or university can decide how to organize, implement, and offer their groupings of HBCU Studies courses. The one course that would remain constant is a 100-flevel "Introduction to HBCU Studies" general education class that all students are required to take during their first year. The course should also concern itself with the flexibility in providing the various departments the opportunity to house and offer the course, based upon the strengths and weaknesses of each individual University. However, the 100-level, "Introduction to HBCU Studies" general education course would have a number of consistent themes such as:

1. Defining HBCU Theory and Leveraging Black College Culture
2. Overview of the HBCU Historical, Political, and Administrative Traditions

3. Social Activities and the Psychology of the HBCU Student
4. HBCU Past, Present, Future, Challenges, and Successes
5. HBCU Statistical Data and Information Systems
6. Comparative HBCU Pedagogy and Critical Thought
7. Post-Graduation HBCU Careers and Alumni Engagement
8. Responsibility of the HBCU Student and Faculty
9. HBCUs and the Community, Diaspora, Nation, and World
10. Black College Infrastructures, Physical Plants, and Architecture.

In all, Black college systems analysis and systems proliferation would be the focus of the "Introduction to HBCU Studies" course and entire HBCU curriculums, which is why I encourage the adoption at Black colleges in particular, en masse. Black colleges need HBCU Studies Departments that drive the HBCU Studies curriculums and work in collaboration with Institutional Research, Innovation, and Effectiveness initiatives. Categorically, the institutions should turn inward and develop united, homespun formulae for carving their futures and predicting and countering crises before the start on automated and collectivized bases where possible.

Though the idea has many fruitful possibilities, I still have numerous questions to answer with regard to fully explaining my current conception of HBCU Studies as an academic discipline that requires a longer format. Nevertheless, I am more than honored to lay out one of many theoretical frameworks for an HBCU Studies minor. The field will need to grow and change as HBCUs transform. Similar to African-American and Women's Studies, an HBCU Studies degree would be useful in numerous professions, businesses, and leadership roles; thus making the degree competitive and valuable on many levels, not just for HBCU students. The more democratized the field is, the more the general public will use critical analysis to further Black colleges and their needs. Similarly, the more arguments HBCU proponents can develop to counter their opponents, the more protected the schools will be. The Black college literature exists. There is a wealth of research and writings on HBCUs. The HBCU Studies programs would join with the library to have a special HBCU Collection on each campus. Faculty could organize targeted course packs for each HBCU Studies class until the textbooks are developed. I urge e-books that are easily updated and shared across campuses. I also envision the end of semester HBCU Studies virtual conferences where technology is leveraged to create socially shared courses between individual classes at different universities. The virtual conferences can serve as places to layout and implement capstone course conclusions and archive ongoing HBCU Studies research.

I know my ideas are novel, but I earnestly believe that HBCUs will always have stunted innovation until the systematic study of Black colleges extends beyond the seasoned researchers that speak to a limited audience. I hope that Black college administrations will evaluate the merits of this proposal and have the boldness to implement an HBCU Studies curriculum. As an academic discipline, HBCU Studies are only a contribution to the long scholarly conversation focused on the purpose of Black colleges and their institutional problems. The active, solution-based HBCU Studies course model is purposed to procure, organize, and advantage Black college consciousness, competitiveness, innovation, and sustainability. HBCU Studies could also be positioned as a protective information center that facilitates the algorithms that serve as the new, high-tech, metrics-based Black college compass and sonar.

CREATING THE NATION'S FIRST HBCU HISTORY COURSE, HIST 349-HBCU HISTORY AT VIRGINIA STATE UNIVERSITY

I am privileged to lay out my ideas for the adoption of HBCU Studies Curriculums en masse, cultivated by the nationally welcomed reception of my role in creating the nation's first HBCU History course—HIST 349-HBCU History at Virginia State University (VSU). Though I personally believed the course was monumental, its national popularity took me by surprise. However, I am eternally grateful to Gwen Dandridge, VSU's Director of Communications, for issuing the initial August 19, 2020 press release regarding the course. I am also appreciative of the numerous media outlets and HBCU community members for their support and outreach regarding the new HBCU class. The creation of HBCU History as a course derived from my growing understanding that Black college history was celebrated, but remained ambiguous and misunderstood. I encountered the same issue with regard to one of my major research specializations, the institutional history of the White House Initiative on HBCUs in Washington, DC. While interning at the office from 2013 to 2015 as a History doctoral student at Morgan State University, through conversations with several Black college patrons, I soon realized the history of the White House Initiative on HBCUs was lacking. In 2016, after completing my dissertation, which serves as the first and only comprehensive history of the White House office that services HBCUs, I came to understand that critical studies on collectivized HBCU history needed improvement. With these factors in mind, upon finishing my history PhD in 2016, I approached my assistant professorships at two Black colleges with great interest in understanding if a course on HBCU History had been created since my time as both an HBCU undergraduate and doctoral student.

During the Fall 2018 semester, my first year as Assistant Professor at VSU, I immediately forwarded my HBCU History course proposal to the curriculum committee, to which they approved. The following semester I decided to teach HIST 343-History of Black Education in the U.S., to further familiarize myself with African-American educational history literature. My goal was to assess whether my initial inclinations remained accurate regarding the deficiencies in the critical study of Black colleges in K-12, higher education, Black History Month commemorations, and other relevant mediums. HBCU history was noticeably missing from the center of African American history, where I argue they belong. My initial reservations resulted from my analysis of three major African-American history survey textbooks. Among them: (1) *From Slavery to Freedom: A History of African Americans, Ninth Edition* by John Hope Franklin; (2) *African Americans: A Concise History,* by Darlene Clark Hine, et al. (3) *Freedom on My Mind*, by Deborah Gray White, et al.[50] I noticed a similar trend in all of the textbooks. From my viewpoint, the HBCU conversations were noticeably shallow, and most prevalent only when discussing Booker T. Washington and W. E. B. Du Bois. While the two men are central features in HBCU history, so are numerous other African-American trailblazers like George Washington Carver, Mary McLeod Bethune, Langston Hughes, Martin Luther King, Jr., Thurgood Marshall, Toni Morrison, Eddie Robinson, and Oprah Winfrey. Notable Black pioneers are centralized in African-American history textbooks, but HBCUs are often trivialized as peripheral, antidotal anomalies. Black college history deserves more analysis and priority in African-American and American History because they single-handedly created the Black middle and upper class while suffering financial and racial duress in the Jim Crow South.[51] I contend the schools were incubators that played two essential roles in post-Civil War America: (1) HBCUs helped to repair the American union by providing the training necessary to sustain the newly freed Black community; (2) Black colleges were responsible for the transformation of enslaved Africans to African Americans. Fostering the conversion of a mostly illiterate, newly freed Black population into the group now described as African Americans is a phenomenal accomplishment. HBCUs' ability to produce with precision, hundreds of thousands of scholarly, dignified, confident, competitive, and determined African-American men and women is worthy of its own widely ascribed, scientific formulation. These schools deserve prizes as prestigious as Presidential Medals of Freedom for what they have endured and provided to this country. Summarily, Black colleges are patriotic institutions, concerned with authenticating American courage, triumph, innovation, and unity.

With a rich story as previously described, HBCU History courses and in-depth textbook discussions of Black colleges are long overdue. I am excited to initiate a movement for the study of HBCU history, thought, and culture through HBCU Studies as a degree field. Though I have yet to conclude the first section of the new HIST-349 HBCU History course, so far the class has progressed well. Recently, exceptional writings on Black colleges' history as a collective have emerged and serve as useful textbooks in the course. The manuscripts include Bobby L. Lovett's (2015) *America's Historically Black Colleges and Universities: A Narrative History, 1837–2009* and Jelani Favor's (2019) *Shelter in a Time of Storm: How Black Colleges Fostered Generations of Leadership and Activism.*[52] The two men's books, in addition to the wealth of targeted studies and articles on HBCUs, are excellent resources for teaching the chronological histories of Black colleges from their nineteenth-century origins, twentieth-century political activism, and twenty-first-century outcomes.

CONCLUSION: TOWARD THE NEXT HBCU FRONTIER

In the near future, it is my sincere hope that HBCUs' long history and prolific contributions usher in a Black College Renaissance through intense, critical, HBCU Studies analysis. I have laid out a vision for institutionalizing, understanding, reprocessing, and leveraging Black college's intellectual property, history, and culture; thereby serving as a form of premeditated inoculation from challenges. I must admit that the racial unrest and political tension of 2020 propelled me and others like the National Basketball Association (NBA) to envision a future beyond systematic racism.[53] Intense protests against racially motivated acts of violence toward African Americans and the unorthodox presidency of Donald Trump led me to question HBCU innovation and sustainability in a changing America. I concluded that remaining quiet or taking refuge in elite HBCU circles are not sufficient. Instead, HBCUs should arm themselves with a vigorous, systematic, rejuvenating, and safeguarding knowledge of their past, present, and future to cross the next frontier in American and African Diasporic history.

NOTES

1. "Virginia State Offers HBCU History Course," Jared Carter Sr., *HBCU Digest*, August 20, 2020, https://www.hbcudigest.com/p/virginia-state-offers-hbcu-history: "Virginia State University Offering a New Course on HBCU History," *Journal of Blacks in Higher Education*, September 4, 2020, https://www.jbhe.com/2020/09/virginia-state-university-offering-a-new-course-on-hbcu-history/.

2. For more information on the creation of interdisciplinary academic programs and their founding justifications see: Lisa R. Lattuca, *Creating Interdisciplinarity:*

Interdisciplinary Research and Teaching Among College and University Faculty (Nashville: Vanderbilt University Press, 2001).

3. Jean Anyon, *Radical Possibilities: Public Policy, Urban Education, and A New Social Movement* (New York: Routledge, 2014).

4. For tuition and fees at all Black colleges, see: White House Initiative on Historically Black Colleges and Universities School Directory, //sites.ed.gov/whhbcu/files/2014/09/HBCU-Directory.pdf.

5. "Virginia State University Possibly Offering Nation's First-Ever History Course on HBCU's," Terrance Dixon, NBC29, last modified September 4, 2020, https://www.nbc29.com/2020/09/04/virginia-state-university-possibly-offering-nations-first-ever-history-course-hbcus/.

6. "Why Choose An HBCU," UNCF, accessed November 10, 2020, https://uncf.org/pages/why-choose-an-hbcu.

7. "How Historically Black Colleges Transformed America," Thurgood Marshall College Fund, accessed November 10, 2020, https://www.tmcf.org/events-media/tmcf-in-the-media/how-historically-black-colleges-transformed-america/.

8. Ibid.

9. "Wholly," Thesurus.com, accessed November 10, 2020, https://www.thesaurus.com/browse/wholly?s=t.

10. "The Challenges Facing HBCU Campuses," PBS, May 26, 2019, https://www.npr.org/2019/05/25/726941875/the-challenges-facing-hbcu-campuses.

11. Thomas Aiello, The Battle for the Souls of Black Folk: W.E.B. Du Bois, Booker T. Washington and the Debate That Shaped the Course of Civil Rights (Santa Barbara, CA: ABC-CLIO, 2016); Marybeth Gasman, *Envisioning Black Colleges: A History of the United Negro College Fund* (Baltimore: Johns Hopkins University Press, 2007), 196–198; Cheryl E. Mango, "High Black Pressure! Major Issues and Controversies that Led to Jimmy Carter's 1980 Creation of the White House Initiative on Historically Black Colleges and Universities" (PhD diss., Morgan State University, Baltimore, 2016).

12. Ibid.

13. Jazmin Goodwin, "Morgan Stanley to Cover Tuition for 60 Students At Three HBCUs," CNN Business, October 22, 2020, https://www.cnn.com/2020/10/22/business/morgan-stanley-hbcu-scholarship-program-12-million/index.html.

14. Oliver O'Connell, "Trump Likens Minneapolis George Floyd Protest to Wartime Berlin," *Independent*, October 30, 2020, https://www.independent.co.uk/news/world/americas/us-election-2020/trump-rally-george-floyd-protest-minneapolis-berlin-world-war-two-b1454966.html.

15. Nicole Chavez, "An HBCU Grad Galvanized Voters in Georgia and Another One is Making History as Vice President," CNN, November 10, 2020, https://www.cnn.com/2020/11/10/us/hbcu-women-kamala-harris-stacey-abrams-trnd/index.html.

16. William K. Watkins, *The White Architects of Black Education* (New York: Teacher's College Press, 2001), xi-xiii.

17. W. E. B. Du Bois, ed., *The College-bred Negro American: A Report of a Social Study Made under the Direction of Atlanta University* (Atlanta: Atlanta University Press, 1900), 100, 18.

18. Ibid.

19. Carter G. Woodson, *The Miseducation of the Negro* (San Diego: The Book Tree, 1933).

20. Ibid., 1.

21. Miller, Kelly. "The Past, Present and Future of the Negro College." *Journal of Negro Education* 2, no. 3 (1933): 413, accessed November 11, 2020. doi:10.2307/2292210.

22. Ibid., 418.

23. Dabney, Thomas L. "The Study of the Negro." *Journal of Negro History* 19, no. 3 (1934): 266, accessed November 11, 2020. doi:10.2307/2714215.

24. Bond, Horace Mann. "The Curriculum and the Negro Child." *Journal of Negro Education* 4, no. 2 (1935): 168. accessed November 11, 2020. doi:10.2307/2292330.

25. Ibid.

26. Benjamin Quarles, "One Shortcoming in Negro Colleges," *Journal of Negro Education* 12, no. 4 (1943): 700–02, accessed November 11, 2020. http://www.jstor .org/stable/2292842; Walter G. Daniel, and Robert P. Daniel, "The Curriculum of the Negro College," *Journal of Educational Sociology* 19, no. 8 (1946): 496–502, accessed November 11, 2020. doi:10.2307/2263572; Wm. F. Brazziel, "Curriculum Choice in the Negro College,"

27. *Journal of Negro Education* 29, no. 2 (1960): 207–9, accessed November 11, 2020. doi:10.2307/2293170; Robert D. Reid, "Curricular Changes in Colleges and Universities for Negroes: Analysis and Interpretation of a Questionnaire Survey," *Journal of Higher Education* 38, no. 3 (1967): 153–60, accessed November 11, 2020. doi:10.2307/1979268.

28. Nathan Hare, "WAR ON BLACK COLLEGES," *Black Scholar* 9, no. 8/9 (1978): 15, accessed November 11, 2020, http://www.jstor.org.vsu.idm.oclc.org/ stable/41067858.

29. Ibid.

30. Ibid.

31. Ibid.

32. J. P. Finlay, "New Name Might Be The New Name for Washington Football," *New York Times*, October 21, 2020, https://www.nbcsports.com/washington/ football-team/new-name-no-name-might-be-new-name-washington-football.

33. Andrew T. Arroyo, and Marybeth Gasman, "An HBCU-Based Educational Approach for Black College Student Success: Toward a Framework with Implications for All Institutions," *American Journal of Education* 121, no. 1 (2014): 57–85, accessed November 11, 2020. doi:10.1086/678112.

34. Ibid., 57.

35. Ibid., 69.

36. Charles H. Curl, "Black Studies: Form and Content," *CLA Journal* 57, no. 1 (2013): 24, accessed November 11, 2020. http://www.jstor.org/stable/44325844.

37. Carlos A. Brossard, "Classifying Black Studies Programs," *Journal of Negro Education* 53, no. 3 (1984): 280, Accessed November 11, 2020. doi:10.2307/2294864.

38. Fabio Rojas, *From Black Power to Black Studies: How A Radical Social Movement Become An Academic Discipline* (Baltimore: Johns Hopkins University Press, 2007).

39. "Biography," Dr. Molefi Kete Asante, accessed November 9, 2020, http://www .asante.net/biography/.

40. Abdul Karim Bangura, *Branches of Asanteism* (New York: Lexington Books, 2019), 2.

41. "The Story of Africa Early History," BBC World Service, accessed November 11, 2020, https://www.bbc.co.uk/worldservice/africa/features/storyofafrica/2chapter2 .shtml#:~:text=The%20first%20theory%2C%20known%20as,are%20ultimately %20of%20African%20descent.

42. "Africana Studies Graduate Programs," National Council of Black Studies Online, accessed November 11, 2020, https://ncbsonline.org/students/as-grad -programs/.

43. Marto Baltodano, Antonia Darder, and Rodolfo D. Torres, eds. *The Critical Pedagogy Reader* (New York: Routledge, 2009).

44. Ronald Barnett, *The Idea of Higher Education* (United Kingdom: Society for Research into Higher Education, 1990), 47.

45. Ashenafi Kebede, *Roots of Black Music: The Vocal, Instrumental, and Dance Heritage of Africa and Black America* (United Kingdom: Prentice-Hall, 1982), 113, 150.

46. Cheryl Mango, "Respectability," In *The World of Jim Crow: A Daily Life Encyclopedia* (Santa Barbara, CA: Greenwood Press, 2019).

47. Billy Hawkins, Joseph Cooper et al. eds. *The Athletic Experience at Historically Black Colleges and Universities: Past, Present, and Persistence* (Lanham, MD: Rowman & Littlefield Publishers, 2015), 189.

48. W. E. B. Du Bois, *The Souls of Black Folk* (New York: Dover Publications, 2012); Woodson, *Miseducation*; Frantz Fanon, *Black Skin, White Masks* (United Kingdom: Grove Press, 2007); E. Franklin Frazier and William Julius Wilson, *Black Bourgeoisie* (United Kingdom: Free Press, 1997); Molefi Kete Asante, *The Afrocentric Idea* (Philadelphia: Temple University Press, 1998).

49. Ibram X. Kendi, *Stamped from the Beginning: The Definitive History of Racist Ideas in America* (New York: Naiton Books, 2016).

50. John Hope Franklin, *From Slavery to Freedom: A History of African Americans, Ninth Edition* (New York: McGraw Hill, 2009); Darlene Clark Hine, et al. *African Americans, Combined Volume: A Concise History* (New York: Pearson Education, 2013); Waldo E. Martin, Deborah Gray White, Mia Bay, *Freedom on My Mind: A History of African Americans, with Documents* (Boston: Bedford/St. Martin's, 2016).

51. "How Historically Black Colleges Transformed America," Thurgood Marshall College Fund.

52. Bobby Lovett, *Historically Black Colleges and Universities: A Narrative History, 1837–2009*, (Mercer University Press, 2015); Jelani Favors, *Shelter in a Time of a Storm: How Black Colleges Fostered Generations of Leadership and Activism*, (University of North Carolina Press, 2019).

53. Marc J. Spears, " 'Black Lives Matter, People': How the NBA's Social Justice Efforts Dominated the Season," *The Undefeated*, October 12, 2020, https://the-undefeated.com/features/how-the-nba-social-justice-efforts-dominated-the-season/.

REFERENCES

"Africana Studies Graduate Programs." National Council of Black Studies Online. Accessed November 11, 2020. https://ncbsonline.org/students/as-grad-programs/.

Aiello, Thomas. *The Battle for the Souls of Black Folk: W.E.B. Du Bois, Booker T. Washington and the Debate That Shaped the Course of Civil Rights* (Santa Barbara, CA: ABC-CLIO, 2016).

Anyon, Jean. *Radical Possibilities: Public Policy, Urban Education, and A New Social Movement* (New York: Routledge, 2014).

Arroyo, Andrew T., and Marybeth Gasman. "An HBCU-Based Educational Approach for Black College Student Success: Toward a Framework with Implications for All Institutions." *American Journal of Education* 121, no. 1 (2014): Accessed November 11, 2020. doi:10.1086/678112.

Asante, Molefi Kete. *The Afrocentric Idea* (Philadelphia: Temple University Press, 1998).

Baltodano, Marto. Darder, Antonia and Rodolfo D. Torres. Editors. *The Critical Pedagogy Reader* (New York: Routledge, 2009).

Bangura, Abdul Karim. *Branches of Asanteism* (New York: Lexington Books, 2019).

Barnett, Ronald. *The Idea of Higher Education* (United Kingdom: Society for Research into Higher Education, 1990).

"Biography." Dr. Molefi Kete Asante. Accessed November 9, 2020. http://www.asante.net/biography/.

Bond, Horace Mann. "The Curriculum and the Negro Child." *Journal of Negro Education* 4, no. 2 (1935): Accessed November 11, 2020. doi:10.2307/2292330.

Brazziel, Wm. F. "Curriculum Choice in the Negro College." *Journal of Negro Education* 29, no. 2 (1960): Accessed November 11, 2020. doi:10.2307/2293170.

Brossard, Carlos A. "Classifying Black Studies Programs." *Journal of Negro Education* 53, no. 3 (1984): Accessed November 11, 2020. doi:10.2307/2294864.

"The Challenges Facing HBCU Campuses." PBS. May 26, 2019. https://www.npr.org/2019/05/25/726941875/the-challenges-facing-hbcu-campuses.Chavez, Nicole. "An HBCU Grad Galvanized Voters in Georgia and Another One is Making History as Vice President." *CNN*. November 10, 2020. https://www.cnn.com/2020/11/10/us/hbcu-women-kamala-harris-stacey-abrams-trnd/index.html.

Curl, Charles H. "Black Studies: Form and Content." *CLA Journal* 57. no. 1 (2013): Accessed November 11, 2020. http://www.jstor.org/stable/44325844.

Dabney, Thomas L. "The Study of the Negro." *Journal of Negro History* 19. no. 3 (1934): Accessed November 11, 2020. doi:10.2307/2714215.

Daniel, Walter G., and Robert P. Daniel. "The Curriculum of the Negro College." *Journal of Educational Sociology*. no. 8 (1946): accessed November 11, 2020. doi:10.2307/2263572.

Du Bois, W. E. B. *The Souls of Black Folk* (New York: Dover Publications, 2012).

Du Bois, W. E. B., editor. *The College-Bred Negro American: A Report of a Social Study Made under the Direction of Atlanta University* (Atlanta: Atlanta University Press, 1900).

Fanon, Frantz. *Black Skin, White Masks* (United Kingdom: Grove Press, 2007).

Favors, Jelani. *Shelter in a Time of a Storm: How Black Colleges Fostered Generations of Leadership and Activism*, (University of North Carolina Press, 2019).

Finlay, JP. "New Name Might Be The New Name for Washington Football." *New York Times*. October 21, 2020. https://www.nbcsports.com/washington/football-team/new-name-no-name-might-be-new-name-washington-football.

Franklin, John Hope. *From Slavery to Freedom: A History of African Americans*, *Ninth Edition* (New York: McGraw Hill, 2009).

Frazier E., Franklin and William Julius Wilson. *Black Bourgeoisie* (United Kingdom: Free Press, 1997).

Gasman, Marybeth. *Envisioning Black Colleges: A History of the United Negro College Fund* (Baltimore: Johns Hopkins University Press, 2007).

Goodwin, Jazmin. "Morgan Stanley to Cover Tuition for 60 Students At Three HBCUs." *CNN Business*. October 22, 2020. https://www.cnn.com/2020/10/22/business/morgan-stanley-hbcu-scholarship-program-12-million/index.html.

Hare, Nathan. "WAR ON BLACK COLLEGES." *The Black Scholar* 9. no. 8/9 (1978): Accessed November 11, 2020. http://www.jstor.org.vsu.idm.oclc.org/stable/41067858.

Hawkins, Billy and Joseph Cooper et al. Editors. *The Athletic Experience at Historically Black Colleges and Universities: Past, Present, and Persistence* (Lanham, MD: Rowman & Littlefield Publishers, 2015).

Hine, Darlene Clark. et al. *African Americans, Combined Volume: A Concise History* (New York: Pearson Education, 2013).

"How Historically Black Colleges Transformed America." Thurgood Marshall College Fund. Accessed November 10, 2020. https://www.tmcf.org/events-media/tmcf-in-the-media/how-historically-black-colleges-transformed-america/.

Kebede, Ashenafi. *Roots of Black Music: The Vocal, Instrumental, and Dance Heritage of Africa and Black America* (United Kingdom: Prentice-Hall, 1982).

Kendi, Ibram X. *Stamped from the Beginning: The Definitive History of Racist Ideas in America* (New York: Naiton Books, 2016).

Lattuca, Lisa R. *Creating Interdisciplinarity: Interdisciplinary Research and Teaching Among College and University Faculty* (Nashville: Vanderbilt University Press, 2001).

Lovett, Bobby. *Historically Black Colleges and Universities: A Narrative History, 1837–2009* (Mercer University Press, 2015).

Mango, Cheryl E. "High Black Pressure! Major Issues and Controversies that Led to Jimmy Carter's 1980 Creation of the White House Initiative on Historically Black Colleges and Universities" (Unpublished PhD diss., Morgan State University, Baltimore, 2016).

Mango, Cheryl. "Respectability." *The World of Jim Crow: A Daily Life Encyclopedia* (Santa Barbara, CA: Greenwood Press, 2019).

Martin, Waldo E. et al. *Freedom on My Mind: A History of African Americans, with Documents* (Boston: Bedford/St. Martin's, 2016).

Miller, Kelly. "The Past, Present and Future of the Negro College." *Journal of Negro Education* 2, no. 3 (1933): Accessed November 11, 2020. doi:10.2307/2292210.

O'Connell, Oliver. "Trump Likens Minneapolis George Floyd Protest to Wartime Berlin." *Independent*. October 30, 2020. https://www.independent.co.uk/news /world/americas/us-election-2020/trump-rally-george-floyd-protest-minneapolis -berlin-world-war-two-b1454966.html.

Quarles, Benjamin. "One Shortcoming in Negro Colleges." *Journal of Negro Education* 12, no. 4 (1943): Accessed November 11, 2020. http://www.jstor.org/ stable/2292842.

Reid, Robert D. "Curricular Changes in Colleges and Universities for Negroes: Analysis and Interpretation of a Questionnaire Survey." *Journal of Higher Education* 38. no. 3 (1967): Accessed November 11, 2020. doi:10.2307/1979268.

Rojas, Fabio. *From Black Power to Black Studies: How A Radical Social Movement Become An Academic Discipline* (Baltimore: Johns Hopkins University Press, 2007).

Spears, Marc J. " 'Black Lives Matter, People': How the NBA's Social Justice Efforts Dominated the Season." *The Undefeated*. October 12, 2020. https://theundefeated .com/features/how-the-nba-social-justice-efforts-dominated-the-season/.

"The Story of Africa Early History." BBC World Service. Accessed November 11, 2020. https://www.bbc.co.uk/worldservice/africa/features/storyofafrica/2chapter2 .shtml#:~:text=The%20first%20theory%2C%20known%20as,are%20ultimately %20of%20African%20descent.

"Virginia State Offers HBCU History Course." Carter Sr., Jared. *HBCU Digest*, August 20, 2020, https://www.hbcudigest.com/p/virginia-state-offers-hbcu-history.

"Virginia State University Offering a New Course on HBCU History." *The Journal of Blacks in Higher Education*. September 4, 2020. https://www.jbhe.com/2020/09 /virginia-state-university-offering-a-new-course-on-hbcu-history/.

"Virginia State University Possibly Offering Nation's First-Ever History Course on HBCU's." Dixon, Terrance. *NBC29*, last modified September 4, 2020. https: //www.nbc29.com/2020/09/04/virginia-state-university-possibly-offering-nations -first-ever-history-course-hbcus/.

White House Initiative on Historically Black Colleges and Universities School Directory. //sites.ed.gov/whhbcu/files/2014/09/HBCU-Directory.pdf.

"Wholly." Thesurus.com. Accessed November 10, 2020. https://www.thesaurus.com /browse/wholly?s=t.

"Why Choose An HBCU." UNCF. Accessed November 10, 2020, https://uncf.org/ pages/why-choose-an-hbcu.

Watkins, William K. *The White Architects of Black Education* (New York: Teacher's College Press, 2001).

Woodson, Carter G. *The Miseducation of the Negro* (San Diego: The Book Tree, 1933).

Chapter 11

Critical Reflections on Race, Social Justice, and Historically Black Colleges and Universities

Felix Kumah-Abiwu

INTRODUCTION

The public awareness and debates that have been intensified in recent times on race and social justice issues in America after the ruthless murder of Mr. George Floyd on May 25, 2020, are renewing important and difficult questions on racial injustice and equity issues that have been overlooked by the mainstream society for decades. There is no question that Americans from different racial backgrounds were traumatized by watching the demise of another human being as we have all seen in the disturbing video of George Floyd's murder. Mr. Floyd, an unarmed African American man, was denied justice, basic human rights, and human dignity as he was killed in public by a white police officer. As many scholar-activists who have dedicated their professional careers to interrogating critical issues of race and social injustice, the unfortunate and public death of Mr. Floyd might be new to some people, but not out of the norm for scholars and other activists who have been exposing the trauma of systemic/institutionalized racism, anti-Blackness, and Back suffering in America.[1]

It is important to also note that the commitment to social change is at the center of focus for scholars engaged in race and social justice works. At the same time, the "race and social justice voyage" can be challenging or quite frankly exhausting, especially when the desired positive social outcomes in our democratic society are slow as discrimination continues to haunt our democratic state, as Michael Hanchard captures well in his book titled, *The Specter of Race: How Discrimination Haunts Western Democracy.*[2] As observed by Michael Hanchard, legal scholar Michelle Alexander in her piece titled, "America, This Is Your Chance: We Must Get It Right This Time or Risk Losing Our Democracy Forever,"[3] made a similar observation on how Americans should be concerned about the weakening of our cherished democracy as we continue to allow racial discrimination to keep haunting and taking deep roots into the fabric of our society and its core institutions. For Alexander, America has been trapped in what she describes as a "cycle of intermittent racial progress followed by fierce backlash and the emergence of new and 'improved' systems of racial and social control."[4] Isabel Wilkerson's recent book *Caste: The Origins of our Discontents* captures the thoughts of many when she describes the racial caste system in America as an old house. According to Wilkerson, "race does the heavy lifting for a caste system that demands a means of human division" . . . and like an old house, "America has unseen skeleton, a caste system that is as central to its operation as are the studs and joists that we cannot see in the physical buildings we call home."[5]

As documented in the extant literature, emancipation, respect, and dignity have always been at the center of the Black struggles for centuries.[6] While it is imperative to recognize the support from allied communities, there is no contention that Blacks have been at the forefront of their struggle for total emancipation. To this end, key questions have been raised in the past and continued to be raised in our contemporary era on the role and place of Historically Black Colleges and Universities (HBCUs) in the discourse on race and social justice issues, especially in this era that has been described as America's reckoning period with race, racism, and social/racial justice issues. For others, HBCUs are not only the embodiment of *Black culture and identity* as these institutions represent one of the core Black institutions across America, but race and racial justice issues are arguably within the "natural domain" of these historic institutions. In essence, pertinent questions need to be asked on how race and social justice issues occupy the intellectual space or domain of HBCUs. In other words, the fundamental questions of interest to be asked are: How integral is race systematically studied and researched at HBCUs? What about critical inquiry into the study of structural racism and racial or social justice issues? Do we have well-resourced academic centers and institutes devoted to the study of race and social justice issues at HBCUs? If so, where are these academic centers or institutes and how well are they doing? If not, why are they lacking for all these years?

These are complex questions that need further scholarly interrogations and answers, which explain the purpose or rationale for this chapter. The chapter explores these questions in our attempt to better understand HBCUs in terms of their focus/study of race, racism, and social justice issues. The rest of the chapter is divided into three sections. The first section provides an overview of the history of HBCUs. Section 2 looks at the conceptual definitions of race, racism, and racial/social justice, and underscores how these concepts connect to the broader discourse of the chapter. The final section integrates the concepts of race, racism, and racial/social justice in addressing the stated research questions. This final section also provides some policy ideas/suggestions on how HBCUs can be well-positioned to serve as strong academic centers for research on race and social justice issues.

HISTORY OF HBCUs: A BRIEF OVERVIEW

Historically Black Colleges and Universities or HBCUs for short, are unique institutions across the United States that emerged from the nineteenth century onward for one main purpose; to educate and provide Black citizens with higher education opportunities following their denial to be educated at mainstream educational institutions.[7] Over one hundred of these institutions exist in the United States and other U.S. territories. For example, there are 101 HBCUs in nineteen states, the District of Columbia (DC), and the U.S. Virgin Islands as of 2018. Out of the 101 HBCUs, fifty-one are public and fifty are private HBCUs.[8] According to Marybeth Gasman, the main goal of HBCUs in educating Black citizens is settled with no ambiguity, but these institutions have also welcomed and continued to welcome students from other races and ethnicity for several decades, to the extent that about 24 percent of students enrolled in HBCUs in 2018 were non-Black students.[9] Some of the notable ones include Howard University in Washington, D.C., Morehouse College in Georgia, Florida A&M University, Xavier University in Louisiana, and Fisk University in Tennessee among many others.[10]

As the literature has underscored, slave owners did not only prohibit enslaved Africans from learning to read and write but Blacks were also denied access to white institutions of higher learning, which necessitated the emergence of HBCUs.[11] Walter Allen and his colleagues argue that factors such as the Emancipation Proclamation, the victory of Northern states over the South during the Civil War, and the Thirteenth Amendment to the U.S. Constitution have all contributed to the establishment of HBCUs.[12] While a majority of HBCUs, especially private ones emerged in the post-Civil War era in many parts of the South, due to the federal support from the Freedman's Bureau program,[13] a few of these institutions served many people of African descent in the pre-Civil War era. Black institutions such as Cheyney State University, which was established in 1837, Lincoln University of Pennsylvania, established in 1854, and Wilberforce University, established in 1856 in Ohio are good examples of the pre-Civil War Black institutions.[14] The Morrill Act of 1890, a land-grant public funding package, also helped to expand public colleges for lower and middle-income Americans, including Blacks across the country.[15]

HBCUs have since their establishment played and continue to play pivotal roles in the upward mobility of Blacks, especially the Black middle class.[16] For example, HBCUs are noted as strong undergraduate serving institutions for African Americans.[17] They are also known for their graduate education in professional fields such as law, medical sciences, engineering, and business administration.[18] The well-known statement by W. E. B. Du Bois on Negro colleges as recounted by Jessica Exkano captures the centrality of these historic institutions. Without the Negro college, as Du Bois noted, Blacks would not have been where they are in terms of their social advancement. For Exkano, Du Bois did not only recognize the need for Blacks to have their own space for "autonomy and self-reflexivity after centuries of oppression," but he also noted that HBCUs provided the venue for Blacks to be educated.[19] In essence, as this chapter concurs with Exkano, HBCUs remain relevant in correcting the centuries of educational inequalities through their strong advocacy of social egalitarianism.[20]

Despite their importance, HBCUs have continued to face many problems and challenges. While some scholars[21] have written on the day-to-day challenges of limited funding and student enrollment issues, other works focused on the influence of Eurocentric ethos on these institutions.[22] For others, these institutions are like other institutions of higher learning in the United States that are also faced with the challenges of student enrollment, limited funding, and the recent impact of the COVID-19 pandemic. We should also note that HBCUs are not monolithic. They differ in size, mission, curricula emphases, traditions, and governance structures.[23]

CONCEPTUAL IDEAS ON RACE, RACISM, AND SOCIAL JUSTICE

Race and Racism

One of the dominant concepts in the social sciences that have continued to evoke intense debates in the scholarly/public domain is the concept of race. Unlike other societies where religion and ethnicity constitute major dividing lines, the American society is largely shaped or divided into racial lines despite the racial advancement made since the Jim Crow era of the 1960s.[24] In her book *Recognizing Race and Ethnicity: Power, Privilege, and Inequality*, sociologist Kathleen FitzGerald argues that race remains a central organizing principle that does not only reflect in the arena of inequality and a subject of ongoing social tensions but race as a factor continues to shape identities and how Americans see themselves.[25] The persistent presence of race is a reminder of W. E. B. Du Bois's statement on the problem of the twentieth century. According to W.E.B Du Bois, as cited in Kathleen FitzGerald's work, "the problem of the twentieth century is the problem of the color-line."[26] Du Bois was not only right, but his prediction has unfortunately continued into the twenty-first century as the American society has not been able to resolve its racial problems. What then is race?

According to Kathleen FitzGerald, "race specifically refers to a group of people that share some *socially* defined physical characteristics, for instance, skin color, hair texture, or facial features."[27] Ethnicity is another important term that is often used with race that might need to be addressed and clarified. It is defined as a group of people that share a common ancestry with shared culture, nationality and or language, with physical appearances not associated with ethnicity.[28] One of the significant elements in the preceding theoretical discussion is the fact that race is a *socially constructed concept* rather than a biological reality. This is because race, as a concept, has undergone changes over time and space. If race were to be biologically real, as FitzGerald argues, the changes with reference to race would not have occurred.[29] For example, groups in the American society such as Irish Americans, Italian Americans, Greek Americans, and Jewish Americans were once not considered whites or members of the white racial group. In other words, the above-mentioned groups were once not considered or seen as whites. While the physical appearances of these groups have not changed, their social standing has, however, changed within the American society which elevated the status of these groups into the racial group of whites.[30] Simply put, race is socially constructed.

Eduardo Bonilla-Silva, who is one of the leading race theorists has also articulated a similar idea on how race is not only a social construct, but race has been a central principle of social organization and a prominent social vessel of group affiliation in the modern era.[31] Another aspect of race relates to racial stratification with hierarchical categories that tend to manifest in either benefits or burdens. The benefits often involve a situation where a racial group is ascribed with a "superior position" in a society with greater access to power (i.e., political, social, economic) and psychological advantages over the group/groups ascribed with an "inferior position."[32] There is no doubt that the socially designed and constructed racial stratification with hierarchical categories have been a burden for people of African descent in particular because of the way they have been historically dehumanized based on their skin color for centuries.[33]

On the concept of racism, Benjamin Bowser's work on the evolution of the concept will be useful to reiterate at this point. According to Bowser, the earliest use of the term racism can be traced to the 1900s edition of the Oxford English Dictionary where the dehumanizing policy toward Native Americans was described as racism.[34] The term was also interchangeably used with "racialism" during the first half of the twentieth century. Bowser observes that racism as a terminology gained further popularity in the mid-1940s with Ruth Benedict's book on *Race and Racism.*"[35] Benedict's work, as recounted by Eduardo Bonilla-Silva, defines racism as incidences of hostilities or ill feelings between groups based on physical differences and characteristics. Racism is also conceptualized as a "dogma that one ethnic group is condemned by nature to congenital inferiority and another group is destined to congenital superiority."[36]

Kathleen FitzGerald's persuasive definition of racism is also worth reiterating. FitzGerald defines racism as "actions, attitudes, beliefs, or behaviors, whether intentional or unintentional, which threaten, harm, or disadvantage members of one racial/ethnic group, or the group itself, over another."[37] She argues that racism tends to manifest in many ways and forms. It can take the form of prejudice. That is a belief system that is not founded on evidence but preconceived notions and stereotypes. Prejudices that are based on false beliefs can be very hard to change even when confronted with contrary evidence of truth, which explains why "prejudice relegates racism to the realm of ideas and attitudes rather than actions."[38]

Bonilla-Silva's discussion of the three standpoints of conceptualizing racism needs to be underscored as well. The first standpoint is that racism consists of a set of ideas or beliefs. Second, those beliefs and ideas about a group or groups are often considered as tending to lead individuals in a society to develop prejudice. Third, the prejudicial attitudes and notions often lead individuals in a society to take real actions that can be discriminatory against other racial groups, especially racial minorities.[39] In fact, social thinker/distinguished philosopher, Polycarp Ikuenobe advanced a similar idea in his work on racism and its subtle forms or manifestations. In the words of Ikuenobe, racism manifests itself when a culture or a social system perpetuates unequal power relations between racial groups that create incentives for people to learn and validate their beliefs and attitudes. In essence, racist ideas and attitudes come through learning and socialization processes in our society.[40]

Joe Feagin's theoretical work on white racial frame provides a further supporting example for the discussion. Feagin defines white racial frame as a centuries-old worldview, set of ideas, and beliefs that involve racial construction of societal reality by some white Americans as the frame that legitimates, rationalizes, and shapes racial inequality in the United States.[41] The frame includes racial prejudices, stereotypes, ideologies, and racial narratives of racial minorities, especially Blacks.[42] Noel Cazenave expanded on these ideas by arguing that the white racial frame is system-sustaining through perceptions, thoughts, feelings, emotions, language, and racialized symbols about racial minorities.[43] This is what Kathleen FitzGerald describes as a worldview that consists of racial beliefs loaded with racial images, verbal utterances, and prejudiced practices which help to justify racism and discriminatory practices.[44]

It is clear, as Benjamin Bowser has argued elsewhere, that no other word, besides prejudice, gained such a popular usage in the United States that describes the decades of social conflicts as did racism in the later years of the twentieth century.[45] It is another reminder of W.E.B Du Bois's famous statement on how the twentieth century, and for that matter the twenty-first century, have become the centuries of the color-line problem.[46] Bowser underscored two other important developments that have popularized the term racism in the twentieth century. The first occurred during World War II, which relates to incidents of anti-Semitism. The second popularization occurred during the civil rights movements of the 1960s in the United States where activists demanded and fought for social justice.[47]

Social Justice

As earlier noted in the introduction section of this chapter, social justice issues have not only continued to dominate public discourses across the United States after the killing of George Floyd by a white police officer in 2020, but scholarly attention on the concept has also increased. While attention on the concept is timely and relevant, scholar-activists with an African-centered perspective on research and activism are likely to respond to the attention debates with enthusiasm and/or exhaustion given the never-ending racial challenges facing Blacks. By definition, social justice, as captured in the work of Suzette Speight and Elizabeth Vera deals with the "elimination of institutionalized domination and oppression."[48] Speight and Vera have advanced Marion Young's conceptual ideas by arguing that social justice is beyond the redistribution of societal benefits such as income and wealth to dealing with institutional and social relations. To these scholars, social justice involves the "degree to which a society supports the elements necessary for a good life."[49] The *good life* argument contains two fundamental elements. First, the element of what Speight and Vera have described as developing and exercising one's capacities and experience in any society. The second deals with participating and determining one's action in relation to society. Put together, social justice involves the "promotion of the values of self-development and self-determination"[50] within a society.

William Cook's study on social justice and its applications to the African American liberation tradition is another important work worth discussing. Drawing on the broader discourse on social justice issues, William Cook recounted James Johnston's definition of social justice as the "formal, informal interaction among people that results in an unbiased community or state."[51] In other words, a social justice state is a place where state actors impartially distribute resources and services toward a *good life* as Suzette Speight, Elizabeth Vera, as well as Marion Young, have articulated. This chapter agrees with the centrality of the nondiscriminatory idea that people can make progress in society to the best of their abilities unhindered.[52] While the nondiscriminatory state idea or what I would describe as a "dreamland state" seems desirable, Michelle Alexander's caution that America's cherished democracy could be lost forever if the country continues to allow systemic and institutional racial discrimination is another important reminder of the complexities of what an ideal social justice state might look like.[53] At the same time, we should be reminded that the intellectual debates on social justice are not new. Social justice issues have always captivated classical thinkers such as Plato, Aristotle, Thomas Aquinas, Immanuel Kant, and thinkers of the Ancient Egyptians. For example, Immanuel Kant was right on point when he observed that actions are morally right if they are motivated by duty without regard to personal motive and self-interest.[54]

From the modern standpoint, most scholars trace the present-day ideas on social justice to John Rawls's work on the theory of justice.[55] Carl Bankston III discusses the origins debate on social justice and noted that the term is closely associated with John Rawls's works. According to Bankston III, two principles that connect to the common understanding of social justice deal with social justice which is often viewed as a matter of redistributing resources to improve the conditions of marginalized groups in a society. Second, the redistribution is considered as a matter of rights (i.e., political, economic, sociocultural) for marginalized groups.[56] Joseph Zajda and colleagues underscored this point on how social justice issues are not only self-evident but critically vital to explore, especially in the quest for creating an egalitarian and just society for everyone.[57] Simply put, the fundamental idea of social justice as advanced in the preceding discussions underscores the centrality of equal rights and equitable opportunities in social, economic, and political spheres for all in society.[58]

HBCUs and Social Justice Issues

Given the continuous struggles for social justice for people of African descent in their quest for emancipation and human dignity[59] and the fact that social justice issues occupy a prominent place in the popular discourses on the Black experience, questions on the role and place of HBCUs in the critical issues of race, racism, and social justice deserve to be explored. In other words, it could be argued that HBCUs are not only the face of Black excellence and progress, but they also embody the spirit of Black identity and experience that reflect the history and culture of Africana people. With the unique role and place of HBCUs in the intellectual tradition of Black struggles and achievements, one wonders how these institutions have systematically devoted resources and intellectual spaces to the study of race, racism, and social justice issues. To put it simply, as a way of reiterating my research question, this chapter seeks to explore these key questions: Do we have well-resourced academic centers and institutes that are devoted to the study of race and social justice issues at HBCUs? If so, where are these academic centers and institutions and how well are they doing? If not, why are these institutions lacking in the first place? This final section examines these questions within the context of race, racism, and social justice issues with some policy ideas and recommendations.

In their work on the legacy of social change, Charles Davis and his colleagues observed that HBCUs have since their inception been the home or epicenter of social justice activities, especially on issues of Black disenfranchisement. In addition to producing most of America's Black professionals such as doctors, lawyers, engineers, and professors, HBCUs have also been instrumental in serving as incubators of student activists throughout the civil rights movement of the 1960s.[60] When thinking about the legacies of HBCUs with respect to serving as incubators for student activism, one does not need not struggle to find prominent personalities such as "Martin Luther King Jr. (Morehouse College in Atlanta, Georgia); Ella Baker (Shaw University in Raleigh, North Carolina); and Bayard Rustin (Wilberforce University in Wilberforce, Ohio, and Cheney University in Cheney, Pennsylvania)."[61]

Charles Davis and his colleagues also discussed the longstanding tradition of organized resistance and collective civic activities of students from HBCUs. They cited the May 26, 1956, case where Wilhelmina Jakes and Carrie Patterson, both Black women students at Florida Agricultural & Mechanical University (FAMU), decided to violate the unjust Jim Crow laws by sitting in the "Whites Only" section of a segregated bus in Tallahassee, Florida.[62] The Tallahassee Bus Boycott of 1956 was another case worth mentioning. According to Davis and his colleagues,[63] the Tallahassee Bus Boycott and the Montgomery Bus Boycott in Alabama were important because of how HBCU students were instrumental to these movements.[64] We should note that Davis and his colleagues are not alone in advancing the argument on the significance of HBCUs as incubators for producing great civil rights leaders. Levon Esters and Marybeth Gasman discussed similar ideas on the role of HBCUs in America's social justice movements. For these scholars, HBCUs are often noted for producing Black professionals in the fields of law, politics, business, and medicine among others, but what is commonly overlooked and rarely discussed is the roles HBCUs have played in inspiring the participation of students in social justice issues.[65] For Esters and Gasman, HBCUs have been able to foster active civic engagement among their students due to their long-standing advantage as Black institutions with strong history and legacy of serving as incubators of civil rights activities. To put it differently, community activism and active civic engagement in social movements and social justice issues have been at the core of HBCUs.[66]

While recognizing the legacy of HBCUs as incubators of producing great leaders of the civil rights movements of the 1960s as well as their recent involvement in new social movements such as the Black Lives Matter, it is significant to ask the critical question of how race and social justice issues are systematically studied at HBCUs. This is where the incubator argument becomes relevant, but it seems like the methods of acquiring civil rights ideas and strategies at HBCUs tend to evolve through what I will describe as "naturally emerged or acquired practices." I argue that the "naturally emerged or acquired practices" of civil rights ideas and strategies at HBCUs were not successfully transformed into well-known academic centers and institutes devoted to the systematic study of race and racial justice issues as expected at HBCUs until recently when a few started to emerge after George Floyd's death.

The seeming lack of well-known academic centers and institutes for the systematic and rigorous study of race, anti-racism, and racial justice/equity issues may have prompted a similar question asked by Langston Clark.[67] Drawing on his personal educational journey and experience at one of the HBCUs, Langston Clark wondered why he did not remember his professors mentioning or critically talking about social justice issues with all the celebrated civil rights leaders with lineage to HBCUs. In his words, Clark notes:

> I wondered, why I did not learn about anti-racist pedagogy at my HBCU. Why did I not learn about culturally relevant pedagogy at my HBCU? And why did I learn about the contributions of the many different people of color to the history of civil rights at my White graduate school, and not my HBCU?[68]

Clark's thought-provoking questions and scholarly lamentation connect well to the central research questions of this chapter and are a reminder of a recent work[69] that explores a similar dilemma on the extent to which African-centered ideas are systematically integrated into the curricula at HBCUs given their natural setting as the "cultural intellectual spaces" that can advance the Afrocentric idea. This might explain why critics are raising questions on why these institutions lack doctoral programs in African

American or Black Studies where the future generation of scholars can be trained. For some, lack of vision from the leadership of many HBCUs could explain the less emphasis on the Afrocentric or African-centered perspective in their curricula.[70] Alan Colon got it right when he raised this question about two decades on why HBCUs presume to produce great leaders of Black communities with many of them knowing very little about their history and culture due to what he describes as the "limited organized exposure to African-centered knowledge" in their curricula.[71] It is apparent that HBCUs need to do more to produce scholars with knowledge of Black affairs as Alan Colon describes it. W. E. B. Du Bois expressed a similar thought several years ago, as captured in Colon's work, that Negro issues need to be a part of the core mission of Black educational institutions.[72]

As the preceding discussions have revealed, HBCUs have been by default creating what I will describe as the "informal cultural spaces" for students to be engaged in racial justice issues since their inception with prominent personalities such as Martin Luther King Jr. of Morehouse College in Atlanta, Georgia, and Ella Baker of Shaw University in Raleigh, North Carolina, among many others.[73] While the significance of the "informal cultural spaces" cannot be discounted, the question of whether HBCUs have academic centers and institutes that are devoted to the study of race and social justice issues needs some answers. Charles Davis and his colleagues captured the above puzzle quite well when they asked: "How should HBCUs continue to support and develop civically engaged advocates for social justice?"[74]

While many HBCUs are taking the needed steps to address some of the social justice issues in their local communities, there are further venues that can still be explored. What are these further venues? This is where I draw on the conceptual ideas of Esters and Gasman in echoing their six recommendations with an emphasis on the creation of social justice centers. Esters and Gasman made their recommendation in 2015 for HBCUs to establish racial and social justice centers, but the call was not given as serious attention as expected. But the attention calculus changed after the massive protests swept across the United States following George Floyd's murder. The next section of the chapter highlights a few examples of the new academic centers and institutes on social justice that were established by HBCUs.

A report published in July 2020 by the esteemed *Journal of Blacks in Higher Education* with the title "Three HBCUs Announce the Creation of New Centers for Racial Justice"[75] not only brought national attention to the creation of these long-awaited centers, but the bold steps taken by these three institutions within a few weeks of each other signaled a new era for HBCUs. In the wake of the massive protests that followed the murder of Mr. George Floyd, a few HBCUs have created new academic centers devoted to racial justice issues. Three of the HBCUs include Shaw University in Raleigh,

North Carolina, which announced the establishment of The Center for Racial and Social Justice.[76] The Center, according to the University, seeks to affect "meaningful social change by supporting engagement around civil and human rights, spiritual formation, discernment, a social justice."[77] Commenting on the creation of the Center, Dr. Paulette Dillard, President of Shaw University, noted that the university has been at the forefront of social justice and civil rights issues throughout its history. The establishment of the new Center, she noted, will honor that legacy/tradition and their commitment to carry on with the tradition of social justice work.[78] The university authorities have also underscored the role of the Ella Baker Institute which was named in honor of alumna Ella Josephine Baker, who played a significant role in the creation of the Student Nonviolent Coordinating Committee (SNCC) on Shaw's campus in the 1960s.[79] Expressing a similar thought on the creation of the new Center, Dr. Valerie Johnson, the co-Director of the Center noted that police reform and restorative justice will be active on the Center's agenda. Dr. Johnson added that their work will focus on the devastating impact of the COVID-19 pandemic on the African American communities as part of the broader discourse on health inequities among the underserved populations in America.[80]

The University of the District of Columbia in Washington, D.C., also established the Institute for the Study and Elimination of White Supremacy in America. Reflecting on the establishment of the Institute, the President of the University, Ronald Mason, noted that "White supremacy cannot have its cake and eat it too." America's progress requires what he describes as a "better business model, one that allows human potential to flourish whatever its color or class."[81]

Dillard University in New Orleans also established a Center for Racial Justice. The Center aims to focus on policing, law enforcement, and community engagement on racial/social justice issues.[82] In a press release issued on June 18, 2020, the University indicated that the Center's establishment is a response to the rising number of police brutality cases in the United States.[83] As a historically Black university, the statement noted that the Center for Racial Justice seeks to bring "systemic change to the way policing is done in communities of color and to promote partnerships with law enforcement including police departments and sheriff's offices, graduate, and professional schools."[84]

CONCLUSION

The year 2020 will go down in history as one of the most challenging years in recent times in terms of the intense public awareness of race and social justice issues. More importantly, the brutal murder of Mr. George Floyd in

Minnesota on May 25, 2020, by a white police officer and the socio-political impact or what could be described as the *George Floyd effect or factor* in galvanizing massive protests against institutionalized racism and systematic injustice will continue to attract scholarly attention. As Michelle Alexander has argued,[85] America's cherished democracy is at greater risk of decay if we continue to allow systemic racial discrimination to keep haunting and taking deep roots in our society and institutions. There is no question that Black communities have continued to face many challenges in our society. At the same time, we are reminded of the courage, strength, and determination of Black freedom fighters, thinkers, and scholar-activists that keep fighting for Black people.

This is where the importance of institutions such as HBCUs that have continued to sustain Black culture and identity need to be underscored. At the same time, pertinent questions have been raised on the extent to which race and social justice issues are systematically studied at HBCUs. The chapter examined these issues by advancing the argument that HBCUs serve as natural settings or domains on critical issues of race, anti-racism, and social justice, but these issues appear not to be systematically studied or institutionalized in the form of academic centers and institutes. The emergence of academic centers and institutes in recent years as part of the *George Floyd effect or factor* represents the right steps for HBCUs. We should note that establishing academic centers and institutes is the first major part of the process. Providing sufficient funding for the running of these academic centers and institutes constitute another important element of the equation. While the record-breaking donations to many HBCUs from large corporations and philanthropists since 2020 are good signs for the future, it is difficult to predict the sustainable nature of what some have described as the "George Floyd inspired donations."[86] There is a need for all Americans who care about social justice and want to see a just society to support the newly established centers and institutes. HBCUs also need to do more in prioritizing the establishment of more academic centers and institutes that will be devoted to a systematic/rigorous study of race and social justice issues.

NOTES

1. Michelle Alexander, "America, This is Your Chance: "We Must Get It Right this Time or Risk Losing Our Democracy Forever." *New York Times*, 2020; Maulana Karenga, *Introduction to Black Studies* (4th ed.) (Los Angeles: University of Sankore Press, 2010).

2. Michael Hanchard, *The Specter of Race: How Discrimination Haunts Western Democracy* (Princeton: Princeton University Press, 2018).

3. Michelle Alexander, "America, This is Your Chance: "We Must Get It Right this Time or Risk Losing Our Democracy Forever." *New York Times*, 2020.

4. Ibid, 1

5. Isabel Wilkerson, Caste: *The Origins of our Discontents* (New York: Randam House, 2020), 17–18.

6. Felix Kumah-Abiwu, "Beyond Intellectual Construct to Policy Ideas: The Case of the Afrocentric Paradigm. *Africology: The Journal of Pan African Studies*, 9, (2016): 23–43, see also Maulana Karenga, *Introduction to Black Studies* (4th ed.) (Los Angeles: University of Sankore Press, 2010).

7. Marybeth Gasman, "The Changing Face of Historically Black Colleges and Universities. Penn Center for Minority Serving Institutions (2013); Kenneth Redd, Historically Black Colleges and Universities: Making a Comeback. *New Directions for Higher Education*, 102 (1998): 33–43; Felix Kumah-Abiwu, "Changing Pathways of Historically Black Colleges and Universities (HBCUs): Any Place for Afrocentric Ideas?" in *Whiteness, Power, and Resisting Change in US Higher Education,* ed. Kenneth R. Roth and Zachary S. Ritter (Palgrave Macmillan, Cham, 2020).

8. Ibid.

9. Ibid.

10. Christopher Brown, "The Declining Significance of Historically Black Colleges and Universities: Relevance, Reputation, and Reality in Obamamerica. *The Journal of Negro Education*, 82, no. 1(2013): 3–19.

11. Walter Allen, Joseph Jewell, Kimberly Griffin and De'Sha Wolf, "Historically Black colleges and Universities: Honoring the Past, Engaging the Present, Touching the Future." *The Journal of Negro Education*, 76, (2007): 263–80.

12. Ibid.

13. Roland Fryer and Michael Greenstone, "The Changing Consequences of Attending Historically Black Colleges and Universities," *American Economic Journal: Applied Economics*, 2 (2010):116–148; Travis Albritton, "Educating our own: The Historical Legacy of HBCUs and their Relevance for Educating a New Generation of Leaders." *Urban Review*, 44 (2012): 311– 331; Robert Palmer and Marybeth Gasman, "It Takes a Village to Raise a Child": The Role of Social Capital in Promoting Academic Success for Black men at a Black College." *Journal of College Student Development*, 49 (2008): 52–70.

14. Redd, "Historically Black Colleges and Universities"; Kumah-Abiwu, "Changing Pathways of Historically Black Colleges and Universities."

15. Seldon Avery, "Taking the Pulse of Historically Black Colleges." *Academic Questions*, 22, (2009): 327–39.

16. Kumah-Abiwu, "Changing Pathways of Historically Black Colleges and Universities."

17. Marybeth Gasman, "Ph.D.'s in African American studies at HBCUs: A Response to Where are They?" *Diverse*. June 18, 2008.

18. Herschelle Challenor, "African Studies at Historically Black Colleges and Universities." *African Issues*, 30 (2002): 24–29.

19. Jessica Exkano, "Toward an African Cosmology: Reframing How We Think About Historically Black Colleges and Universities." *Journal of Black Studies*, 44, no. 1 (2013): 63–80.

20. Ibid.

21. Albritton, "Educating our own: The Historical Legacy of HBCUs"; see also Marybeth Gasman, "The Changing Face of Historically Black Colleges and Universities." Penn Center for Minority Serving Institutions (2013); Mikyong Kim and Clifton Conrad, "The Impact of Historically Black Colleges and Universities on the Academic Success of African American Students. *Research in Higher Education*, 47, no. 4 (2006): 399–427.

22. Ibid.

23. Alan Colon, "Black Studies: Historical Background, Modern Origins and Development Priorities for the early Twenty First Century," *Western Journal of Black Studies*, 27 (2003):145– 56.

24. Kathleen FitzGerald, *Recognizing Race and Ethnicity: Power, Privilege, and Inequality* (New York: Routledge, 2014).

25. Ibid.

26. Ibid., 4

27. Ibid., 9

28. Ibid., 9

29. Ibid., 21

30. Ibid., 21

31. Eduardo Bonilla-Silva, "The Essential Social Fact of Race." *American Sociological Review*, 64, no. 6 (1999): 899–906.

32. Ibid.

33. Kumah-Abiwu, "Beyond Intellectual Construct"; Karenga, *Introduction to Black Studies.*

34. Benjamin Bowser, "Racism: Origin and Theory." *Journal of Black Studies*, 48, no. 6 (2017): 572–90.

35. Ibid.

36. Eduardo Bonilla-Silva, "Rethinking Racism: Toward a Structural Interpretation." *American Sociological Review*, 62, no. 3 (1997): 465- 480.

37. FitzGerald, "Recognizing Race and Ethnicity," 10.

38. Ibid.

39. Bonilla-Silva, "Rethinking Racism."

40. Polycarp Ikuenobe, "Conceptualizing Racism and its Subtle Forms." *Journal for the Theory of Social Behaviour*, 4, no 2 (2011):161–181, see also Felix Kumah-Abiwu, "Media Gatekeeping and Portrayal of Black Men in America." *Journal of Men's Studies* 28, no. 1(2020): 64–81.

41. Joe Feagin, *The White Racial Frame: Centuries of Racial Framing and Counter-Framing* (New York, NY: Routledge, 2013), see also Kumah-Abiwu, "Media Gatekeeping and Portrayal of Black Men."

42. Ibid.

43. Noel Cazenave, "Joe R. Feagin: The Social Science Voice of Systemic Racism Theory," in *Systemic Racism: Making Liberty, Justice, and Democracy Real*, ed. Ruth

Thompson-Miller and Kimberly Ducey (New York, NY: Palgrave Macmillan, 2017): 17–40.

44. FitzGerald, *Recognizing Race and Ethnicity.*

45. Bowser, "Racism: Origin and Theory."

46. Ibid.

47. Ibid.

48. Suzette Speight and Elizabeth Vera, "A Social Justice Agenda: Ready or Not? *The Counseling Psychologist*, 32, no.1 (2004): 109–118, see also Marion Young, *Justice and the Politics of Difference* (Princeton, NJ: Princeton University Press, 1990).

49. Ibid., 111

50. Ibid., 111

51. William Cook, "Social Justice Applications and the African American Liberation Tradition," *Journal of Black Studies,* 50, no. 7 (2019): 651–81.

52. Ibid.

53. Alexander, "America, This is Your Chance."

54. Joseph Zajda, Suzanne Majhanovich and Val Rust, "Introduction: Education and Social Justice," *Education and Social Justice*, 52 (2006): 9–22.

55. John Rawls, *A Theory of Justice* (Cambridge, MA: Harvard University Press, 1971).

56. Carl Bankston III, "Social Justice Cultural Origins of a Perspective and a Theory," *The Independent Review*, 15, no. 2(2010): 165–78.

57. Zajda, Majhanovich and Rust, "Introduction: Education and Social Justice."

58. Cook, "Social Justice Applications and the African American Liberation Tradition," see also Alexander, "America, This is Your Chance."

59. Kumah-Abiwu, "Beyond Intellectual Construct"; Karenga, *Introduction to Black Studies.*

60. Charles Davis III, Felecia Commodore and Kyah King, "Lest We Forget: Continuing Historically Black Colleges and Universities' Legacy of Fostering Social Change," *Diversity and Democracy* (Association of American Colleges and Universities), 22, no. 4 (2020)

61. Ibid.,1.

62. Ibid.

63. Ibid.

64. Ibid.

65. Levon Esters and Marybeth Gasman, "HBCUS' Role in The Social Justice Movement," *HBCU Lifestyle,* October 5, 2015.

66. Ibid.

67. Langston Clark, "Standing in The Gap: A Social Justice Ethnography of a Historically Black PETE Program," *Journal of Negro Education*, 89, no. 3(2020): 215–32.

68. Ibid., 215

69. Kumah-Abiwu, "Changing Pathways of Historically Black Colleges and Universities."

70. Gasman, "Ph.D.'s in African American studies at HBCUs"; Challenor, "African Studies at Historically Black Colleges and Universities."

71. Alan Colon, "Black Studies and Historically Black Colleges and Universities: Towards a New Synthesis," *Out of the Revolution: The Development of Africana Studies*, ed. Delores Aldridge and Carlene Young (MD: Lexington Books, 2000), 287–313.

72. Ibid.

73. Davis III, Commodore and King, "Lest We Forget: Continuing Historically Black Colleges and Universities' Legacy."

74. Ibid., 1

75. *Journal of Blacks in Higher Education.* "Three HBCUs Announce the Creation of New Centers for Racial Justice." July 3, 2020. Accessed August 27, 2021 https://www.jbhe.com/2020/07/three-hbcus-annouce-the-creation-of-new-centers-for-racial-justice/.

76. Ibid.

77. The Center for Racial and Social Justice (Shaw University). Accessed August 26, 2021, https://crsj.org/about/

78. *Journal of Blacks in Higher Education.* "Three HBCUs Announce the Creation of New Centers for Racial Justice."

79. Michael Perchick, "Shaw University Announces the Creation of The Center for Racial and Social Justice. June 30, 2020. Accessed August 20, 2021, https://abc11.com/shaw-university-the-center-for-racial-and-social-justice-u-raleigh/6285496/.

80. Ibid.

81. *Journal of Blacks in Higher Education.* "Three HBCUs Announce the Creation of New Centers for Racial Justice."

82. Ibid.

83. Dillard University Press Release (June 18, 2020). Accessed September 4, 2021, https://dillard.edu/communications/news/center-for-racial-justice.php.

84. Ibid.,1

85. Alexander, America, "We Must Get It Right this Time or Risk Losing Our Democracy."

86. Liz Schlemmer, 2021. "Nation's Largest HBCU Sees Record-Breaking Donations." Accessed September 8, 2021, https://www.npr.org/2021/05/01/992480703/nations-largest-hbcu-sees-record-breaking-donations.

REFERENCES

Albritton, Travis. "Educating Our Own: The Historical Legacy of HBCUs and their Relevance for Educating a New Generation of Leaders." *Urban Review* 44 (2012): 311– 31.

Alexander, Michelle. "America, This is Your Chance: "We Must Get It Right this Time or Risk Losing Our Democracy Forever." *New York Times*, June 8, 2020. Accessed August 25, 2021, https://www.nytimes.com/2020/06/08/opinion/george-floyd-protests-race.html.

Allen, Walter, Joseph Jewell, Kimberly Griffin, and De'Sha Wolf. "Historically Black Colleges and Universities: Honoring the Past, Engaging the Present, Touching the Future." *The Journal of Negro Education*, 76, (2007): 263–280.

Bankston III, Carl. "Social Justice Cultural Origins of a Perspective and a Theory," *The Independent Review* 15, no. 2(2010): 165–178.

Bonilla-Silva, Eduardo. "Rethinking Racism: Toward a Structural Interpretation." *American Sociological Review* 62, no. 3 (1997): 465– 480.

Bonilla-Silva, Eduardo. "The Essential Social Fact of Race." *American Sociological Review* 64, no. 6 (1999): 899–906.

Bowser, Benjamin. "Racism: Origin and Theory." *Journal of Black Studies* 48, no. 6 (2017): 572– 590.

Brown, Christopher. "The Declining Significance of Historically Black Colleges and Universities: Relevance, Reputation, and Reality in Obamamerica." *The Journal of Negro Education*, 82, no. 1(2013): 3–19.

Cazenave, Noel. "Joe R. Feagin: The Social Science Voice of Systemic Racism Theory," in *Systemic Racism: Making Liberty, Justice, and Democracy Real*, eds. Thompson-Miller, Ruth and Kimberly Ducey. New York: Palgrave Macmillan, 2017.

Challenor, Herschelle. "African Studies at Historically Black Colleges and Universities." *African Issues* 30, (2002): 24–29.

Clark, Langston. "Standing in The Gap: A Social Justice Ethnography of a Historically Black PETE Program." *The Journal of Negro Education* 89, no. 3(2020): 215–232.

Colon, Alan. "Black Studies and Historically Black Colleges and Universities: Towards a New Synthesis," in *Out of the Revolution: The Development of Africana Studies*, ed. Aldridge Delores, and Carlene Young. MD: Lexington Books, 2000.

Colon, Alan. "Black Studies: Historical Background, Modern Origins and Development Priorities for the early Twenty First Century." *Western Journal of Black Studies* 27(2003):145–56.

Cook, William. "Social Justice Applications and the African American Liberation Tradition." *Journal of Black Studies* 50, no. 7 (2019): 651–681.

Davis III, Charles, Commodore, Felecia, and King, Kyah. "Lest We Forget: Continuing Historically Black Colleges and Universities' Legacy." *Diversity and Democracy* (Association of American Colleges and Universities), 22, no. 4 (2020). Accessed August 28, 2021, https://www.aacu.org/diversitydemocracy/2020/summer/davis

Dillard University Press Release (June 18, 2020). Accessed September 4, 2021, https://dillard.edu/communications/news/center-for-racial-justice.php

Esters, Levon and Gasman, Marybeth. "HBCUS' Role in The Social Justice Movement," *HBCU Lifestyle*, October 5, 2015. Accessed August 27, 2021, https://hbculifestyle.com/hbcu-social-justice-movement/

Exkano, Jessica. "Toward an African Cosmology: Reframing How We Think About Historically Black Colleges and Universities." *Journal of Black Studies* 44, no.1(2013): 63–80.

Feagin, Joe. *The White Racial Frame: Centuries of Racial Framing and Counter-Framing* (New York, NY: Routledge, 2013).

FitzGerald, Kathleen. *Recognizing Race and Ethnicity: Power, Privilege, and Inequality*. New York: Routledge, 2014.

Fryer, Roland, and Michael Greenstone. "The Changing Consequences of Attending Historically Black Colleges and Universities," *American Economic Journal: Applied Economics* 2 (2010): 116–48.

Gasman, Marybeth. "The Changing Face of Historically Black Colleges and Universities." Penn Center for Minority Serving Institutions (2013). Accessed August 27, 2021, http://repository.upenn.edu/gse_pubs/335.

asman, Marybeth. "Ph.D.'s in African American studies at HBCUs: A Response to Where are They?" *Diverse*. June 18, 2008. Accessed August 20, 2021, https://www.diverseeducation.com/opinion/article/15091687/phds-in-african-american-studies-at-hbcus-a-response-to-where-are-they.

Hanchard, Michael. *The Specter of Race: How Discrimination Haunts Western Democracy*. Princeton: Princeton University Press, 2018.

Ikuenobe, Polycarp. "Conceptualizing Racism and its Subtle Forms." *Journal for the Theory of Social Behaviour* 4, no. 2 (2011): 161–81.

Journal of Blacks in Higher Education. "Three HBCUs Announce the Creation of New Centers for Racial Justice." July 3, 2020. Accessed August 27, 2021 https://www.jbhe.com/2020/07/three-hbcus-annouce-the-creation-of-new-centers-for-racial-justice/.Karenga, Maulana. *Introduction to Black Studies* (4th edition). Los Angeles: University of Sankore Press, 2010.

Kim, Mikyong, and Clifton Conrad. "The Impact of Historically Black Colleges and Universities on the Academic Success of African American Students." *Research in Higher Education*, 47, no. 4 (2006): 399–427.

Kumah-Abiwu, Felix. "Beyond Intellectual Construct to Policy Ideas: The Case of the Afrocentric Paradigm. *Africology: The Journal of Pan African Studies* 9 (2016): 23–43.

Kumah-Abiwu, Felix. "Media Gatekeeping and Portrayal of Black Men in America." *Journal of Men's Studies* 28, no.1 (2020): 64–81.

Kumah-Abiwu, Felix. "Changing Pathways of Historically Black Colleges and Universities (HBCUs): Any Place for Afrocentric Ideas?" in *Whiteness, Power, and Resisting Change in US Higher Education: A Peculiar Institution*, eds. Kenneth Roth and Zachary Ritter (Cham, Switzerland: Palgrave Macmillan, 2021).

Palmer, Robert, and Marybeth Gasman. "It Takes a Village to Raise a Child": The Role of Social Capital in Promoting Academic Success for Black men at a Black College." *Journal of College Student Development*, 49 (2008): 52–70.

Perchick, Michael. "Shaw University Announces the Creation of The Center for Racial and Social Justice." June 30, 2020. Accessed August 20, 2021, https://abc11.com/shaw-university-the-center-for-racial-and-social-justice-u-raleigh/6285496/

Rawls, John. *A Theory of Justice*. Cambridge, MA: Harvard University Press, 1971.

Redd, Kenneth. "Historically Black Colleges and Universities: Making a Comeback." *New Directions for Higher Education*, 102 (1998): 33–43.

Seldon, Avery. "Taking the Pulse of Historically Black Colleges." *Academic Questions*, 22 (2009): 327–39.

Speight, Suzette, and Elizabeth Vera. "A Social Justice Agenda: Ready or Not?" *Counseling Psychologist*, 32, no.1 (2004): 109–18.

Schlemmer, Liz. "Nation's Largest HBCU Sees Record-Breaking Donations." Accessed September 8, 2021, https://www.npr.org/2021/05/01/992480703/nations -largest-hbcu-sees-record-breaking-donations.

The Center for Racial and Social Justice (Shaw University). Accessed August 26, 2021, https://crsj.org/about/.

Wilkerson, Isabel. *Caste: The Origins of our Discontents*. New York: Random House, 2020.

Young, Marion. *Justice and the Politics of Difference*. Princeton, NJ: Princeton University Press, 1990.

Zajda, Joseph, Suzanne Majhanovich, and Val Rust, Val. "Introduction: Education and Social Justice," *Education and Social Justice* 52 (2006): 9–22.

Index

About the Editors

Alem Hailu is an Associate Professor of African Studies at Howard University. He completed graduate studies at Syracuse University, where he obtained a PhD in Social Science and an MA in Social Science and an MA in Public Administration at the Maxwell School of Citizenship and Public Affairs. He has worked in various academic, public and nongovernmental institutions. He has been engaged in the development, public policy, and human security initiatives in Africa and the Global South. He has also developed partnership projects for governmental and nongovernmental institutions as well as international organizations. A strong believer in collaborative work between academic, governmental, and public/private institutions of learning and public policy organizations, Dr. Hailu has organized international conferences on themes ranging from race and xenophobia, war, violence, and terrorism to Interdisciplinary responses to the challenges of technological changes involving the impact of social media, technology and cross-border flows of ideas and goods across the Continent and the world. Dr. Hailu's education and work are informed by the imperatives for developing new approaches to confronting the challenges of global inequality, conflict, and social displacement within the framework of formulating global policy responses in an increasingly interconnected world.

Sabella Ogbobode Abidde is a professor of political science and member of the graduate faculty at Alabama State University. He is the editor of two ongoing book series: Lexington Books' *African Governance, Development, and Leadership Series*, and Springer Nature's *Africa-East Asia International Relations Series*. Dr. Abidde is an interdisciplinary scholar with a BA in international relations and an MSC in educational administration from Saint Cloud State University Minnesota, an MA in political science from Minnesota State University Mankato Minnesota, and a PhD in African Studies, World Affairs, Public Policy, and Development Studies from Howard University. His scholarship includes published volumes on Africa, Latin

America, and the Caribbean. His forthcoming books are on the contest and contestations between China and Taiwan in Africa. Professor Abidde is a member of the Association of Global South Studies (AGSS); the African Studies & Research Forum (ASRF); the Latin American Studies Association (LASA); the Caribbean Studies Association (CSA); and a lifetime member of the American Association for Chinese Studies (AACS).

Mohamed Saliou Camara is a professor in the Department of African Studies at Howard University. He earned an MA and a PhD from Northwestern University in History on a Fulbright Scholarship, a DES in Philosophy from the University of Conakry, and an Advanced Professional Degree in Journalism from the University of Dakar. He taught at Embry-Riddle Aeronautical University where he also served as Director of the McNair Scholars Program, Speaker of the Faculty Senate, and Associate Vice President for Academics. Previously, Camara served as Associate Chair of the Department of Philosophy at the University of Conakry, a journalist for the National Radio Television of Guinea, and president of the University Press of Conakry. He is the author of *His Master's Voice: Mass Communication and Single-Party Politics in Guinea under Sékou Touré*; *Le Pouvoir politique en Guinée sous Sékou Touré*; *The Development of a Trans-National Region in West Africa*; *Political History of Guinea since World War Two*; *Knowledge and Theory of Knowledge in the African Experience*; *Historical Dictionary of Guinea* (5th Edition); and *Health and Human Security in the Mano River Union*.

About the Contributors

Ivon Alcime is an associate professor of communication in the Department of Communications at Alabama State University. He received his BA in philosophy in 1997, his MA in organizational communication in 2004, and his PhD in intercultural communication from Howard University in 2012. His research and publication focus on intercultural communication, intercultural listening, and conflict management.

Tamika Baldwin-Clark is an assistant professor of social work at Prairie View A&M University. She earned her BA in Sociology from the University of Michigan, her MSW from Michigan State, and her PhD in Social Work from Morgan State. She has studied and worked in the field of social work, both internationally and domestically, for over a decade, and previously taught graduate courses online at the University of Nevada-Reno. Some of her other positions include being a foster care worker in Detroit, a therapist at Baylor College of Medicine, and a care manager in London, UK. Tamika is a licensed clinical social worker supervisor and a licensed chemical dependency counselor. She has practiced in the areas of gerontology, child welfare, substance use, and mental health.

Carla Monette Brown is a PhD candidate in the Public and Social Policy program at Saint Louis University. Carla received a Masters's degree in Public Administration (MPA) from Clark Atlanta University and a Bachelor of Science in Business Administration from the University of North Carolina at Greensboro. Her research focuses on public policy issues including social justice, race, minority relations, and civil and human rights. Carla is currently looking at small-town responses to the unjust treatment of Blacks. Overall, Carla has a passion for equality and the advancement of civic engagement.

Rico Devara Chapman received his PhD in African Studies from Howard University. He is currently an associate professor of history at Clark Atlanta

University. He also serves as assistant dean of the School of Arts and Sciences and Director of the Humanities PhD program. His most recent book is titled *Student Resistance to Apartheid at the University of Fort Hare: Freedom Now, A Degree Tomorrow* (Lexington, 2016).

Patrice W. Glenn Jones began her career as a high school English teacher and radio-air personality in Jacksonville, Florida. After several years in the K–12 arena, she focused her career on higher education. The veteran educator and author love teaching at the university level and proudly champions servant leadership as the Executive Director of Online Education and Programs at Alabama State University (ASU). Before joining ASU, Dr. Glenn Jones served as a virtual learning educational consultant while maintaining an assistant professorship at Embry-Riddle Aeronautical University-Worldwide. She holds a Doctor of Philosophy in educational leadership from Florida A&M University, a specialist degree in information science and learning technology from the University of Missouri–Columbia, and a master's degree in English from the University of North Florida. Some of her research interests include factors that impact Black American student achievement, learning in virtual ecologies and positive psychology.

Elizabeth Carmel Hamilton, PhD, is an art historian and assistant professor at Fort Valley State University whose research is focused on African American art and Afrofuturism. Currently, she is working on a book manuscript: *Charting the Afrofuturist Imaginary in African American Art: The Black Female Fantastic* (Routledge Press). Elizabeth's work has been published in *Nka: The Journal of Contemporary African Art*, *African Arts*, and the *International Review of African American Art*. She completed her doctorate at the University of Florida's School of Art and Art History. Before that, she received a Bachelor of Fine Arts degree from the University of Wyoming.

Felix Kumah-Abiwu is an associate professor in the Department of Africana Studies at Kent State University. He is also the founding director of the Center for African Studies at Kent State. He received his PhD in Political Science from West Virginia University. He also studied at Ohio University and the Legon Centre for International Affairs & Diplomacy, University of Ghana. His research focuses on the politics of development, elections/democratization in Africa, African security/international relations, Black males/public education, narcotics policy, and African-centered theories. In addition to his published book, scholarly book reviews, and several book chapters, Dr. Kumah-Abiwu's scholarly articles have also appeared in the *Commonwealth Journal of International Affairs (The Round Table)*, *Journal of Pan African Studies*, *West Africa Review*, *International Journal of Public Administration*,

Urban Education, Journal of Men's Studies, Journal of Economics/Sustainable Development, and *Commonwealth & Comparative Politics*.

Cheryl E. Mango is an assistant professor of history at Virginia State University Petersburg, VA. She holds an MA in History (Louisiana Tech University, 2012), and a PhD in History (Morgan State University, 2016). Dr. Mango is the author of "Black Radicalism, Black Consciousness, Black History, Black Liberation, Black YouTube: A New Age Revolution." In *From Slavery to Liberation: The African American Experience*, edited by Joshua Farrington and Gwen Graham. (Richmond: Eastern Kentucky University Libraries, 2020). "Afrocentricity and Religion," in Douglas Thomas and Temilola Alanamu, editors, *African Religions: Beliefs and Practices through History* (Santa Barbara CA: ABC-CLIO). She was a 2014–2015 intern at the White House Initiative on Historically Black Colleges and Universities U. S. Department of Education, Washington, D.C.

Regina M. Moorer is an assistant professor of political science at Alabama State University. Her research agenda and pedagogical approach intentionally center on race and gender. She pays particular attention to how intersections of gender and race influence policy implementation and the political experiences of women of color.

Carlos Morrison is a professor of communication in the Department of Communication at Alabama State University. He received a PhD in Intercultural Communication and African American Communication from the Kathy Hughes School of Communication at Howard University in Washington, DC in 1996. Dr. Morrison teaches courses in both Communication Studies and Mass Communications. His research area focuses on Black popular culture, African American rhetoric, and the rhetoric of social movements.

Tabitha S. M. Morton is an assistant professor of political science at Prairie View A&M University. She earned her PhD in Political Science from Texas A&M University with concentrations in public administration, public policy, race, ethnicity, and gender politics. Her work is based on evaluating and creating policies and making recommendations on rectifying disparities on issues that affect minority communities. A significant portion of her research uses theories from public administration to address the racial and gender disparities in public and higher education. Her work also includes examining the current trends in minority education and creating research models that improve that ability to predict future trends, often including non-traditional variables.

Ashla Hill Roseboro is an assistant professor of communications media in the Department of Communications at Alabama State University. She received her PhD in Communication, Culture, and Media Studies and her graduate certificate in Women's Studies from Howard University. She also holds a BA from James Madison University (BA) and an MS from Virginia State University. Her research areas focus on women in media, organizational communication and digital media. Recently, she released a book chapter on the topic of "Historically Black Colleges and Universities Access to Digital Media: An Intersectional Content Analysis of Black Women Social Entrepreneurs." She was the founder and host of a television show on the NBC Comcast local channel in Manassas, Virginia.

D. Caleb Smith is a PhD candidate in the History Department at Tulane University. Smith has served as an instructor of record in the university's History Department and Center for Public Service. He has taught courses on the United States and African American history. Aside from his historical studies, Smith has taught courses on social justice and community engagement. He is also a past recipient of the Andrew Mellon Graduate Fellowship in Community Engagement.

Tiffany D. Thomas is the program coordinator and assistant professor of community development at Prairie View A&M. She is an expert in community engagement and outreach targeted in African American neighborhoods and communities. She specializes in philanthropy, community needs assessments, and leveraging HBCUs for engaged research design and practice. She is affiliated with the University of Kentucky Lexington Community Lab and most recently received a Transformational Presidential grant from Texas A&M University to support a design, build, and engagement project in urban and rural Texas communities. Her work is featured in the *Community Development Journal*, *Local Development*, and *Society, Contemporary Issues in Social Justice*, and the forthcoming book *Black Women and Public Health* and a special of the *Journal of Social Policy and Public Administration*.

Oscar Williams, PhD, Ohio State University, is an associate professor of Africana studies at the University at Albany in New York. His specialty is African American History, with a focus on American Slavery, the Civil Rights & Black Power Movement, African American Literature, African American Intellectual History, and Black Conservatism. His book, *George S. Schuyler: Portrait of a Black Conservative*, is the first published biography of the

African American journalist for the *Pittsburgh Courier*. His current research project is a biography of Dr. John Manuel Gandy, who served as President of Virginia State University from 1914 to 1943.

www.ingramcontent.com/pod-product-compliance
Lightning Source LLC
Chambersburg PA
CBHW022311280326
41932CB00010B/1063